Social Justice and Israel/Palestine

Foundational and Contemporary Debates

Social Justice and Israel/Palestine

Foundational and Contemporary Debates

Edited by
Aaron J. Hahn Tapper and
Mira Sucharov

UNIVERSITY OF TORONTO PRESS
Toronto Buffalo London

© University of Toronto Press 2019
Toronto Buffalo London
utorontopress.com
Printed in Canada

ISBN 978-1-4875-8807-6 (cloth)   ISBN 978-1-4875-8806-9 (paper)

∞ This book is printed on acid-free, 100% post-consumer recycled paper with vegetable-based inks.

Library and Archives Canada Cataloguing in Publication

Title: Social justice and Israel/Palestine: foundational and contemporary debates / edited by Aaron J. Hahn Tapper and Mira Sucharov.
Names: Hahn Tapper, Aaron J. (Aaron Joshua), editor. | Sucharov, Mira, editor.
Description: Includes bibliographical references and index.
Identifiers: Canadiana 20190085622 | ISBN 9781487588069 (paper) | ISBN 9781487588076 (cloth)
Subjects: LCSH: Arab-Israeli conflict—1993– | LCSH: Social justice.
Classification: LCC DS119.76 .S63 2019 | DDC 956.05/3—dc23

We welcome comments and suggestions regarding any aspect of our publications—please feel free to contact us at news@utorontopress.com or visit our internet site at utorontopress.com.

North America
5201 Dufferin Street
North York, Ontario, Canada, M3H 5T8

2250 Military Road
Tonawanda, New York, USA, 14150
ORDERS PHONE: 1–800–565–9523
ORDERS FAX: 1–800–221–9985
ORDERS EMAIL: utpbooks@utpress.utoronto.ca

UK, Ireland, and continental Europe
NBN International
Estover Road, Plymouth, PL6 7PY, UK

ORDERS PHONE: 44 (0) 1752 202301
ORDERS FAX: 44 (0) 1752 202333
ORDERS EMAIL: enquiries@nbninternational.com

Every effort has been made to contact copyright holders; in the event of an error or omission, please notify the publisher.

University of Toronto Press acknowledges the financial assistance to its publishing program of the Canada Council for the Arts and the Ontario Arts Council, an agency of the Government of Ontario.

Canada Council
for the Arts

Conseil des Arts
du Canada

ONTARIO ARTS COUNCIL
CONSEIL DES ARTS DE L'ONTARIO
an Ontario government agency
un organisme du gouvernement de l'Ontario

Funded by the
Government
of Canada

Financé par le
gouvernement
du Canada

Canada

MIX
Paper from
responsible sources
FSC® C016245

Contents

Contents

Part II. Contemporary Debates

About the Editors

Aaron J. Hahn Tapper is the Mae and Benjamin Swig Professor in Jewish Studies and the founding director of the Swig Program in Jewish Studies and Social Justice at the University of San Francisco, where he has been since 2007. He has been an educator for more than two decades; his primary academic interest is the intersection between identity formation, social justice, and marginalized groups. His previous books include *Muslims and Jews in America: Commonalities, Contentions, and Complexities* (Palgrave Macmillan, 2011), which he co-edited with Reza Aslan, and *Judaisms: A Twenty-First-Century Introduction to Jews and Jewish Identities* (University of California Press, 2016). During the 2013–14 academic year, Aaron was a Fulbright Senior Scholar in Australia. Affiliated with the University of Melbourne and Monash University, he traveled around the country conducting research on how Indigenous communities—Aboriginal and Torres Strait Islanders—have received former prime minister Kevin Rudd's political apology, delivered in February 2008. He is currently writing a book on this research.

In addition, he is the executive director of the Center for Transformative Education, an educational initiative aiming to create empowering educational programs to help societies achieve their potential, which he co-founded in 2008.

Mira Sucharov is an associate professor of political science at Carleton University in Ottawa, Canada, where she is a provost teaching fellow and where she teaches courses on Israel/Palestine, foreign policy analysis, op-ed writing, and political identity and graphic novels. She is a four-time teaching award winner, most recently having received the 2017 OCUFA award for teaching excellence—the highest university teaching award in Ontario. She is the author of *The International Self: Psychoanalysis and the Search for Israeli-Palestinian Peace* (SUNY Press, 2005), *Public Influence: A Guide to Op-Ed Writing and Social Media Engagement* (University of Toronto Press, 2019), and various articles on pedagogy, Israel/Palestine, and reflections on being a scholar-blogger. Her many op-ed pieces have appeared in *Haaretz, The Forward, The Globe and Mail, The Toronto Star, The Ottawa Citizen, The Daily Beast, Huffington Post,* and *The Canadian Jewish News*. She is the founding co-chair of the Jewish Politics Division at the Association for Jewish Studies, and is currently co-editor, along with Chaya Halberstam, of *AJS Perspectives*. She is currently working on a memoir manuscript tracing how a North American scholar's identity becomes embedded in the topic of the politics of Israel/Palestine.

Acknowledgements

In two previous books, I thanked a long list of people who played a positive role in shaping me and my work, recognizing friends, family, and professional mentors and colleagues going back as far as preschool. Echoing these earlier acknowledgements and adding to them regarding this project in particular, I'd like to thank my colleagues at the University of San Francisco, where I have taught since 2007, in particular those in the Swig Program in Jewish Studies and Social Justice as well as the Department of Theology and Religious Studies. My friend and colleague in the Swig JSSJ program, Oren Kroll-Zeldin, has been a significant confidante and ally, especially when it comes to anything related to Israel/Palestine. As this book is partially the outgrowth of my work at USF as well as in various conflict resolution and transformation programs, I want to thank the hundreds of students and participants who have helped me develop my understanding of conflict and social justice. Thanks also go to Jennifer Derr, Joshua Schreier, and Lior Sternfeld. My sincere apologies if I have inadvertently forgotten anyone; this does not reflect a lack of gratitude but rather a failed memory.

Thank you also goes to my immediate family—Mom, Dad, Shelly, Stone, Susan, Michael, Lisi, Jacob, Jen, Alice, Jack, Becky, Hanan, Talia, Elisheva, Debby, Andy, Sam, and Nathan. Among those who have moved on to other realms, thank you Grammie and Grampie, Grandfather Abraham and Grandmother Janet, Bubbe and Zaydeh, Aunt Isabel, and David. Peace be with you all.

Finally, I am grateful to my partner, Laurie, and the love and profound support she has given me and continues to give me, especially in terms of my efforts to grow professionally. You are my best friend and I love you. As to my two not-so-little-anymore little ones, Isaiah Everett and Delilah Yareyach, you are the lights of my life, the joys of the deepest parts of my soul, and the reason I do what I do in the world. Laurie, Isaiah, and Delilah (+ Bu and Lamington Sparkle), I love you with all my heart, soul, and being.

—Aaron J. Hahn Tapper, San Francisco

There are so many people who have helped—directly and indirectly—in inspiring this project.

Thank you to my colleagues at Carleton University's political science department and in the Faculty of Public Affairs who have provided a supportive atmosphere for my teaching and research interests. My wonderful doctoral student and teaching assistant, Lena Saleh, has been a superb help in the delivery of my Israel/Palestine course. My many students over the years have continually challenged me to think about the dynamics of the Israeli-Palestinian relationship—and politics more broadly—in new ways.

Aside from the talented contributors to this book, thanks goes to many friends colleagues—too numerous to name—who continue to enrich my understanding of Israel/Palestine. I would particularly like to thank the members of the Israel/Palestine pedagogy group on Facebook, part of my broader social network which is in large part concerned with discussing and debating Israel/Palestine issues from various vantage points, and Brent Sasley, a contributor to this book who deserves special mention for being a longtime trusted friend and source of professional insight.

The Association for Jewish Studies, the International Studies Association, the Middle East Studies Association, and the Association for Israel Studies have all provided fertile ground over the years for panels and roundtables in which I've participated on the topic of teaching Israel/Palestine.

My family—parents, siblings, aunts, uncles, cousins, and late grandparents, and especially my wonderful husband and awesome kids—is a continuous source of love, support, and inspiration for which I am forever grateful.

—Mira Sucharov, Ottawa

For this book in particular, huge gratitude goes out to Mat Buntin, our editor at University of Toronto Press, who helped us nurture the initial idea and oversaw every stage of writing, reviewing, and production with timely, creative, and sage advice. Christine Robertson led the production team deftly and efficiently: Terry Teskey, our excellent copy-editor, Gordon Mance, our very fine proofreader, and Pierre Joyal, who helpfully compiled the index. Marketing manager Cheryl Noseworthy and her colleagues in sales and marketing brought the book from manuscript to market with insight and creativity.

Special thanks goes to Lena Saleh, who helped with careful and insightful editing towards the end of the drafting phase, and to the Faculty of Public Affairs at Carleton University for a research productivity bursary that helped bring the project to completion. Two external reviewers provided helpful feedback at various stages.

Most of all, we'd both like to thank the many contributors who gave of their time and wisdom to share their scholarly and ethical takes on an issue that continues to breed suffering over there and polarization over here. We hope this book contributes to justice and understanding.

—Aaron J. Hahn Tapper and Mira Sucharov

Introduction

The Israeli–Palestinian conflict is all too often taught and studied through an informational and explanatory lens: what happened and why? Although the reasons behind this approach are sound, it is equally important to examine ways in which the what, how, and why behind this seemingly intractable conflict can—and will—lead to its ultimate end. By examining the Israeli-Palestinian relationship through the lens of social justice, an interdisciplinary perspective that places concepts such as rights, justice, and oppression at the forefront, this book aims to de-exceptionalize this ostensibly exceptional conflict, empowering readers to understand ways to end the suffering and injustice that plague those living in Israel/Palestine and beyond.

Before going any further, however, it is critical to lay out just what we mean by "social justice," or, in this specific case, "social justice education." One common misconception is that social justice education is akin to social diversity education. The latter idea, though valuable, actually is an approach focusing on an appreciation of social differences. In contrast, social justice education takes social diversity and goes much deeper, focusing instead on understanding the social and power dynamics that result in some groups having privilege, status, and access while other groups are disadvantaged, oppressed, and denied access. Additionally, it commonly pays attention to ways to eliminate oppression (Griffin, 2007).

The Book's Primary Goal

The primary goal of this book is to offer a more nuanced and sustained discussion of some of the sensitive, controversial, and contested issues that often plague discussions around Israel/Palestine. Although we recognize that many have sought to metaphorically barricade their conversations against the seeping in of politics and activism (despite the fact that, by definition, this is not possible), and we ourselves have experienced that impetus at certain times, we aim to counter an avoidance approach. This is especially germane now, in the age of social media, where these debates are omnipresent. Put another way, this book endeavors to help readers navigate these waters, offering tools to serve critical enquiry regarding some of the more vexing issues of this conflict. At the end of the day, we want readers to question answers more than answer questions.

The Book's Structure: Foundational and Contemporary Debates

The chapters of this book contain a series of complex and topical debates helping readers make sense of some of the most foundational and contemporary ideas around the politics of the Israeli-Palestinian conflict. Each chapter considers one topic, represented by two or three essays offered in conversation with one another. Together, these essays advance different perspectives; in some cases they are complementary and in others they are oppositional. The eight chapters are each introduced by a short framing essay, with the first four covering various foundational issues and the last four addressing more contemporary themes.

Foundational Debates. Chapter 1, "Narratives," with essays by George E. Bisharat, Alan Dowty, and Samia Shoman, presents various scholarly and activist approaches to the interpretation of narratives in the context of Israel/Palestine. Is there a difference between communal narratives, facts, and truth? If so, what is it? Are monolithic group narratives more analytically useful, or should we take care to uncover differences within each community? Do certain narratives about the conflict serve to highlight particular worldviews and subsequent policy options, thus foreclosing other possibilities?

Chapter 2, "Self-determination," with essays by Brent E. Sasley, Ran Greenstein, and Thea Renda Abu El-Haj, assesses the concept of self-determination in the case of Jewish Israelis and Palestinians. Does self-determination necessarily mean state sovereignty? Can Israel's desire to maintain a Jewish demographic majority be justified according to contemporary international norms? What should be the role of Palestinian refugees in assessing just outcomes? Is the conflict about rights for the people currently living in Israel/Palestine, or should those who live outside the land also be taken into account? Is territorial compromise the most suitable way to address the demands of self-determination?

Chapter 3, "Settler Colonialism," addresses the debate over settler colonialism as an appropriate framework for interpreting the history of Israel/Palestine. An essay by Sam Fleischacker and a second by As'ad Ghanem and Tariq Khateeb consider whether the settler-colonial framework is the best model for understanding Israel/Palestine or whether the competing nationalisms paradigm is better. Preferencing one analytical model over another means that one category is better suited than another for historical and contemporary comparison. Which model one adopts also guides analysts and officials towards certain policy inferences regarding what is most appropriate and what is most just.

Chapter 4, "International Law," tackles an array of international legal issues, including the use of force as laid out in international humanitarian law, the legality of the occupation and of the West Bank settlements, and religious rights in Jerusalem. Three essays, by Michael Lynk, Lisa Hajjar, and Miriam F. Elman, lay out particular legal arguments for assessing these issues, as well as the status of the occupation and the nature of the sporadic Israel-Hamas conflicts.

Contemporary Debates. Chapter 5, "Refugees and Displacement," begins the contemporary debates section, with three essays on the topic of displacement and dispossession. Roula El-Rifai describes the role of third-party countries (in her case, Canada) in facilitating Israeli-Palestinian negotiations on the Palestinian refugee issue; Shayna Zamkanei traces the debate over possible restitution for the Jewish refugees who were displaced from Arab-majority countries from the 1940s onwards; and Safa Aburabia turns the lens on the Palestinian Bedouin citizens of Israel, showing how the legacy of dispossession since the *Nakba*—meaning catastrophe, this term is used to signify the exile of Palestinians from their land that occurred between 1947–49—has continued through current state planning policies, and has shaped the ways that Bedouin communities have resisted.

Chapter 6, "Apartheid," addresses the debate over whether the apartheid label, which is used increasingly in Palestine solidarity activist circles, is an appropriate way to describe Israel's military occupation of the West Bank and Gaza. With Oren Kroll-Zeldin presenting one essay and Zeina M. Barakat and Mohammed S. Dajani Daoudi another, each puts forth an argument for why the label is or is not applicable to Israel/Palestine.

Chapter 7, "Intersectional Alliances," looks at how the conflict has been exported globally, how marginalized groups have sought out solidarity with one another, and how the concept of intersectionality, including overlapping oppressions, has played a role in the politics of Israel/Palestine. Joey Ayoub traces ways that African American activists have formed transnational alliances with Palestinians; Aziza Khazzoom examines the possibility of cooperation and solidarity between Mizrahim (Jews of Middle Eastern and North African descent) and Palestinians in Israel/Palestine; and Yousef Munayyer describes the evolving US-Israel relationship, suggesting that Israel is coming to be perceived less as part of the liberal and democratic order, and more as a representative of authoritarianism and ethnocracy.

Chapter 8, "BDS (Boycott, Divestment, and Sanctions)," comprises three essays by Tom Pessah, Rachel Fish, and Amjad Iraqi. Each lays out a case either for or against BDS as a set of tactics, considering sub-issues such as attempts in the US, Israel, and elsewhere to legislate against BDS; what the implications of these attempts are for justice in the region; whether or not BDS is an anti-Semitic movement; and if a generalized academic culture has contributed to what staunch advocates of Israel see as the BDS movement's unfair targeting of Israel.

As these 22 essays demonstrate, assessing the conflict in Israel/Palestine in the context of social justice is not a straightforward task. While each author has clear ideas about the best route towards justice, sometimes the standards of measurement differ. Authors disagree on specific elements such as the interpretation of law, how to weigh individual human rights in the context of collective identity, which academic and activist categories best apply, and what the role of territorial compromise should be. Through each chapter, readers will be able to ascertain an array of convergences and divergences regarding these eight foundational and contemporary topics, and thus be able to discern the core arguments at play. Ideally, this will help readers to determine the strengths and weaknesses of each position, deepening their understanding of the history and politics of Israel/Palestine. Ultimately, we hope that this book will help readers to gain a deeper understanding of the relationship between Israelis and Palestinians in order to see a path forward—towards justice for all.

Reference

Griffin, P. (2007). "Oppression Lecture Slide Show," Teaching for Diversity and Social Justice: An Introduction to Theoretical Concepts and Vocabulary. In M. Adams, L.A. Bell, & P. Griffin (eds), *Teaching for Diversity and Social Justice* (2nd ed.) New York, NY: Routledge.

the best route towards justice sometimes is confronted w/ the standards of measurement that differ.

PART I

Foundational Debates

one
Narratives

One of the ways a community's collective memory survives—especially over the course of numerous generations—is through the telling and retelling of a master narrative (or narratives), what scholar Ilana Pardes (2002) calls a "national biography." Narratives capture a set of experiences that the members of a community—including their ancestors—are said to have undergone together. Virtually all communities engage in this.

In fact, all of us are storytellers—narrators—in our own right. As individuals, we engage in this activity during our daily routines, whether at work, school, or someplace else. We do it when meeting someone for the first time, such as on a date or when applying for a job. In all of these moments we recycle stories—scripts—about who we are. Sometimes, we even make things up (Hahn Tapper, 2016, pp. 13–14).

We do this as individuals through basic statements we make about ourselves: I go to primary school. I am a college student. I bag groceries. I am a mechanic. I live on the street. I am an exciting person and you should spend more time with me. I am a skilled laborer and you should hire me. We also do this as larger groups, even societies: Our nation fights for freedom and protects us. Our state only protects some of us. Our country is built on a commitment to life, liberty, and the pursuit of happiness. Along the way, we edit these personal and communal narratives, adding pieces here, subtracting pieces there. The script is never fixed. Through this process, individual and group identities are created and re-created. Narratives, and the identities they help construct, also shape boundaries often tied to political action (Hahn Tapper, 2016, pp. 13–14; Sucharov, 2005).

As in all intercommunal conflicts, narratives are central to the Israeli–Palestinian conflict. Jewish Israelis, Palestinians, scholars, activists, and countless other groups and individuals approach this conflict through the lens of particular perspectives, specific narratives. The topic of communal narratives underpins the first chapter of this book because it arguably plays more of a role in this conflict than any other issue. In fact, the theme of narratives—both how Palestinians and Jewish Israelis understand themselves and how scholars and activists understand them—undergirds every other topic in this book.

The first of the three essays in this chapter, Alan Dowty's "Competing Narratives and Social Justice," argues that the more intense the controversy, the more a "competing narratives approach" seems relevant. Dowty contends that in studying conflicts such as the Israeli-Palestinian conflict, each group's "real feelings and thoughts" should be laid out for the other. Presenting things using each group's own words allows "the full intensity of the confrontation" to be conveyed, "something that may be diluted in second-hand accounts." But, he says, we must go further. We need to look not just at the competing dominant narratives between Jewish Israelis and Palestinians, but also at the way dominant voices of one group use extremist voices of the other as validation (e.g., dominant Palestinian narratives citing Jewish Israeli extremists as the "real face" of the Jewish enemy). There are also other competing subnarratives within the Jewish Israeli and Palestinian communities.

The second essay, George E. Bisharat's "Six Useful Pasts," begins by remarking that the most common narrative regarding Israel/Palestine "is deeply pessimistic, emphasizing the conflictual aspects of Jewish-Palestinian Arab relations." This pessimism, he contends, has locked most of us into the belief that the only suitable solution is separation, more commonly known as the "two-state solution." What would happen, he asks, if instead we brought other aspects of history into the foreground? Because the past is not static or monolithic, we need to open our eyes to multiple versions of it, look at the role intentionality plays in choosing what to highlight, and underscore the way power shapes perceptions of it. He goes on to offer six historical periods that suggest that separation is not the only possible outcome. Instead, he argues for the possibility of a single state for all Israelis and all Palestinians.

The third and final essay in this chapter, Samia Shoman's "Beyond Two Sides," maintains that parties in the Israeli-Palestinian conflict will only be able to move towards a resolution if they use a "multiple narratives framework." Beginning by laying out the relationship between facts, perspectives, narratives, and truth, Shoman acknowledges those historical facts that most people can agree on. She then uses two case examples linked to the Israeli-Palestinian conflict to illustrate the way a multiple narratives approach can be embraced: the 1948 war and US president Trump's 2017 recognition of Jerusalem as Israel's capital, accompanied by his decision to move the US embassy from Tel Aviv to Jerusalem.

All three essays discuss the need to reexamine narratives about the Israeli-Palestinian conflict. All three authors challenge the idea that dominant discourses about Israel/Palestine should merely be accepted, passed on, and regurgitated, instead suggesting that reapproaching these narratives—as well as the mundane ways in which they are regenerated—will finally bring the Israeli-Palestinian conflict to a just and peaceful end.

References

Hahn Tapper, A.J. (2016). *Judaisms: A Twenty-First-Century Introduction to Jews and Jewish Identities.* Oakland, CA: University of California Press.

Pardes, I. (2002). "Imagining the Birth of Ancient Israel: National Metaphors in the Bible." In D. Biale (ed.), *Cultures of the Jews: Mediterranean Origins* (vol. 1, pp. 9–41). New York, NY: Schocken.

Sucharov, M.M. (2005). *The International Self: Psychoanalysis and the Search for Israeli-Palestinian Peace.* Albany, NY: State University of New York Press.

Competing Narratives and Social Justice

ALAN DOWTY

Perhaps it is possible to present controversial issues in the classroom using such careful language that neither side could find fault with the formulation. But would such a neutral account convey the primal force of the controversy? Why not embrace controversy, giving the oppositional viewpoints full voice, and allow listeners to sort out the claims and counterclaims for themselves?

Many of the classroom books on the Arab–Israeli conflict adhere to a model of neutrality, at least in form. These books usually offer a detailed account of the conflict over time, focusing on historical facts that are relatively undisputed. Where judgment over interpretations of these events is offered, it is usually in the form of brief descriptions of the positions of both sides. There are also introductory texts that focus more explicitly on broader analytical issues and thus take on questions of social justice, and of right and wrong. These more judgmental accounts often favor the arguments of one side or the other, whether this is acknowledged explicitly or not; only a few of them work on the model of competing narratives presented in full force with all of the resulting contradictions, leaving the reader to make his or her own judgment.

The sharper the controversy, the more the competing narratives approach seems relevant. Encountering competing narratives between and within parties to a conflict is, first of all, a step towards *authenticity*, towards contact with the real feelings and thoughts of the adversaries. The voices of those engaged reflect, we assume, their own preoccupations and perceptions better than the words of an outside observer, however impartial. The narratives of the clashing parties are also more likely to convey the full *intensity* of the confrontation, something that may be diluted in second-hand accounts. It is also likely that focus on the participants' perspectives will serve as a measure of *intractability*, when those most closely involved resist proffered remedies and solutions that seem so logical and uncomplicated from a distance. To take the case at hand, it is very instructive that the idea of a binational state—a solution that would involve a single, democratic political entity encompassing all of what is now Israel, the West Bank, and Gaza, and where all individuals would live and vote equally, and central government powers would be shared between the two sides—is not part of the narrative of any of the core parties on either side (Dowty, 2017, pp. 260–62).

Finally, looking closely at competing narratives reminds us that there is also *variability* within each side of the conflict. There is a "mainstream" narrative: factions and movements within each side typically share common perceptions about the nature of the conflict and social justice issues attached to it. But there are also variants of this narrative that may differ widely, especially on preferred policies and solutions. There are, in other words, competing narratives within, as well as between, the two primary sides.

This chapter reveals, therefore, that a hard look at the competing narratives of parties to a conflict is essential to understanding its roots and the chances of resolution, and may also be the most useful—or even necessary—first step in studying the conflict. Such an approach takes into account the importance of variant narratives on both sides, as emphasized by Samia Shoman's essay (this volume). It does not rule out emphasis on positive narratives of past conciliation, as put forward by George E. Bisharat's essay (this volume). Instead it puts such "useful pasts" in perspective along with other elements of historical relationships. Finally, it does not negate the necessary role of critical analysis of the claims made by conflicting parties, once a fair-minded understanding of their narratives is established.

With all of this in mind, how does this approach apply to Jewish/Israeli and Arab/Palestinian perspectives in relation to the Israeli-Palestinian conflict?

The Historical Dimension

Both Israeli and Palestinian dominant narratives employ a historical perspective measured in millennia. Though the immediate conflict began only at the end of the nineteenth century, their respective narratives should be understood within a broad historical sweep.

Jewish history, rooted in the Hebrew Bible, goes back some 4,000 years to the patriarch Abraham. For much of this time, its center was the Holy Land (also called the Land of Israel or *Eretz Yisrael*). As many Jews see their history, the Jewish role in bringing monotheism to the world was at the center of their survival as a people. The themes of exile from and return to the Land of Israel are embedded in biblical history and Jewish consciousness, well before the dispersion that took place under Roman rule in the first two centuries CE. Centers of Jewish life shifted from Mesopotamia to Spain to eastern Europe. During this long history, the idea of a "Return to Zion" remained alive, giving rise sporadically to movements towards that goal.

Persecution of Jews as a minority was a constant thread in this history. When a new vicious anti-Semitism erupted in 1881 in Tsarist Russia, home to roughly half the world's Jews, the response was similar to that in the past: four million Russian Jews fled the region. A small number of them, perhaps 2 per cent, fled to the Palestinian provinces of the Ottoman Empire. Influenced by the currents of nationalism and the nation-state model then sweeping Europe, these settlers concluded that the only solution to the age-old problem of anti-Semitism was the establishment of a Jewish national home or state. As for possible conflict with the existing population, the prevailing view among the Jewish settlers was that they would bring the benefits of modern civilization to the Arab inhabitants *as individuals*, but that there were no Arab/Palestinian people with a national claim to the territory. This perception reflected the absence of an Arab nationalist movement, which did not become a significant force until shortly before World War I.

This narrative was reinforced during the first half of the twentieth century by waves of Jewish refugees fleeing persecution, primarily from Russia, Poland, and Germany. It culminated in the Holocaust, the killing of one-third of the Jewish people, creating (in many Jewish eyes) a compelling humanitarian case for a Jewish state. The Holocaust essentially ended the debate among Jews over the need for a Jewish place of safety. It also brought about a surge of support from the United States and western European nations that had failed to prevent the Holocaust. The founding of Israel, only three years after the end of World War II, made this compressed period one of the most dramatic and fateful in Jewish history. Jews, in summary, saw themselves as a persecuted people asserting their right to equal standing among nations by a return to their historic homeland.

The Arabs are also heirs to a long history, going back to the ninth century BCE. But it was the rise of Islam in the seventh century CE that made the Arabic language and civilization one of the major actors on the world stage. For several centuries Arabs, at the core of the Islamic world, experienced a Golden Age as Europe passed through the Dark Ages. This period also gave rise to a bitter history of conflict between the Christian West and the Muslim East, marked by the Crusades (eleventh to thirteenth centuries CE), which were seen by most Arabs as a sustained assault by barbarians on the more advanced Islamic civilization. When a resurgent Europe began successfully penetrating and subjugating the Middle East in the nineteenth and twentieth centuries, Arabs and other Muslims viewed this as intrusion by an alien civilization.

By the early twentieth century, Arabs in the Palestinian areas of the Ottoman Empire were beginning to develop a distinct identity and a common resistance to the Jewish settlers who began arriving in the 1880s. They tended to see the Zionist newcomers as part of the general wave of European colonialism that penetrated most of the Middle East in the late nineteenth and early twentieth centuries. The Jewish settlers, coming primarily from Russia, were seen as Europeans, and their presence was seen as part of the overall threat to the Arab and Muslim world from the West (Dowty, 2019).

As Arabs saw it, the British imposed their Mandate on Palestine under the humiliating premise that Arabs were not capable of self-government, and furthered the growth of the Jewish presence against the will of the Arab majority, thus laying the groundwork for establishment of a foreign entity in the heart of the Arab world. They explained the defeat of Arab forces by the new State of Israel in 1948–49 as a result of the international (mainly Western) support for Zionism as well as the corruption and ineffectiveness of Arab governments in the fight against Western imperialist forces. Palestinians, in short, saw themselves as an indigenous people fighting against illegitimate colonial intruders representing an alien and unwelcome civilization.

The Claims of Justice

With such dominant historical perspectives, it is hardly surprising that narratives of the two sides clash fundamentally on claims of national rights and just solutions. Jewish claims emphasize a unique historic tie to the land, extending over more than three millennia. This link has been widely recognized by international institutions and national governments. In the near future Israel will be home to more than half the world's Jews, fulfilling its restoration as the center of Jewish life.

But should ancient history be a guideline for modern territorial arrangements? The mainstream Jewish narrative maintains that there is no statute of limitations on rectifying a historic injustice—in this case, the original dispersion of Jews from their homeland. It was historic circumstances, not a lack of yearning or expiration of just claims, that delayed this restoration until the last century. Other peoples have returned to their homelands after generations or centuries; is the Jewish claim weaker simply because it is more ancient?

The mainstream Palestinian narrative rests on the fact that Palestinians were the indigenous population when the first Zionists arrived. Had they possessed control of their own destiny—the right of self-determination— they would surely have blocked Jewish immigration. In today's world, forced demographic change, sometimes termed "ethnic cleansing," is universally condemned. Palestine had been predominantly Muslim in religion, and almost entirely Arab in language and culture, for many centuries.

Only the onslaught of Western imperialism, according to this narrative, created the conditions under which Zionist settlers could gain a foothold, and eventually displace the existing culture and population. Just as other peoples have liberated themselves from colonial rule elsewhere in the world, Palestinians feel that they have a natural right to fight for basic human rights in their own homeland.

These two mainstream narratives seem to exist in total isolation from each other. It is easy to imagine people, in good faith, being persuaded of the justice of either narrative—especially if they have not been exposed to the other. It is natural to suppose that if one side is right, the other must be wrong. But reality does not always provide such simple solutions. Tragedy, it has been said, is in fact the clash of right with right—though it is useful to be reminded, as Bisharat's essay (this volume) points out, that narratives contain both conciliatory and conflictual elements.

One of the striking aspects of these two mainstream narratives, each examined in its own terms, is that both sides have legitimate reason to think of themselves as victims. Jewish history is a history of persecution, culminating in what many consider to be the worst genocide in modern human history. Although this persecution was not perpetrated by Muslims or Arabs, there is a tendency to see Arab attacks of today as a continuation of historic hatred of Jews. For Palestinians, their very identity centers on their suffering as a people, mainly at the hands of Jews. For both, the very real grievances from past suffering inevitably color their attitudes towards remission and reconciliation.

In any face-to-face conflict, victims often see the other side only as the victimizer. They are not conditioned to consider how their own actions may, in fact, be creating new victims. There is a sense that their suffering frees them from legal and moral constraints and justifies any action taken to end that suffering. This creates a near-perfect formula for perpetuating a conflict long after initial grievances have faded away.

Moderates and Extremists

Once the basic mainstream narratives are identified, it is important to note that there is in fact a spectrum of narratives on either side. The discussion above identifies common threads to the dominant positions taken by Jewish Israelis on the one hand and Palestinians on the other, but there are variant narratives on both sides. For the most part, this divergence deals less with how the other side is perceived than with the question of what policies and actions should be adopted.

The Jewish Zionist movement was divided, almost from its earliest days, between those who advocated an integrationist position—actively taking on the Arabs as partners—and those who advocated separatism on grounds that the new Jewish community in Palestine should develop without dependence on the existing population. Intermediate positions called for cooperation with Arabs based on liberal institutions or on socialist programs. Common to all of these variants was, of course, the assumption that in the end the Arab community would have to accept the presence of a Jewish-majority society to which they would have to adjust, willingly or not. The competing narratives in Israel today, vociferously debating such controversial issues as the future of West Bank Jewish settlements, can be traced back to these early divisions between different Zionist camps.

Palestinians were also divided in their approach to Zionism and the new Jewish settlements. As early as 1899, the Mufti of Jerusalem, Muhammad Tahir al-Husayni, advocated the use of violence against Jewish settlers in order to force them out (Mandel, 1976, p. 41). During the British Mandate period (1922–48) there were fierce arguments among Palestinians over military versus nonmilitary means of opposing the project of a Jewish national home, culminating in a full-scale uprising inspired by another mufti, Haj Amin al-Husayni (Muhammad Tahir's son). Following the *Nakba* (disaster) of 1948–49, Palestinians organized themselves into a variety of newly structured movements representing different ideological and strategic positions, most of them only loosely unified by the early 1970s under the umbrella organization of the Palestine Liberation Organization (PLO). Finally, beginning in the 1980s, new radical Islamist movements—primarily Hamas—challenged the secular basis of existing Palestinian groups and, on religious grounds, rejected any solution to the conflict that included formal recognition of Israel. Hamas rejectionism was essentially a return to those earlier versions of the Palestinian narrative that had refused to negotiate on the basis of recognition of Israel and coexistence with the Jewish state that had emerged in 1948.

By 1993, the PLO leadership had agreed to mutual recognition, leading to the Oslo peace process. Though Israelis and PLO representatives continued to cast doubt on the other side's genuine devotion to a two-state solution, this marked the first time in the history of the conflict that mainstream positions among accredited leaders overlapped sufficiently to make a final resolution seem attainable.

But in this focus on dominant and variant narratives, what is the place of the extremists on both sides? If we define extremism as the belief that one's own cause is so righteous that it justifies any means, no matter how violent or immoral, it is clear that extremists have played a major role in the course of the conflict. (Consider, for example, the assassination of Yitzhak Rabin or the 1972 Munich massacre.) By definition, extremists part ways with the mainstream narrative of their own public, but they cannot be left out of the picture.

What makes best sense, perhaps, is to see extremists as an important element in the dominant narrative *of the other side*. Both sides tend to see the extremists of the other side as representatives of the "real face" of the enemy, commonly magnifying their overall importance in this process. To the extent that the extremists on the other side are prominent—Hamas suicide bombers on one side, violent West Bank Jewish settlers on the other—each validates the more uncompromising aspects of one's own narrative. It is common for both sides to minimize the importance of extremists among their own ranks, claiming (sometimes accurately) that their role is marginal. But by the same token, these extremists, whatever their real importance, play a disproportionate role in the perceptions of the other side.

Is Judgment Possible?

At this point it is reasonable to ask whether a focus on narratives does not leave us without any means of deciding between wildly conflicting claims. If all narratives are valid as expressions of deeply held convictions, then how can anyone judge one way or another? The best answer, perhaps, is to see the analysis as a matter of stages. The first stage is to understand the parties to the conflict as they see themselves, both as a collective and in terms of internal differences. In doing this, we, as observers, strive to appreciate the authenticity, intensity, intractability, and variability of the narratives that guide those most intimately involved in the conflict. We try to encompass the complexity of the analytic and ethical issues involved, and to rid ourselves of simplistic notions that make sense only when one is far removed from the actual "field of battle."

Once we have done this, it is then legitimate and even essential to look for tools to analyze and critique the narratives examined. Competing narratives do not involve only different subjective points of view, which may be neither right nor wrong. They also involve disputes over basic facts, where objective judgment can be brought to bear. It is good to sow confusion in the minds of those who come with fixed ideas that are not rooted in close observation by presenting them with contrary ideas and claims that they had not yet considered. But confusion is not an end in itself; it needs to be followed by demonstration of the role that impartial critical analysis can play in examining the claims of both sides.

A ready case in point is the creation of the Palestinian refugee issue in 1948–49. Since that time, widely conflicting numbers have been put forth; a student left with such contradictions would understandably be at a loss. But we have historians, such as Benny Morris (1988), whose primary research has sought to narrow the range of debate over basic facts. That this work has been criticized by partisans of both sides testifies to its relatively nonpartisan nature.

The Israeli-Palestinian conflict will not be resolved by agreement over historical rights or claims of victimhood. But it seems clear that the point of departure should be an understanding of the parties to the conflict, or, in common terms, "where they are coming from." Only in this way can we understand the complexity of real-world clashes of right against right, and begin to look for solutions that will be built on historical legacies and are mindful of the subjective realities of the adversaries.

Alan Dowty is a professor emeritus of political science at the University of Notre Dame, where he has been based since 1975. He is a graduate of Shimer College and the University of Chicago, where he received his PhD in 1963. In 1963–75 he was on the faculty of the Hebrew University in Jerusalem, where he served as executive director of the Leonard David Institute for International Relations and as chair of the Department of International Relations. From 2003 to 2006 he was the first Kahanoff Chair Professor of Israel Studies at the University of Calgary, in Canada, and from 2005 to 2007 he was president of the Association for Israel Studies. Among his books are *The Jewish State: A Century Later* (University of California Press, 1998, 2001) and *Israel/Palestine* (4th ed., 2017). In 2017 he received the annual Lifetime Achievement Award in Israel Studies from the Association for Israel Studies and the Israel Institute.

References

Dowty, A. (2017). *Israel/Palestine* (4th ed.). Cambridge, UK: Polity.

Dowty, A. (2019). *Arabs and Jews in Ottoman Palestine: Two Worlds Collide*. Bloomington, IN: Indiana University Press.

Mandel, N.J. (1976). *The Arabs and Zionism before World War I*. Berkeley, CA: University of California Press.

Morris, B. (1988). *The Birth of the Palestinian Refugee Problem Revisited*. Cambridge, UK: Cambridge University Press.

Six Useful Pasts

GEORGE E. BISHARAT

Many believe that our past serves to structure, if not wholly determine, our present. Were we asked to explain the current condition of our society, for example, the past is the first place we would normally look. We would isolate particular events and identify historical forces that have brought us to our current state. We might point to specific pivotal moments where, had things gone differently, we might have taken a different turn but, considering what in fact happened, were impelled inevitably to where we find ourselves. Frequently our sense of possibility for the future is constrained, if not defined, by our senses of the past and the present.

The version of the past that is most often remembered when it comes to Israel/Palestine is deeply pessimistic, emphasizing the conflictual aspects of Jewish-Palestinian Arab relations. The subtext is that the cause of this conflict lies in the essential beings of the two peoples who have been locked in a hateful blood feud for centuries. The response of many has been to assume that whatever has been will continue to be; that nothing can effectively be done to end endemic bloodshed and strife, and thus nothing is, in fact, done to move towards resolution.

I challenge this sense of the past and seek to unchain us from the perception of a past that determines the present and also dictates the future. Instead I argue in favor of *pasts*—plural—that leave space for both contingency and human agency—more specifically, our agency. Remembering different pasts is a key step in imagining different futures because doing so helps us challenge our assumptions about the inevitability of the present and shakes our sense that observed realities express or reflect eternal verities. Hope, for those of us not content with current realities in Israel/Palestine, lies in disrupting an image of the past that imprisons and limits our imaginations and liberating ourselves to instead "remember the future."

Let me commence with some propositions about how we commonly think about the past.

First, there is no "Past," as such, with a capital "P." By this I do not mean that there is no objectively ascertainable past nor any reason to privilege one narrative (a construction of the past by a conscious being) over another. Indeed, it is both possible and necessary to differentiate between truthful and accurate renditions of the past and untruthful and even mendacious versions.

For example, it was commonly claimed after the Palestinian *Nakba* (disaster) that the leaders of the Arab armies that intervened in the fighting in Palestine ignited by the UN Partition Plan for Palestine in 1947 had ordered, via radio broadcasts, that Palestinian civilians flee to facilitate their military operations against the forces of the nascent Israeli state. This was part of an official Israeli propaganda campaign that obscured Israel's expulsions of Palestinian refugees and attempted to shift blame to the Arab states and to diminish Israel's moral responsibility to accept the right of Palestinian refugees to return to their homes.

This narrative was false. Painstaking examination by Erskine Childers (1973) of the transcripts of radio broadcasts in the region, monitored and recorded by the BBC, revealed that Arab leaders, in fact, pleaded with Palestinian civilians to remain in their homes. While I agree with Alan Dowty (this volume) that understanding different narratives of parties to a conflict can be a step towards resolution, and with Samia Shoman (this volume) that ignoring the respective "truths" of another can perpetuate conflict, to me it is imperative that such false narratives be debunked and discarded. The persistence of false narratives is a hindrance to understanding and hampers the achievement of peaceful reconciliation.

Second, while there may be no "past" as such, there are multiple pasts—a nearly infinite number of them. Imagine, for a moment, all of the events that were occurring at 12:37 p.m. on 22 July 1946, when the militant right-wing Zionist Irgun bombed the King David Hotel in Jerusalem, killing ninety-one people. Several blocks away, my father's family (including my uncles Emile and George, who had left the King David Hotel around 12:10 p.m. that same day) were sitting down to lunch. Elsewhere in the city, other individuals were drinking coffee, reading the newspaper, doing laundry, gossiping with neighbors, picking fruit—all of the multitude of things that people did in the normal course of a day in Palestine at that time. All of these events are part of the past, as they actually occurred, and their truth, in many cases, can be verified.

Third, all pasts are pasts for something. Behind each past is an intentionality that guides our selection of what events are memorable. It is not by mistake that the bombing of the King David Hotel has been recorded in many history books, while my family's lunch that July day was not, even though each actually occurred and was equally part of the past. All such choices are made with a purpose, whether spoken or unspoken. Were our purpose, for example, to document Palestinian cuisine, my family's lunch on 22 July 1946 would have far more relevance than the explosion that occurred that same day a few kilometers from their home.

Fourth, the frequent effect of a rendition of the past is to both naturalize the present and provide guidance for future conduct. The present comes to be seen as the inevitable consequence of the past, especially as the product of impersonal, superhuman forces in which none of us truly had much choice. Why? Because our choices are human, fallible, and contestable, while the "march of history," as it is sometimes called, is no more contestable than the weather. It simply *is*. The telling of a particular past, therefore, has the capacity to defuse resistance, particularly from its victims. Why resist something over which, like a hurricane or earthquake, humans exercise no control?

A telling of the past also implies a logical, if not mandatory, next step. Renowned scholar Edward Said (1995), in describing Israel's policies towards the city of Jerusalem, referred to this as a process of projection in which establishing acceptance of a vision of the city and its history as the eternal capital of the Jewish people was a vital precedent to the actual physical transformation of the city to match that vision.

As this example demonstrates, many pasts—let us call them "public pasts"—are deployed not to command individual behaviors, but to legitimate broad public actions and policies taken by states and their groups, which have fateful impacts on others.

This differentiates pasts from, for example, faith. Everyone has the right to his or her private belief. But pasts, when elevated to public status and put to the service of some against others, have winners and losers. That is why we cannot indulge false or misleading pasts, such as the aforementioned fabrication regarding Arab radio broadcasts in 1948. Hundreds of thousands of Palestinians were denied their right to return to their homes on the strength of the false claim that Arab leaders caused their flight.

However, our confidence that the past provides wise guidance for the future is often misplaced. We may think we know, by a linearly presented sequence of facts, why certain events transpired. But in selecting those facts we simultaneously obscure others, not only the many other events that transpired at the same time and may well have exercised unrecognized influences, but also contingencies: what almost happened, or what very well could have happened, that would have led to a changed course of history. What if, for example, British private Henry Tandey had executed Adolph Hitler in their claimed encounter on a World War I battlefield instead of sparing him? While understanding historical causation is a worthy goal, we must be cautious not to trust our abilities too much in this area.

Fifth and finally, which pasts are consistently recorded is considerably shaped by power. As Nigerian writer Chimamanda Ngozi Adichie (2009) stated regarding "stories" (which are essentially the same as a telling of the past or narratives): "How they are told, who tells them, when they are told, how many stories are told, are really dependent on power." There are, of course, many forms of power (financial, military, political, moral), but power is decisive in elevating some pasts to canonical status while erasing others.

Political Zionism (the nineteenth-century European-based movement to create a Jewish state) has, virtually since its inception, enjoyed a decisive power differential in communicating its narratives in the West. Think back now to the widely accepted past of Israeli-Palestinian relations, that which emphasizes conflict and violence: this is exactly the past one would tell to support the Israeli government's oppressive policies towards Palestinians and to dissuade external actors from intervening to transform current dynamics in the region. After all, if Palestinians were irrevocably hostile towards and bent on annihilating Israeli Jews, who could blame the Israeli government from doing whatever it took to oppose that terrible outcome? In the face of this implacable mutual hatred, the only imaginable future other than more of the same would be one of separation.

But what if our project were different? What if our starting point were recognition that Israeli Jews and Palestinian Arabs will never be truly separated, as they are now irrevocably intermingled in both Israel and the Occupied Palestinian Territories? Only genocide or ethnic cleansing could bring about such a separation, and neither, despite the fears of both sides, seems likely. No political force is capable of uprooting approximately 600,000 Israeli settlers (and counting) from the West Bank (including East Jerusalem), and no Palestinian state with meaningful sovereignty can be established in the remaining land.

Like it or not, Israel has defeated the drive for a separate Palestinian state. Meanwhile, all indications are that the *de facto* single-state system that has functioned since 1967 will continue to do so indefinitely. Yet it is both morally unacceptable and ultimately threatening to both peoples for the current power relations—in which Israeli Jews control virtually everything and Palestinian Arabs nothing—to continue.

What if we acknowledged a future of coexistence in a single state but instead insisted that the terms be altered from ethnic privilege to equal rights? Rather than chasing the mirage of the two-state solution—something the international community has done in vain for nearly three decades—would a single state based on equal rights not provide a framework for maximizing rights for the greatest number of Israeli Jews and Palestinian Arabs (Bisharat, 2008)? Are there pasts that would be useful to recall that would support this kind of future of coexistence and mutual respect? I think the answer is yes.

Let me suggest six useful pasts—useful in relation to this emancipatory project—while identifying elements from each that could support an alternative future based on mutual dignity and accord.

Muslim-Jewish Relations in Medieval Andalusia

As chronicled by Maria Rosa Menocal (2002) in *Ornament of the World*, eighth-century Andalusia witnessed an unprecedented flowering of arts, culture, philosophy, and the sciences under the Muslim Umayyad dynasty—a brilliant civilization enabled by genuine religious tolerance among Muslims, Christians, and Jews. Their achievements suggest the promise of cultural synergy and the potential fruits of mutual tolerance. For the many Israeli Jews and Palestinian Arabs who might wish simply to be rid of one another, medieval Andalusia is a healthy reminder that a future together can be greater than one apart.

Arab-Jewish Relations in Ottoman Palestine

If the example of Muslim-Jewish relations in medieval Andalusia seems too distant, Arab-Jewish relations in Ottoman Palestine are less so, and thus should be of particular interest in our search for useful pasts. Indeed, there are at least two positive elements we can glean from this period.

First is the notion of "civic Ottomanism" that emerged in the early twentieth century, expressed in the words of young Jewish lawyer Shlomo Yellin: "In the Ottoman Empire the different peoples are equal to one another and it is not lawful to divide according to race; the Turkish, Arab, Armenian, and Jewish elements have mixed one with the other, and all of them are connected together, molded into one shape for the holy *vatan*" (quoted in Campos, 2011, p. 2). In the relatively recent past, both Jews and Arabs living in Palestine enjoyed a form of citizenship that delinked ethnicity and rights, and instead promoted a supranational sense of belonging and identity. That same conceptual move may be necessary in the future if Jews and Arabs—Jewish Israelis and Palestinian Arabs—are to live together in a regime of equal rights.

Second, the Ottoman millet system afforded religious communities considerable internal communal autonomy, modeling the possibility of living a Jewish or Christian or Muslim life in Palestine without monopolizing sovereignty.

Arab-Jewish Relations in the Arab World Prior to 1948

Before Israel's establishment in 1948, Jewish communities thrived in Arab-majority countries from Morocco to Iraq. Most were culturally assimilated, speaking Arabic and eating foods nearly indistinguishable from those of their Christian and Muslim Arab neighbors. While typically excluded from governing authority, and occasionally victims of either official or popular persecution, most Arab Jews—a term commonly used by Jews pre-1948—saw themselves as citizens of their countries and held every expectation of remaining so (Levy, 2008).

These communities were severely destabilized upon Israel's creation. These Jews became the objects of official and popular suspicion, leading to discriminatory policies and legislation against them by some Arab regimes. Some Arab Jews adopted Zionism, leaving their homes in Arab-majority countries to emigrate to Israel. Communal violence against Jewish communities broke out in a number of Arab-majority countries, forcing many Jews to flee to Israel, Europe, or North America.

While the near demise of most Arab Jewish communities is a dispiriting legacy, their centuries of secure and peaceful existence should not be forgotten. For Palestinians, who might be tempted to see Israeli Jews only as European colonizers, Arab Jews are a reminder of Jewish indigeneity in the Middle East. While bitter memories cannot simply be wiped away, a reservoir of cultural affinities between Arab Jews and Palestinian Arabs remains to be tapped.

Arab-Jewish Relations under the British Mandate

The British Mandate is an important period for two reasons, the first of which is rooted in the prevailing notion of Palestinian citizenship. In this time and place, Jews, Christians, and Muslims were all "Palestinians" by virtue of residing in Palestine, not by virtue of ethno-religious identity. None of these three groups had control of state power, nor did any of them have institutionally based privileges.

Second, living memories of friendship and accord between individual Jews and Palestinian Arabs persist from this period. My grandfather and grandmother, for example, harbored Jewish neighbors in their Jerusalem home during the riots of 1929. As a young man my father acquired his enduring love of Western classical music as a member of a mixed Jewish-Palestinian listening group.

I suspect that many, if not most, Palestinian Arab and Jewish families have similar direct, personal experiences of friendship and kindness between one another from the Mandate era. Differences—in language, cultural style, background, education, and more—are not intrinsically inimical to mutual respect and accord. In the right set of circumstances, Jews and Palestinian Arabs may again appreciate each other for all of their endearing qualities.

Arab-Jewish Relations in Israel/Palestine, 1993–2000

There was a brief interlude following the signing of the Oslo Accords in 1993 and before the unsuccessful final status negotiations at Camp David in 2000—followed only weeks later by the outbreak of the second

Intifada—when significant optimism prevailed among both Palestinians and Jewish Israelis that a genuine and lasting peace was near. Israeli soldiers had withdrawn from most Palestinian population centers in the Occupied Territories and a nascent Palestinian government had begun to take shape. For the first time in decades, Palestinians of the West Bank and Gaza were able to walk the streets of many of their towns and villages without regularly encountering Israeli soldiers.

Calm was never entirely complete, but tensions deflated palpably, as the entire region exhaled a collective sigh of relief with peace seemingly on the horizon. While travel restrictions still barred Palestinians living in the Occupied Territories from traveling across the Green Line, Israelis shopped in Palestinian towns of the West Bank for fresh produce, took their cars for repair in Qalqilya, enjoyed weekend ventures to the Palestinian-operated casino in Jericho, and further exploited a relaxed regional atmosphere to visit Jordan, Turkey, and other Arab- or Muslim-majority countries.

This period demonstrated how quickly tensions between Palestinians and Jewish Israelis could dissipate once immediate fears were abated. For Israeli Jews, it also offered a glimpse of what benefits lie ahead for them once they are no longer seen as oppressors of the Palestinians and gain the regional acceptance that has long eluded them.

White-Black Relations in Post-Apartheid South Africa

Post-apartheid South Africa may seem a strange past to cite in building a future of mutual respect and accord between Israelis and Palestinians. But there is no reason that Palestinians and Israelis need only look at their own pasts. It is also feasible to learn from the pasts of others.

What are the useful takeaways from post–apartheid South Africa? First, that fundamental structural transformations of societies are possible, even where prior institutions have the appearance of permanence. In 1981, few in South Africa predicted that apartheid would end within a decade—and yet it did. Second, the bloodbath that many white South Africans sincerely feared upon the establishment of democratic rule with a black majority did not unfold. The elimination of antidemocratic structures need not, therefore, be accompanied by vengeance, and instead can be managed peacefully.

Reassembling Shards of Pasts into a Future of Peace and Freedom

My point here is not that any of these pasts provide full-blown models for reconciliation between Palestinians and Jewish Israelis. They surely do not. Each of these pasts had (and has) contradictory elements, and I have been deliberately cherry-picking the most positive features of complex realities. Yet this is not different than the unacknowledged cherry-picking that highlights the conflictual elements of Palestinian-Israeli interests. I acknowledge my selections and my reasons for them: to promote the possibility of better future relations between peoples who are destined to live together, like it or not.

Neither is it easy to shed the dominant image of the past as one riddled by violence and conflict. That image is not lacking its truths, and it is, in many ways, compelling. But those of us who share an emancipatory commitment are not without resources. These six useful pasts accentuate values of tolerance, cultural syncretism, and dynamism that are far more in tune with contemporary sensibilities and moral commitments—notwithstanding the recent resurgence of white nationalism in the United States and some parts of Europe. They remind us of other futures—more hopeful, optimistic, and edifying of humanity—and thus unchain our hearts from the shackles of a heartless past.

George E. Bisharat was a public defender in San Francisco before joining the University of California, Hastings, faculty in 1991. Professor Bisharat studied law, anthropology, and Middle East studies at Harvard, and authored a book about Palestinian lawyers working under Israeli military occupation in the West Bank. He writes and speaks frequently on the Middle East, both for academic audiences and for major media sources in the United States and abroad. After taking emeritus status in 2015, Bisharat, as "Big Harp George," has recorded three blues albums that earned award nominations and critical acclaim.

References

Adichie, C.N. (2009). "The Danger of a Single Story." TED Talk. Retrieved from https://www.ted.com/talks/chimamanda_adichie_the_danger_of_a_single_story?language=en

Bisharat, G. (2008). "Maximizing Rights: The One State Solution to the Palestinian-Israeli Conflict." *Global Jurist, 8*(2), 1–36. https://doi.org/10.2202/1934-2640.1266

Campos, M.U. (2011). *Ottoman Brothers: Muslims, Christians, and Jews in Early Twentieth-Century Palestine.* Palo Alto, CA: Stanford University Press.

Childers, E. (1973). *Wordless Wish: From Citizens to Refugees.* Belmont, MA: Association of Arab-American University Graduates.

Levy, L. (2008). "Historicizing the Concept of Arab Jews in the *Mashriq.*" *Jewish Quarterly Review, 98*(4), 452–69. https://doi.org/10.1353/jqr.0.0024

Menocal, R.M. (2002). *The Ornament of the World: How Muslims, Jews, and Christians Created a Culture of Tolerance in Medieval Spain.* New York, NY: Little, Brown.

Said, E. (1995). "The Current Status of Jerusalem." *Jerusalem Quarterly, 45,* 57–72.

Beyond Two Sides

SAMIA SHOMAN

I have spent a great deal of my life ... advocating the rights of the
Palestinian people to national self-determination,
but I have always tried to do that with full attention paid to the
reality of the Jewish people and what they
suffered by way of persecution and genocide.
—*Edward Said, leading Palestinian American intellectual, professor of
literature, Columbia University (American Task Force on Palestine, 2005)*

When Israelis ask me about the Palestinians, I tell them they
live like us, they suffer like us, they laugh and cry like us.
They are just like us, but they suffer more than us.
—*Dr Zvi Bentwich, founder of Israel's first and largest AIDS clinic, member
of Physicians for Human Rights (American Task Force on Palestine, 2005)*

Palestine/Israel, and all it encompasses, is described by scholars and
educators, politicians and civilians, in different ways: a war, an intractable
situation, and, most popularly, a conflict. Yet, deducing the histories of the
parties involved is not a simple task. Although the most common way to
structure what international communities commonly call the Arab- or
Palestinian-Israeli conflict is through a dichotomous lens, as one side versus
another, such an approach does not reflect this conflict's complicated nature,
which is rooted in—and should be taught as—a multiple narrative framework. Such an approach not only allows us to consider multiple narratives
simultaneously, but also creates the space to understand that narratives are
not always developed in opposition nor that there is a singular narrative that
represents all Palestinians and Israelis. Narratives of Palestinians' and Israelis'
common humanity and their willingness and desire to live in peace with
one another, as reflected in the quotes above, are often overshadowed or
silenced by the dominant narrative of Palestinians and Israelis as enemies.
But Palestine/Israel is more than a conflict that pits two peoples against one
another. In fact, until it is understood using a multiple narratives framework,
opportunities for a true and lasting peace will remain elusive. A multi-
perspectival approach creates an opportunity for us to imagine a different
future for Palestinians and Israelis, possibly one entirely untethered from the
notion of *conflict*.

Introduction to a Multiple Narratives Framework

One way to understand a multiple narratives framework is through four in-terrelated concepts: fact, perspective, narrative, and truth. A *fact* is something that has actually occurred. It is known by tangible observation or genuine testimony, and is widely accepted. *Perspective* is a particular attitude towards or way of thinking about something, such as an individual's or a group's point of view. By combining facts with perspectives, which are subjective, individuals or groups create a *narrative*, a story a party believes or tells in order to explain how a set of facts or events are connected to each other. *Truth* is an interpretation of facts based on one's own perspective. Truth is something an individual creates for themself; a belief one holds to be true after considering the narrative(s) one has learned.

One example to help clarify these terms, showing how they build upon one another, is found in the ways different people refer to Palestine/Israel. Some use "Israel" exclusively, others use "Palestine," and some both. For example, imagine a Palestinian woman today who was born in 1942. She can point to a map from 1947 and prior where the region is labeled "Palestine." This is her evidence of the fact that supports her perspective. Even though more recent maps found in many American textbooks (and arguably most countries and organizations in the world) officially recognize the region as Israel, this woman will continue to say she is from Palestine. Her truth, de-veloped through the narrative of her life, is that the land is and always will be Palestine. Now picture someone who today identifies as an Israeli Jew. Born in 1950, they can point to a map where their country, Israel, is located. To this person, though at one point in time Palestine may have existed, it no longer does. Only Israel can be found on this person's map. This is their truth.

The multiple narratives framework supports learning both of these nar-ratives, as well as those of people whose truth is that the region is both Palestine *and* Israel. Instead of seeing these two narratives in opposition to one another—positioning people to have to choose one as right and one as wrong—the multiple narratives approach pushes us to examine experiences more deeply, to see the complexity of life rather than its alleged simplicity, thereby encouraging us to move beyond the all too common dichotomy of Palestine or Israel.

How Truth Is Created

Currently, approximately 6.22 million Palestinians and 6.34 million Jewish Israelis live in Palestine/Israel. These are facts. Within these 12.56 million lives are particular narratives relative to personal and collective experiences. Shaped, in part, by historical facts, these narratives reflect different truths. Generally speaking, societies equate fact with truth. But in this situation, like many others, truth has been produced in relation to the interpretation of facts, most commonly rooted in personalized understandings of reality. Palestinians and Jewish Israelis have often used their truths in place of historical facts; these distinct storylines are used to maintain particular perspectives on history linked to each one's perceived reality. Additionally, there are external stakeholders who have their own truths: Palestinians and Jews living in the diaspora, and others who find themselves in solidarity with one group, enraged by the ongoing situation, or confused about the history altogether. The influence of these groups on the events of the region also moves us beyond a dichotomous conflict.

As Ilan Pappe (2017) writes, "Constructed fallacies about the past and the present in Israel and Palestine hinder us from understanding the origins of the conflict. Meanwhile, the constant manipulation of the relevant facts works against the interests of all those victimized by the ongoing bloodshed and violence" (p. ix). When narratives are monolithic, an individual's truth can also be, using Pappe's language, a constructed fallacy. Stakeholders use such narratives to defend actions that contribute to creating and maintaining the conflict in isolation from other narratives. As Pappe suggests, as long as such fallacies continue to be created and disseminated, historical facts remain hidden. A basic consequence is that stakeholders continue to deny, or feign ignorance about, widely accepted facts, blinding them to the experience of the other or to an openness to accept that more than one truth exists.

If narratives and the truths that develop from them continue to be pitted against one another, then Palestine and Israel will continue to be viewed as a dichotomous conflict, stripped of its nuances and complications and reduced to what Alan Dowty (2017) describes as a "zero-sum game: whatever one side gains comes at the expense of the other (gains and losses thus total zero)" (p. 5).

Considering how truths are formed, and specifically how they are commonly distinct from historical facts, is central to using a multiple narratives framework. If all stakeholders move beyond their own constructed truths, it may be a step towards finding and internalizing cross-communal—and common—historical experiences, and thus a refocus on a shared humanity. Without this, there will be no solution to this conflict.

Understanding and accepting that there are multiple narratives—which in turn have led to varying truths—is imperative. But debating truths in the Palestine/Israel conflict undergirds any possibility for a true and sustainable peace. When truth is considered to be synonymous with fact, and the nuances of experiences and language are not analyzed or contextualized, the historical record becomes distorted. In the case of Palestine/Israel, this has led to the grave consequence we see today: a fractured region physically carved up by a noncontiguous wall that separates more than 12 million people living vastly different lives while holding vastly different truths, with little to no regard of the reality of the other.

Applying a Multiple Narratives Framework

When we apply a multiple narratives approach to two instances in the politics and history of Palestine/Israel—the events of 1948 and US president Trump's 2017 declaration recognizing Jerusalem as Israel's capital and the new home of the US embassy—we see how the Palestinian-Israeli conflict is more than a mere binary. Instead, we learn about several different narratives in which Palestinians and Jews inside and outside of the region share the same truths, as evidenced, for example, in George E. Bisharat's "Six Useful Pasts" (this volume). This is significant since dominant narratives consistently pit Palestinian and Jewish-Israeli truths against one another, creating a scenario where one imagines a victor and loser, a victim and oppressor. Once we are willing to accept that there are more than two sides to this conflict, then the potential for peace will commence.

Applying a Multiple Narratives Framework to 1948: The State of Israel and the Palestinian *Nakba*

It seems appropriate to use 1948 as an anchor to apply this framework as this is when the State of Israel was established and the interrelated Palestinian *Nakba* occurred. If all stakeholders do not acknowledge what happened in 1948, the current status quo will continue. Dowty alludes to this in "Competing Narratives and Social Justice" (this volume) when he describes how the victims often only see the other side as the victimizer. Over decades, as these divergent narratives developed, spread, and became accepted as truth, roadblocks to peace emerged.

One basic fact about 1948, which many if not most agree upon, is that Palestinian villages were destroyed in the making of Israel. *Al-Nakba* began with this erasure and displacement. In *Learning Each Other's Historical Narrative*, Sami Adwan and Dan Bar-On (2003) quote Moshe Dayan, former chief of staff of the Israeli Defense Forces, to describe what happened:

> Jewish villages were built on the remains of Arab villages. You don't even know the names of these Arab villages and I don't blame

you because the geography books no longer exist. It is not only
geography books that no longer exist, but also the Arab villages
themselves disappeared. For Nahalal was established on the site of
Ma'loul, Kibbutz G'vat on the site of Jebbata, Kibbutz Sarid in the
place of Khneifes....There is not one place built in the country that
did not have a former Arab population. (p. 28)

There is a lack of consensus regarding the actual number of villages destroyed, but the majority of historians put the number between 418 and
530. While Jamil Fayez (2005, p. 6) notes that 452 villages were ethnically
cleansed, creating 800,000 refugees, Pappe (2017, p. 64) says, "In a matter
of 7 months, 531 villages were destroyed and eleven urban neighborhoods
emptied." It is well documented that Palestinians were intimidated into
fleeing by Israeli military forces, including episodes such as the April 1948
Deir Yassin massacre, when 254 Palestinian civilians were killed by the militant right-wing Zionist Irgun. Many Israeli military leaders, such as David
Ben-Gurion, Israel's first prime minister, are on historical record supporting the intentional goal to physically move Palestinians: "With compulsory
transfer we would have a vast area for settlement.... I support compulsory
transfer. I don't see anything immoral in it" (Morris, 2001, p. 144). And yet at
the same time, as recently as 2016, Israeli historian Benny Morris contended
in *Haaretz*, "In 1947–1948 there was no prior intention to expel the Arabs,
and during the war there was no policy of expulsion. There are clearly Israel-
hating 'historians' like Ilan Pappé and Walid Khalidi, and perhaps also Daniel
Blatman … who sees the Haganah's Plan Dalet of March 10, 1948, as a
master plan for expelling the Palestinians. It isn't."

While there are multiple narratives, and therefore constructed truths,
about 1948, the fact is that on 14 May 1948 the State of Israel was officially
declared to exist, setting off a series of long-lasting consequences. Jews worldwide were extended a legal birthright to immigrate to Israel, a safe haven
following the Holocaust and the persecution they had faced for centuries
prior. This truth, more commonly known as the "Law of Return," is based in
historical facts. However, even though the notion of a "birthright" is a legal
fact according to the Israeli government, not all people accept that Jews have
this right—or should have this right—by virtue of being Jews.

For Palestinians, this Jewish birthright has come at their expense. For
those Palestinians who became refugees in 1948, their truth is that they have
a birthright guaranteed by their ancestors and the unfulfilled UN Resolution
194—also passed in 1948—which declares that Palestinian refugees wanting
to return to their homes should be allowed to do so at the earliest possible
date. (Those who choose not to return are entitled to compensation for

the loss of or damage to their property.) The Palestinian birthright has a factual base, since it is well documented that at least 750,000 Palestinians lost their homes and land between 1947 and 1949. Since the UN Resolution was passed, the State of Israel has ignored it; concurrently, Jews continue to exercise their birthright and immigrate to Israel while Palestinians are denied this same right, both as laid out in Israeli law.

Today, Palestinians and Jews have multiple narratives about birthright. While each community's dominant narratives may position them as existing in opposition to one another, not all of them are. In fact, when the narratives are analyzed more closely, one can see that often the ones said to be in opposition are actually those internal to the Palestinian and Jewish communities, respectively, as Dowty argues (this volume).

For example, the Palestinian political leadership of Fatah understands the right of return to be potentially negotiable, while Hamas and the Palestinian-American organization Al-Awda ("the return" in Arabic) see it as nonnegotiable. The Israeli government does not support any Palestinian right of return, whereas the International Jewish Anti-Zionist Network does. Such examples reflect how when we move beyond dichotomous narratives, we see Palestinian and Jewish narratives converge. This is one of the places where hope is born.

Although Jews and Palestinians had lived together in relative peace for decades prior to 1948, the events of that year created starkly different realities. Because they were focused on their loss, many Palestinians were unable to internalize what Jews in Europe had experienced during the Holocaust. Similarly, Jews emigrating to Palestine were not cognizant of the losses that Palestinians endured for this newfound Jewish freedom. Meanwhile in Palestine—at the same time—there were communities of Jews and Palestinians that continued to live as neighbors. But this is not a popular fact, since it interrupts the dominant narrative of two enemy populations whose survival is portrayed as mutually exclusive. Bisharat (this volume) supports our remembering this often-ignored narrative as one of the six useful pasts that could help Palestinians and Jews imagine a more hopeful future. If these multiple narratives were more widely taught, the idea of Palestine/Israel as dichotomous would begin to wane.

Another example from 1948 that illustrates why we must learn multiple narratives lies in the explanation for why Palestinians left their villages right before and after Israel was declared a state. The popular narrative among Jewish Israeli leaders is that Palestinians fled their villages willingly at the directive of Arab leaders. According to Pappe (2017), "The official Israeli line, however, has not changed for years: the Palestinians became refugees because their leaders, and the leaders of the Arab world, told them to leave Palestine before the Arab armies invaded and kicked out the Jews, after which they could then return. But there was no such call" (p. 54). Although several historians support this assertion, others do not. Historians like Morris, Pappe, and Khalidi have each created a narrative based on historical facts from 1947–48. Each narrative conveys a varied truth. But if one learns or accepts only one truth, they will have an incomplete and inaccurate picture of history.

Truth, Trump, and Jerusalem

The pattern of truth-making and the consequences it can have were quite evident on 6 December 2017, when United States president Donald Trump recognized Jerusalem as the capital of Israel: "I have determined that it is time to officially recognize Jerusalem as the capital of Israel.... [T]hrough all of these years, presidents representing the United States have declined to officially recognize Jerusalem as Israel's capital." One of many things Trump failed to mention was that no previous president had gone this far largely because it is well documented in political peace negotiations (which various US governmental negotiating teams were usually involved in) that Palestinians and Israelis themselves would decide the status of Jerusalem. The following day, Israeli prime minister Benjamin Netanyahu, validating Trump's truth, said, "Jerusalem has been the capital of the Jewish people for 3,000 years. It has been the capital of [the State of] Israel for nearly 70 years.... Jerusalem has been the focus of our hopes, our dreams, our prayers for 3 millennia. We're profoundly grateful for the president for his courageous and just decision to recognize Jerusalem as the capital of Israel and to prepare for the opening of the US Embassy here" (*Straits Times*, 2017).

Since Trump's Jerusalem declaration, people worldwide have weighed in with their own truths. Palestinian president Mahmoud Abbas reacted by calling Jerusalem the "eternal capital of the State of Palestine" (Al-Jazeera, 2017). Many members of the European Union countered Trump's declaration as well. In a statement published on their official website, the American-based nongovernmental association Jewish Voice for Peace said: "This move is counter to international law and is a clear attempt by Israel and the U.S. to consolidate Israeli annexation of land. This move is reckless, endangering the lives of Palestinians and Israelis on the ground" (2017).

In other words, since there is no international agreement that Jerusalem is the capital of Israel, and thus this is not a widely accepted fact, this declaration reflects Trump's truth (as well as Netanyahu's) above others. To the contrary, on 21 December 2017, 128 countries voted against his declaration in the United Nations, while 35 countries abstained and 9 offered their support.

Examples of additional multiple narratives that have become truths for various people in Palestine/Israel are seemingly endless: the Separation Barrier/Wall in the West Bank is for security and safety, a method of control, or built to expropriate Palestinian land for Israeli settlements; Israeli soldiers are the guardians of security or brutal oppressors, leaving out the Refuseniks, Israeli youth who refuse to serve in the military on moral grounds; Palestinian suicide bombers are murderers, martyrs, or psychologically desperate. As long as there are narratives that are delegitimized by the truths of another, the cycle of misunderstandings, denials, and dichotomies will continue. As narratives of confrontation and violence remain dominant—in contrast to the examples outlined by Bisharat (this volume)—peace will remain, at best, a mere hope.

Need for Multiple Narratives

As mainstream media and education systems continue to perpetuate the idea of a dichotomous conflict, Palestinians, Israelis, and the international community often fail to recognize that there are multiple narratives between and within various stakeholder groups directly involved with the conflict. In the absence of analyses of multiple narratives, widely accepted historical facts have been replaced by reductionist truths, creating and maintaining roadblocks to peace. This essay began with two quotes that illustrate the power of what can happen when Israelis and Palestinians recognize one another's truths: they find their common humanity, thus recognizing their shared right to live in safety and security. This is what will lead to peace. And although Palestinian and Israeli governments are not currently paving the path to peace, this potential remains, whether among Palestinians, Israelis, or another group altogether.

Samia Shoman is a Palestinian-American educator and administrator in the San Francisco Bay Area. Having taught high school social science for sixteen years, she currently serves as the manager of English learner and academic support programs at San Mateo Union high school district. She has lectured in the College of Ethnic Studies—Arab and Muslim Ethnicities and Diaspora Program and the Health Education Department at San Francisco State University, and has taught administrators in training for Cal State East Bay. Over the last ten years, she has facilitated multiple professional learning sessions for educators across the United States on teaching the Palestinian-Israeli conflict through a multiple narratives approach. She received her bachelor's degree in political science and minor in Spanish from UC Davis, a master's in education from San Francisco State University, and a PhD in education, organization, and leadership from the University of San Francisco.

References

Adwan, S., & Bar-On, D. (2003). *Learning Each Other's Historical Narratives*. Beit Jallah, PNA: Peace Research Institute in the Middle East.

Al-Jazeera. (2017). "Mahmoud Abbas Lambasts Trump's Decision on Jerusalem." Retrieved from https://www.aljazeera.com/news/2017/12/mahmoud-abbas-lambasts-trump -decision-jerusalem-171206184655902.html

American Task Force on Palestine. (2005). *Palestine-Israel 101: A Two State Solution*. Washington, DC. Retrieved from https://www.slideshare.net/tranceking/israel -palestine-101

Fayez, J. (2005). *Lest the Civilized World Forget the Colonization of Palestine*. New York, NY: Americans for Middle East Understanding.

Jewish Voice for Peace. (2017, December 6). "JVP Responds to Trump's Announcement of Jerusalem as Israel's Capital and Plan to Move U.S. Embassy" [press release]. Retrieved from https://jewishvoiceforpeace.org/jvp-responds-to-trumps-announcement-of -jerusalem-as-israels-capital-and-plan-to-move-u-s-embassy/

Morris, B. (2001). *Righteous Victims: A History of the Zionist-Arab Conflict, 1881–2001*. New York, NY: Vintage Books.

Morris, B. (2016, 23 October). "'Ethnic Cleansing' and Pro-Arab Propaganda." *Haaretz*. https://www.haaretz.com/opinion/.premium-ethnic-cleansing-and-pro-arab -propaganda-1.5452143

Pappe, I. (2017). *Ten Myths about Israel*. London: Verso Press.

Straits Times. (2017, December 7). "Israel's Benjamin Netanyahu Hails Trump's Jerusalem Declaration as 'Historic.'" Retrieved from https://www.straitstimes.com/world/ middle-east/israels-benjamin-netanyahu-hails-trumps-jerusalem-declaration-as -historic

Trump, D. (2017, December 6). "Statement by President Trump on Jerusalem." The White House. Retrieved from https://www.whitehouse.gov/briefings-statements/ statement-president-trump-jerusalem/

two
Self-Determination

Most ethno-national groups want to be in control of their own affairs in some way, whether through a sovereign state of their own or through another political arrangement that protects their civil and human rights. This chapter brings together three essays that seek to lay out the most just expression of self-determination for Jews and Palestinians in the context of Israel/Palestine. All three authors agree that the current status quo, embodied in the occupation of the West Bank and Gaza, is unjust. They differ—explicitly, in the ways they lay out specific proposed policy outcomes, and implicitly, in their discussion of refugees—as to whether a two-state solution, whereby Israel would retain its current national character and demographic composition and a sovereign Palestinian state would emerge in the West Bank and Gaza, would be the best outcome. Concurrently, they present different ideas as to whether Palestinian refugees should be allowed to return to their pre-1948 lands (meaning the area encompassed by Israel, the West Bank, and Gaza), or only to a nascent Palestinian state (to be established in the territories Israel captured in, and has occupied since, 1967, where Palestinians were living).

The core disagreements come down to whether and to what extent one sees Israel as responsible for the *Nakba*; whether and to what extent enabling a state (i.e., Israel) to maintain its demographic majority and self-defined national character is fair and reasonable; and whether and to what extent one sees the current asymmetry of power between Israelis, who have an independent country, and Palestinians, who do not, as requiring the privileging of certain outcomes over others.

Brent E. Sasley's essay calls for a two-state solution whereby Israel would withdraw from the West Bank, making way for a Palestinian state there and in Gaza. This, he says, would be the most just for the greatest number of people, and would allow for self-determination for both Israelis and Palestinians. Accordingly, Sasley sees Israel's desire to maintain an ethnic majority (while ensuring full rights for Palestinian citizens of Israel, who make up approximately 20 per cent of the population) as a reasonable and understandable expression of Jewish self-determination. He supports his argument by pointing to the "basic legal fact of the contemporary international system, namely, that the state rather than people is the highest form of political authority. These states are divided not just geographically," he writes, "but on the basis of different identity communities. This fits with the demands of both Jews and Palestinians who ... demand their own state in which their own identities are

31

privileged." Sasley's essay represents what's known outside of Israel as a "liberal Zionist" position, and what's represented in Israel by the labor Zionist, or "left Zionist," political parties such as Labor and Meretz.

By contrast, Ran Greenstein lays out what he sees as the fundamental problem with the Zionist project in the context of indigeneity. "Recognizing Jews in general as a national group should raise no particular concern for anyone outside of the group," he contends. "But when the site selected for the exercise of self-determination and statehood is an inhabited country, and the process of building the 'national home' leads to the dismantling of the national home of another group already residing there, political conflict is inevitable." As such, he sees a two-state solution as insufficient for bringing about justice: "Even if the 1967 occupation is brought to an end and an independent Palestinian state is established (and this seems less likely now than ever), it would do nothing to change the discrimination practiced against Palestinian citizens [of Israel] or the exclusion of the 1948 refugees and their descendants." He concludes his essay by proposing a set of guidelines that could structure equal relations between Jewish Israelis and Palestinians, including those who currently reside and formerly resided in Israel/Palestine, and their families.

In the third essay, Thea Renda Abu El-Haj emphasizes the lack of rights currently experienced by Palestinians, including Palestinian refugees. With a foundation rooted in an awareness of settler colonialism, she argues that "any discussion of self-determination must begin from an acknowledgement that Palestinians have lived with a deficit of rights even before 1948." In particular, she addresses the importance of spotlighting the issue of refugee return. "Understanding the place of Palestinians in the diaspora, within the broader context of displacement brought about by a settler-colonial dispossession, means that they must be included in the right to self-determination, including the possibility that they may wish to return to their and their recent ancestors' homeland." She contends that all Palestinians, wherever they reside, must "be meaningfully involved in decision-making about their future."

These three essays cut to the heart of what are among the most pressing questions in the Israeli-Palestinian conflict. Central to the Zionist idea is that the State of Israel should remain a safe haven for Jews worldwide who may wish to immigrate there. This is currently embodied in Israel's "Law of Return," which allows virtually any Jew in the world to become an Israeli citizen, and upheld by the Israeli desire to maintain a Jewish majority in the country. Palestinians and their supporters, however, view these policies, and the intentions undergirding them, as intensely problematic, especially in light of the simultaneous barring of the return of Palestinian refugees.

The essays also ask to what extent this is a conflict between two national groups who simply need to engage in territorial compromise (what has roughly become the international consensus of the "two-state solution" upon which decades of on-and-off political peace negotiations have been based), or whether this sort of proposed division of the territory into two states for two peoples misses two fundamental pieces of the social justice puzzle: the rights of Palestinians who currently live elsewhere due to the *Nakba*, and the status of Palestinian citizens of Israel, some of whom see their rights as unable to be fulfilled in a country that understands itself to be a Jewish state.

Identity-Based States and the Israeli-Palestinian Conflict

BRENT E. SASLEY

Among scholars and students of the Israeli-Palestinian conflict who criticize the two-state solution,[1] some argue that instead of political rights for specific peoples (i.e., self-determination and statehood for specific ethno-national communities), there should be a focus on human rights for all peoples, which means eschewing separate states in favor of a single state with shared sovereignty (either in the form of a binational state, which gives both peoples communal autonomy, or a unitary state, which abjures any separate group rights). The latter does not entail any specific political arrangement but in practice is often used to argue in favor of a one-state solution that encompasses all of what is today Israel, the West Bank, and the Gaza Strip. This assumption is problematic, however, for three reasons. First, a single state in the entire area will repeat the mistake critics point to regarding contemporary Israel: that the state privileges one ethno-national population (Jews) at the expense of another (Palestinians). A single state will mean a majority Palestinian population and a minority Jewish population, and thus simply reverses the contemporary conditions that critics rightly condemn. That is, a Palestinian majority will seek to enshrine privileges for itself at the expense of the Jewish minority.

Second, an emphasis on rights of entire peoples regardless of what state they already live in leads to a conflation between Israel within the Green Line on the one hand and the West Bank and Gaza Strip on the other. Yet the former is a sovereign country while the latter is a region occupied and controlled by Israel. These different and separate political conditions pose different problems of rights. For example, ending the Israeli occupation of the West Bank does not require attending to the inequality that exists between Jewish and Palestinian citizens of Israel.

Third, focusing only on human rights for peoples ignores the basic legal fact of the contemporary international system, namely, that the state rather than people is the highest form of political authority. These states are divided not just geographically, but on the basis of different identity communities. This fits with the demands of both Jews and Palestinians, who, as discussed below, each demand their own state in which their own identities are privileged.

Thea Renda Abu El-Haj and Ran Greenstein (this volume) succinctly lay out the historical developments that led to the contemporary condition of Israel and Palestine. But their emphasis on history neglects a number of contemporary conditions that must be accounted for when thinking about best solutions to the Israeli-Palestinian conflict. Historical events are not necessarily useful on their own as a vehicle for resolving contemporary political disputes. A fair and just solution to this and to other conflicts does not require a reversal of past events, but a careful assessment of the needs and interests of people in "the now," moving forward from today based on current facts on the ground. For example, the stories of persecution that begin Abu El-Haj's essay (this volume) are similar to those told of Jews in Europe, America, and the Middle East before 1948. This chapter argues that the most effective resolution is and has been self-determination—a separate state for separate peoples.

The argument here is that in order to achieve as much justice and fairness for the greatest number of people as possible, a two-state solution—a State of Israel dominated by Jews and a State of Palestine dominated by Palestinians—is the most appropriate solution. This would also reflect contemporary reality, given the disposition of the two populations, and would not require forced removal from homes or population transfers. Finally, it fits into the contemporary world and its existing legal patterns.

This essay begins by discussing the state as the primary, if not only, vehicle through which peoples' twenty-first-century political aspirations can be realized. Next it examines the case for self-determination of peoples, including Jews and Palestinians. The third section addresses the question of minority rights. The conclusion summarizes the overall argument.

The Modern Nation-State

A state is a legal-bureaucratic entity that contains both governing institutions and boundaries that mark the geography of the state (i.e., the physical area demarcating where the state's authority beings and ends). It also entails official recognition by other states, represented by an exchange of state-appointed representatives, such as ambassadors, and membership in international organizations like the United Nations.

A nation, by contrast, is a sociocultural concept, which defines a group of individuals bound together by a set of ascriptive characteristics such as language, religion, shared history and cultural practices, ethnicity or race, and so on. A social group like this also exists because group members identify as part of the group; they share the same collective memories and emotional reactions when other members of the group, whom they may not even know, are attacked (Sasley, 2011; Smith & Mackie, 2008; Tajfel, 1981). The modern nation-state, then, generally refers to a state whose borders encompass a specific nation.

The modern state, in its legal-political-bureaucratic form, emerged out of the European experience. Different forms of political authority had long existed in Europe, and indeed around the world: empires, kingdoms, city-states, tribal confederations, and more. But in the medieval period in Europe, the hierarchy that marked both the temporal and the religious worlds meant that there was no equality: every individual or entity owed fealty to an individual or entity above it. Under these conditions political authority was diffused, across the macro level (e.g., between regional lords and the Catholic Church) and the micro level (e.g., between different types of local lords and clerics). Over time, these various entities were consolidated into increasingly distinct units with centralized forms of governance. By the seventeenth and eighteenth centuries, this consolidation became associated with the notion of sovereignty (Krasner, 1993): the state became the highest form of authority both within its borders and in relation to other states.

The immediate origins of modern nationalism that created the nation-state lie in the seventeenth century, but it was a series of events in the eighteenth century, such as the French Revolution, and the nineteenth century, such as the unifications of Germany and Italy, that laid the foundation for our contemporary understanding of the political rights of identity communities. These events were predicated on the idea that these communities were tied together by a set of ascriptive characteristics and emotional markers that constituted a separate and distinct social group that had the right to self-determination, that is, the right to a state that represented and reflected that specific identity.

In the period since then, this recognition has been expanded across the globe. At the end of World War I, the breakup of the Ottoman, Russian, and Austro-Hungarian empires led to the emergence of several new entities explicitly created for the purpose of providing self-determination for different peoples. Later, the decolonization process that marked the 1950s, 1960s, and 1970s was as much about asserting a specific form of nationalism as it was about throwing off colonial control.

As the Europeans expanded across the globe, they either exported their systems to the regions they came to control, such as in the Middle East where new states were formed that conformed to European expectations; or extant entities were reshaped to conform to European standards as a way to become both more modern and more competitive, such as in Japan and Turkey.

Due to the migration of peoples around the world over time there are almost no pure nation-states left in the world. Some states, such as Canada and the United States, have several nations within their borders, including indigenous communities that lived in these territories before modern states were formed there. Some nations, such as the Jews or the Armenians, live scattered among several states even while some live within their own Jewish or Armenian state. And some nations, such as Kurds, Rohingya, and Palestinians, do not have a state, and so some live in and identify with different countries. In short, the dominant form of the modern state is one that includes more than one nation, or people. (This raises the problem of minority rights, of course, which is discussed below.)

That said, most states are dominated by one social group or identity community. This hegemonic group typically established the state or came to control it over time. Its members occupy most positions in the government, the political system, the economy, and so on. The state's symbols often reflect that group's own history or sense of identity, while national holidays, educational curriculum, legal and political norms, and so on reproduce the dominant group's perception of what is appropriate for the state. To take only a handful of examples: this is the case in Germany, where ethnic Germans are in control; in Turkey, governed by ethnic Turks; in Hungary, dominated by ethnic Hungarians or Magyars; and in Iraq where Arabs are predominant.

This description applies not just to states where citizenship has historically been based on blood or kinship (which constitutes the majority of states in the international system), but also to liberal democracies whose concept of citizenship is tied to loyalty to a set of ideas and institutions, such as Canada and the United States. In both countries, white Christians from Europe moved to the region and constructed a state by suppressing the indigenous peoples already living there and recasting political boundaries and authority on the basis of their Christian-European heritage (Sucharov, 2013; Resnick, 2005).

This also applies across time. While many nation-states emerged in Europe during the eighteenth, nineteenth, and early twentieth centuries, new states tied closely to a specific identity community have continued to emerge both in Europe and elsewhere. In Europe and Asia, the collapse of the Soviet Union in 1991 led to the creation of fifteen new countries, all of them tied to one specific social group with dominance over others. In 1993, Czechoslovakia peacefully separated into the Czech Republic, under the control of the majority Czechs, and Slovakia, dominated by ethnic Slovaks. In the mid-1990s, Yugoslavia broke violently apart, leading to the establishment of several different states, most of them populated primarily by one ethno-national group. In 2002, with the help of the international community, Timor-Leste seceded from Indonesia. The population of Timor-Leste is a mix of indigenous peoples but with a shared historical experience that ties them together. And in 2011 the Republic of South Sudan seceded from Sudan and become an independent country on the basis of both being ethnically and religiously different from Sudan. The ongoing process of the creation of new states has continued on the basis of citizens' demands for separation on the basis of identity.

In the twenty-first century the state is still the predominant actor in the international system. It is the highest form of political authority. Certainly, there are other actors in the system—international organizations, transnational religious or social movements, multinational corporations, nongovernmental organizations, and more. Some of them can undermine the authority of specific states at certain moments, and some might be stronger than certain weak states. In addition, in particular places social groups hold the loyalty of citizens more than the state itself. In Iraq, for example, since the American invasion in 2003 sectarian groups have placed the importance of their own communities above the Iraqi state. But even in such cases, dissatisfaction often emerges out of the concern that the state does not adequately represent those groups' needs; their response has been either to try to form a new state (e.g., Kurds) or to ensure that the state is oriented specifically towards them (e.g., Shi'ites in Iraq).

Greenstein (this volume) writes that rights are vested in people, not in states. Yet in light of the above discussion, this is an incomplete argument. At the same time that the nation-state emerged, the rights of citizens were also being expanded and codified. In the Euro-Anglo context, the French and American revolutions were explicitly about citizens' rights. But it was the state that provided and protected those rights. In addition, many of those rights were about protecting citizens from certain activities by the state. In other words, the state was recognized as the ultimate authority but whose power had to be limited in certain areas. To speak of peoples' rights without also speaking of the state is to paint only half of the picture.

Conditions for Self-Determination

The practice of self-determination (the attainment of statehood for a specific ethno-national community) is constrained by the realities of politics in a given country. While common practice and international standards accept that ethno-national communities have the inherent right of self-determination, the conditions in place in a specific country might not allow for such a right to be fully realized. Put another way, by the twenty-first century the boundaries of the modern state system were widely recognized. This does not mean that they cannot change; but any change is difficult, if not unlikely, unless certain conditions are first met.

First, the inhabitants of the country must want and approve of the self-determination. Ideally, citizens would vote "yes" in a referendum or poll for separation or secession, in order to garner as much support as possible and to ease the transition. In South Sudan, for instance, almost 99 per cent of the people voted in a referendum to separate. In some cases, though, independence is driven by political leaders while the broader population is indifferent or opposes such a process. For example, the dissolution of Czechoslovakia was not widely supported at the time, yet no serious movement to reverse the breakup exists. This serves as a form of passive acceptance.

Second, the political, financial, and security conditions might not be viable for a group to become independent. Not every group that wants to be independent *can* become independent. There might, for example, be a web of laws and regulations that tie a community to a larger state, a set of strictures too difficult to counter. A community might owe too much money to a central government. Its economy might be too small to survive on its own; and if the state from which it seceded decides not to maintain an economic union, it would be irresponsible to secede.

Third, political rights can be realized in forms other than self-determination. Varying degrees of autonomy, for example, might be appropriate for specific communities and countries. In Canada, the province of Quebec has considerable autonomy in language rights; the provincial government has passed a set of laws requiring French to be given greater prominence in education and advertising. Although these laws have faced challenges in the Supreme Court of Canada, many have been upheld. In Belgium, the country is divided into both language communities and geographic regions. The former, comprised of French-, Dutch-, and German-speaking communities, have considerable autonomy in the area of language while the latter have degrees of autonomy in areas such as education, housing, and some economic development.

The trend in Israel and Palestine repeats this pattern of demands for separate self-determination. Public opinion polls of Israeli citizens (Jews and Palestinian Arabs) and of Palestinians in the West Bank and Gaza consistently highlight the demand for separation and independence.[2] For instance, an overwhelming majority of Israeli Jews do not want to share equal political rights in a state with another ethno-national community. This complicates majority-minority relations in Israel (see Sasley & Waller, 2017, chap. 7). But majorities of Arab citizens of Israel also regularly contend they want to remain in the Israeli state, but with an end to discrimination against them. For their part, Palestinians in the West Bank and Gaza, also by large majorities, unfailingly demand a state that reflects Palestinian identity only.

Minority Rights

Abu El-Haj's focus in this volume on recent conceptualizations of universal rights excludes the interest that peoples have in promoting their own identity. Since the state remains the vehicle for achieving, maintaining, and expanding rights, ethno-national communities have insisted that the state serve as the vehicle for their identity. But as noted above, states with hegemonic identities often create political and legal problems for minority groups that do not share the same identity as the hegemonic community.

According to Abu El-Haj and Greenstein (this volume), discrimination against the Palestinian Arab minority in Israel must be considered as part and parcel of the conflict between Israel and Palestinians in the West Bank and Gaza. While they are correct that Jewish-Arab relations in Israel are often shaped by the conflict (e.g., Frisch, 2011), they also mean that the internal discrimination in Israel against the Arab minority should be resolved in the same way as the Israeli occupation of the West Bank—that is, as an end to Israel and the creation of a single state in the area. Thus no distinction is made between Palestinian citizens of Israel and Palestinians under Israeli control in the West Bank.

But because Israel is a sovereign country, any discrimination or inequality that exists within its borders is as much an internal issue as is racism against African Americans in the United States, the imbalance in allocation of resources in favor of non-indigenous populations over indigenous peoples in Canada, or the Turkish suppression of the cultural practices of its Kurdish minority. It is worth repeating, too, that public opinion surveys of the Arab minority in Israel demonstrate high levels of interest in remaining within Israel if Palestine becomes independent, even as they recognize their struggle against discrimination and alienation.

If one hallmark of the modern state system is the existence of minorities within countries dominated by one hegemonic ethnic community, then how majority communities have dealt with minority communities in their midst has varied across the world and over time. In Iraq, for example, although the minority Kurds were kept out of the central government, they were also given considerable autonomy (following a number of rebellions). In Canada and the United States, indigenous communities have considerable autonomy in local government and economic policy, and carry their own identity cards, which are separate from "normal" citizenship markers such as passports. In Turkey, the Kurds have long been marginalized; in the twentieth century the central government tried to stop Kurds from using Kurdish in media and in educational settings.

In short, the question of how states controlled by one majority deal with minority communities within their borders is an open one, but it is a common policy dilemma that tends to make up a considerable portion of legal and political activity concerning those minorities. There is, then, nothing unusual about dilemmas of discrimination against Palestinian Arab citizens in Israel. Addressing this inequality does not require erasing the State of Israel.

Conclusion

The claim for self-determination by ethno-national communities is a strong one, rooted in long-standing practice and international legal networks. It also highlights the range of issues that accompany any such effort. The Israel-Palestine case is therefore not unique, and we can look for many examples around the world for comparison and to draw on for ideas.

But the discussion also makes clear that self-determination under specific conditions is the ideal solution to situations in which different ethnic communities live together unhappily. A two-state solution would satisfy each community's own desires and needs, comport with international law and long-standing practice, and fit into the way in which the modern state system has been constructed.

While there are certainly valid criticisms one can direct towards both the modern state system (e.g., the very idea that the state itself should be the highest form of political authority in the world), these are separate from thinking about how to resolve the Israeli-Palestinian conflict in the fairest way that meets both peoples' needs.

Brent E. Sasley is an associate professor of political science at the University of Texas at Arlington, where he teaches Israeli politics, Middle East politics, and international relations. His research focuses on how language, emotions, and collective memories shape identity and foreign policy. His most recent book, co-authored with Harold Waller, is *Politics in Israel: Governing a Complex Society* (Oxford University Press, 2016).

Notes

1 The most common understanding of the two-state solution, and the one used as the basis for the argument here, is of a predominantly Jewish state (Israel) and a predominantly Palestinian state (Palestine), each with a minority of Palestinian Arabs and Jews, respectively.

2 On Israeli citizens, see the Israel Democracy Institute's monthly Peace Index (http://www.peaceindex.org/defaultEng.aspx). On Palestinians, see the Palestinian Center for Policy and Survey Research (http://www.pcpsr.org/en).

References

Frisch, H. (2011). *Israel's Security and Its Arab Citizens*. Cambridge, UK: Cambridge University Press.

Krasner, S. (1993). "Westphalia and All That." In J. Goldstein & R. Keohane (eds), *Ideas and Foreign Policy* (pp. 235–64). Ithaca, NY: Cornell University Press.

Resnick, P. (2005). *The European Roots of Canadian Identity*. Peterborough, ON: Broadview Press.

Sasley, B.E. (2011). "Theorizing States' Emotions." *International Studies Review*, *13*(3), 452–76. https://doi.org/10.1111/j.1468-2486.2011.01049.x

Sasley, B.E., & Waller, H.M. (2017). *Politics in Israel: Governing a Complex Society*. Oxford, UK: Oxford University Press.

Smith, E.R., & Mackie, D.M. (2008). "Intergroup Emotions." In M. Lewis, J.M. Haviland-Jones, & L. Feldman Barrett (eds), *Handbook of Emotions* (3rd ed., pp. 428–39). New York, NY: Guilford Press.

Sucharov, M. (2013). "Imagining Ourselves Then and Now: Nostalgia and Canadian Multiculturalism." *Journal of International Relations and Development*, *16*(4), 539–65. https://doi.org/10.1057/jird.2012.23

Tajfel, H. (1981). *Human Groups and Social Categories: Studies in Social Psychology*. Cambridge, UK: Cambridge University Press.

The Right to National Self-Determination and Israel/Palestine

RAN GREENSTEIN

In this essay I discuss the right to national self-determination with a focus on its application in the context of Israel/Palestine. I outline historical moves that shaped the ways in which the nation-state emerged in the twentieth century as a universal norm, based on self-determination as its principle of legitimacy. After addressing two important documents, written a century ago, that have served to entrench this principle, I attempt to draw out the implications for developments in Israel/Palestine from the time the documents were written to the present.

Historical Background

In the course of World War I (1914–18), the Russian, Austro-Hungarian, German, and Ottoman empires collapsed due to combinations of defeats in the battlefield and internal rebellions. Of particular relevance here was the Arab Revolt of 1916–18, which played a role in the demise of the Ottoman Empire. It was entangled with one of three sets of promises made by the British during the war: the Hussein-McMahon correspondence of 1915, which promised Arab independence in the region; the Sykes-Picot agreement of 1916, which planned the division of the region into British and French spheres of influence; and the Balfour Declaration of 1917, which asserted British support for a "national home for the Jewish people" in Palestine.

The subsequent history of the Middle East involved a combination of all three promises: from the Ottoman Empire several Arab countries were carved out and eventually gained independence in the following decades. Palestine was an exception, but it too became a distinct entity destined for a separate existence.

The conceptual basis for the postwar developments was provided by two documents. The first, written by Vladimir Lenin (1914), asserted the right of nations to self-determination and statehood: "the tendency of every national movement is towards formation of national states." Therefore, "we must inevitably reach the conclusion that the self-determination of nations means the political separation of these nations" (chap. 1).

Referring to multinational empires, Lenin (1914) called for "complete equality of rights for all nations; the right of nations to self-determination" (chap. 10). Specifically, this applied to groups occupying a distinct territory within a larger political framework that was imposed on them, such as

43

Ukrainians and Poles in the Russian and Austro-Hungarian empires, and to nations dominated by the British and French colonial empires. In 1916 Lenin formulated that point as a call on workers to "demand freedom of political separation for the colonies and nations oppressed by 'their own' nation."

Towards the end of the war, in 1918, US president Woodrow Wilson outlined fourteen principles to guide a peace plan, including "a free, open-minded, and absolutely impartial adjustment of all colonial claims, based upon a strict observance of the principle that in determining all such questions of sovereignty the interests of the populations concerned must have equal weight with the equitable claims of the government whose title is to be determined."

In the following year, Article 22 of the Covenant of the League of Nations, in whose establishment Wilson played a key role, asserted that "certain communities formerly belonging to the Turkish Empire" should be granted "existence as independent nations," though they required "administrative advice and assistance by a Mandatory" until they became fully ready for that. It added: "the wishes of these communities must be a principal consideration in the selection of the Mandatory" (League of Nations, 1924).

The result of all of these decisions was a proliferation of independent nation-states in Europe and the Middle East, though many of these states contained large ethnic and religious minorities. In the Middle East, the formation of new states, and moves towards territorially based identities and movements, clashed with the rise of an Arab nationalist movement that promoted pan-Arab political identity and institutions.

A second stage in the development of the nation-state as a universal political form came with the collapse of colonial empires in the wake of World War II. Decolonization gave rise to dozens of new states in Africa and Asia. Following the establishment of the United Nations in 1945, in 1960 that body produced the UN Declaration on the Granting of Independence to Colonial Countries and People. The declaration opposes "the subjection of peoples to alien subjugation, domination and exploitation" and asserts that "all peoples have the right to self-determination; by virtue of that right they freely determine their political status and freely pursue their economic, social and cultural development" (United Nations, 1960, pts 1 and 2).

The Case of Palestine/Israel

As part of the Ottoman Empire until 1917, and a British-ruled territory until 1948, Palestine met the definition of a territory whose population was entitled to self-determination, as did all its neighbors. But which nation was the subject of that right? The answer seemed simple: at the end of the war the vast majority of the population (over 90 per cent) were Arabic-speaking

Muslims and Christians who had started to refer to themselves collectively as Palestinian Arabs at the beginning of the twentieth century. Jewish residents were a small minority, with no concentrated demographic presence in any part of the country, and therefore with no valid claim to political independence in the country on their own.

But the 1917 Balfour Declaration, followed by the British Mandate, changed the picture. Instead of addressing the concerns of local Jewish communities, the declaration promoted "a national home for the Jewish people" to be located in that geographical area. The term "the Jewish people" was not defined precisely but was commonly interpreted to mean the entire array of Jewish communities throughout the world, irrespective of their specific conditions. The "Jewish people" (in the singular) was seen as a coherent group entitled to collective rights, rather than a multitude of diverse communities with a wide range of political preferences in their many different countries of residence (Jewish people in the plural). Despite its geographical dispersion, that group was granted a claim to a specific territory from which most of its members were absent and to which local residents (most of whom did not belong to the group) formulated their own claims, based on overwhelming physical presence and long-term family, community, and historical links.

We have to realize the implications of the Balfour Declaration in introducing a radical political and conceptual change: (1) it redefined the Jewish people as a unified political subject instead of a heterogeneous set of ethnic-religious communities with disparate concerns in relation to each one's specific circumstances, as they had been until then; and (2) it redefined Palestine as a site for the realization of the political aspirations of the "Jewish people," bypassing and marginalizing the concerns of the majority of the land's residents, including Jewish communities there and elsewhere. In both respects the Balfour Declaration reflected the recently formulated ideas of the Zionist movement, which was at the time a minority tendency among Jews globally as well as in Palestine itself. The declaration's commitment not to "prejudice the civil and religious rights of existing non-Jewish communities" did not amount to recognition of the political rights of the group comprising the overwhelming majority of the population, Palestinian Arabs.

The definition of Jews as a nation with a political claim to Palestine was a novel idea. Jews regarded the Land of Israel as the *symbolic* anchor of their identity, but the land was first targeted *politically* for purposes of immigration and settlement in the late nineteenth century. For political Zionists, Jews needed a state of their own to guarantee their safety, and Palestine was the obvious location for it, given the centuries-old connection to this land.

But were Jews indeed a "nation," did their safety require an independent state, and was Palestine a legitimate place for it?

Most political Zionists answered all three questions in the affirmative. But other responses were more common among Jews, at least until 1948. In the beginning of the twentieth century, most European Jews saw themselves as members of the Jewish people despite the loose links between their widely dispersed communities. But they did not envisage a common future in their own national territory. Rather, they aimed to integrate themselves in their countries of residence and become equal citizens. Immigration to democratic countries with good economic prospects was viewed by many as the best solution. Nationalism and statehood in Palestine had limited appeal compared to the promise of religious freedom and individual prosperity in western Europe, the Americas, and South Africa.

Palestine already was an inhabited country. Exercising Jewish self-determination in a territory in which they were a small minority, and of recent origin at that, was bound to clash with the rights of existing residents who naturally saw their own claims—derived from their continued historical presence in the land—as superior.

The question of political rights was a constant theme during the Mandate period (1920–48). Addressing Britain's contradictory commitments—preparing the country for independence, and building the "Jewish National Home"—the Royal Commission of Enquiry of 1937 concluded that these two issues "have proved irreconcilable; and, as far ahead as we can see, they must continue to conflict. To put it in one sentence, we cannot—in Palestine as it now is—both concede the Arab claim to self-government and secure the establishment of the Jewish National Home" (Palestine Royal Commission, 1937, p. 347).

A decade later, in 1947, a similar conclusion was reached by the UN Special Committee on Palestine (UNSCOP), which asserted that "the claims to Palestine of the Arabs and Jews, both possessing validity, are irreconcilable." Hence, partition of the country was "the only means available by which political and economic responsibility can be placed squarely on both Arabs and Jews" (United Nations, 1947, chap. 6, recommendation 2, clause 7). This became the foundation for the notion of two states for two distinct nations.

The Two-State Solution

The discourse of symmetry—two nations, two peoples, two states, two sets of historical rights, two valid claims to self-determination based in the same territory—remains powerful. Yet it must be subjected to a critical examination.

The first question has to do with indigeneity: do immigrant settlers have the same right to self-determination as indigenous people? Palestinian Arabs can demonstrate a continuous presence in the country stretching over many centuries. Most Israeli Jews trace their origins in the land to the twentieth century, with a few who go back earlier. This difference in possessing deep physical roots calls for some distinctions, but what should they be?

Of greater concern are the boundaries of the "nation" with the right to self-determination. The case of Palestinians seems straightforward: they are Arabic-speaking residents of the country, Muslims and Christians whose ancestors had lived in the country long before World War I. Other Muslims and Christians and Arabic speakers do not qualify for such right without a concrete link to the country. The case of Israeli Jews seems different: Jews who have lived in the country for any length of time qualify as part of the Israeli-Jewish Hebrew-speaking people, but what about other Jews who do not live there and never have?

Zionist ideology regards them as potential citizens who have not yet enacted their right to return to their homeland. But such Jews are not residents of the territory at present, nor do they share characteristics that normally serve to define a nation: common language, territory, or economic life, despite their sense of belonging to the same group of people. Should self-determination be reserved for Israeli Jews—a territorially identified group of people—or to all Jews, whatever their actual links to the country?

A related issue: the notion of "return" is central to claims to self-determination. For Palestinians it is the right of return for those in their community who became refugees as a result of the 1948 ethnic cleansing, as well as their descendants, now comprising more than 50 per cent of their total population; for Jews it is the law of return that grants every Jew in the world the right to move to Israel and become a citizen. This surface similarity disguises a profound difference: for Palestinians return means going back to the same building, plot of land, village, or town in which they or their immediate ancestors used to live; for Jews it means moving to a new country in which neither they nor any of their known ancestors had ever lived, although they share a sense of having their historical roots there. It means going to a "homeland" in an abstract ideological sense, not to a concrete location or physical site to which they have any familial relationship.

The ideological nature of the concept of "return to the homeland" means that Jewish self-determination in Israel/Palestine does not refer to independence from colonial rule or secession from a foreign regime as in other cases. Rather, it is the formation of a new state through the gathering of disparate people who share religious and ethnic sentiments but no direct living experiences. This is not to deny the sense of nationalism unifying Jews in Israel *today*, but to question whether what is involved is self-determination of an already-existing national group.

The core issue here is not theoretical definitions but practical politics. Recognizing Jews in general as a national group should raise no particular concern for anyone outside of the group. But when the site selected for the exercise of self-determination and statehood is an inhabited country, and the process of building the "national home" leads to the dismantling of the national home of another group already residing there, political conflict is inevitable.

This need not be the case if the nation is open to members of all groups, in the same way that all residents of France can join the French nation regardless of religious or ethnic origins, and all immigrants to the United States or Canada can become part of the American or Canadian nation, sharing equal citizenship, regardless of their diverse backgrounds. But the nation-state of the Jewish people, as Israel is officially defined, is open only to people with a Jewish ethno-religious background. It does not recognize a nationality of a civic nature, open to all citizens alike. It gives preference to Jewish immigrants over and at the expense of the rights of indigenous non-Jewish people.

This is a situation with few if any equivalents at present. Many states incorporate some ethnic or religious symbols into their notions of citizenship, and may practice some informal preference for members of some groups. But the degree to which a regime of systematic ethnic domination is institutionalized in Israel (Adalah, 2018), combined with the forcible eviction of much of the indigenous population and its displacement and replacement by recently arrived settlers, are unique outside of the context of the colonial era, which was coming to an end after World War II. Over the years, most states that had emerged out of a colonial encounter normalized their situation by granting the descendants of settlers and indigenous people equal rights and incorporating them fully into the body politic. Israel, in contrast, continues to entrench Jewish domination throughout its sphere of control and is doing that in an intensified manner, albeit differentially in relation to various segments of the Palestinian population.

Sasley's argument (this volume) that this is common practice is wrong. To be sure, cases of ethnic or national oppression (Tibetans in China, Kurds in Turkey, Basques in Spain) exist, but the denial of self-determination to these groups is normally accompanied by the offer—indeed the imposition—of common citizenship in order to facilitate their cultural assimilation into the dominant group. Palestinians under Israeli control are offered neither assimilation and equal citizenship nor independence, but rather permanent marginalization. A recent spate of legislative proposals and acts denies non-Jewish citizens a place in the state's definition as the nation-state of the Jewish people exclusively, demotes the official status of the Arabic language, entrenches the existing practice of maintaining and creating Jewish-only communities, and reinforces the specific Jewish character of state symbols. Even if the 1967 occupation is brought to an end and an independent Palestinian state is established (and this seems less likely now than ever), it would do nothing to change the discrimination practiced against Palestinian citizens or the exclusion of the 1948 refugees and their descendants.

Having said that, we must recognize that over the years an Israeli-Jewish national identity has developed alongside a Palestinian-Arab national identity, and each can serve as a foundation for the right to self-determination on an equal basis, as a starting point towards solving the issue in all its aspects. Yet when full membership in the political community is open to all Jews (even if they and their ancestors never set foot in the territory and have no relationship to anyone living there), and closed off to all noncitizen Palestinians (even if they and their ancestors were born there and have relatives living there), serious challenges follow.

Without addressing this fundamental imbalance—what Thea Renda Abu El-Haj (this volume) refers to as "deficit of rights" and "citizenship gaps"—the notion of two states for two peoples remains inadequate as a political solution for the country. It is not a matter of a border dispute that can be resolved by shifting lines on a map. It has to do with the ways in which definitions of citizenship, national identity, and political rights are handled by the state.

Sasley's claims (this volume) that Israel and the 1967 occupied territories are two separate issues, and that the rights of Palestinian citizens of Israel is an internal matter, do not stand up to scrutiny, as Abu El-Haj (this volume) asserts. The entire range of relations between the State of Israel and different segments of the Palestinian-Arab people (1948 refugees, 1948 citizens, 1967 occupied subjects in Gaza, the West Bank, and East Jerusalem) has been shaped by the same historical process. We cannot look at any one component without considering the others, which is not to say that all aspects of the situation can be resolved in one political big bang.

Conclusion

What does this mean for the prospects of equality and dignity for national groups, advocated by Lenin and Wilson a century ago? The following principles may serve as a guide:

- There are two national groups in the historical territory of Israel/
  Palestine, Israeli Jews and Palestinian Arabs. Self-determination
  should be restricted to residents, current and former, and their family
  members.
- Members of each group should be entitled to political equality as
  individuals as well as recognition of their collective rights to practice
  their religions, speak and be educated in their languages, and develop
  their cultures.

- Each should have the right to form political institutions and shape the nature of the state or states in which they live, as long as they adhere to universal democratic norms and civil and human rights for all. Principles of redress for past injustices may be applied in this context.
- As a transitional arrangement, extended over time if people so wish, separate states may be maintained in agreed boundaries. Each state should maintain equality for all its citizens regardless of ethnic, religious, and national origins.

Ran Greenstein is an associate professor of sociology at the University of the Witwatersrand, Johannesburg, South Africa. He has written from a comparative perspective on history, society, and politics in Israel/Palestine and South Africa. He has published *Genealogies of Conflict: Class, Identity, and State in Palestine/Israel and South Africa to 1948* (Wesleyan University Press, 1995), *Comparative Perspectives on South Africa* (Macmillan, 1998), and *Zionism and Its Discontents: A Century of Radical Dissent in Israel/Palestine* (Pluto, 2014). His forthcoming book is *Identity, Nationalism, and Race: Anti-Colonial Resistance in South Africa and Israel/Palestine* (Routledge, 2019).

References

Adalah. (2018, April 16). "Adalah Reports to UN on Israel's Systemic Discrimination against Palestinians." Retrieved from https://www.adalah.org/en/content/view/94811

League of Nations. (1924). *The Covenant of the League of Nations.* The Avalon Project. Retrieved from http://avalon.law.yale.edu/20th_century/leagcov.asp

Lenin, V.I. (1914). "The Right of Nations to Self-determination." *Marxists Internet Archive.* Retrieved from https://www.marxists.org/archive/lenin/works/1914/self-det/ch01.htm

Lenin, V.I. (1916). "The Socialist Revolution and the Right of Nations to Self-determination." *Marxists Internet Archive.* Retrieved from https://www.marxists.org/archive/lenin/works/1916/jan/x01.htm

Palestine Royal Commission. (1937). *Palestine Royal Commission Report: Presented by the Secretary of State for the Colonies to Parliament by Command of His Majesty.* London, UK: His Majesty's Stationery Office.

United Nations. (1947). *United Nations Special Committee on Palestine: Report to the General Assembly.* United Nations Information System on the Question of Palestine. Retrieved from https://unispal.un.org/DPA/DPR/unispal.nsf/0/07175DE9FA2DE563852568D3006E10F3

United Nations. (1960, December 14). *UN Declaration on the Granting of Independence to Colonial Countries and People.* Resolution 1514. Retrieved from http://www.un.org/en/decolonization/declaration.shtml

Wilson, W. (1918, January 8). "President Woodrow Wilson's Fourteen Points." The Avalon Project. Retrieved from http://avalon.law.yale.edu/20th_century/wilson14.asp

Considering Rights and Self-Determination in Light of Injustice and Unequal Power

THEA RENDA ABU EL-HAJ

Consider the following three stories:

Beirut, 2009

I'm sitting in a room with over 100 educators from UNRWA (United Nations Relief and Works Agency for Palestinian Refugees) schools located in two of Lebanon's Palestinian refugee camps. As part of a workshop, my colleagues and I have engaged the group in a poetry-writing exercise. Participant after participant reads aloud their "Where I am from" poems narrating rich portraits of the Palestinian villages and towns from which they, their parents, or their grandparents were forcibly expelled during the *Nakba* ("catastrophe" in Arabic). These places—a majority of which were destroyed by the nascent State of Israel—remain alive in the memories and narratives of these Palestinians and their families who all aspire to return to their homes in Palestine, even generations later. Narrated along with these memories and aspirations are other stories: of living in what have become permanent refugee camps; and of cycles of violent conflict—civil war and Israeli invasions—that have left myriad family members dead or permanently disabled.

Lydda/Lod, 2008

Samira Khateeb (a pseudonym) has flown from the United States (where she was born and raised) to visit, for the first time since she was two, her family in her parents' village in the occupied West Bank. She is wholly unprepared for the nine-hour isolation and interrogation by Israeli officers at Ben Gurion International airport. She is finally released, shaken and terrified by her first encounter with the powerlessness of detention. This would prove to be only one of many subsequent lessons—learned at Israeli checkpoints and during night-time Israeli raids of her village—about what it means to live without rights in the face of unqualified power.

East Jerusalem, 2013

I am visiting with my father's cousin and his wife. We sit in the garden in the family home in which he was born a few years before the establishment of the State of Israel. I am hearing the story of this cousin's still-unresolved court case. He is fighting to retain his residency permit, without which he will be denied the right to remain in Jerusalem. A brief stint to work outside the country violated new regulations that Israel put in place for Palestinian residents of East Jerusalem, who must demonstrate that Jerusalem is and has continuously been their "center of life" to be "allowed" to maintain their residency, to work and live where they were born.

I begin with these stories to illustrate concretely the everyday experiences of living without the right of self-determination: the principle that all people have the right to "freely determine their political status and freely pursue their economic, social and cultural development" (UNGA, 1960). It is not enough to consider questions and principles of self-determination and rights in the abstract, or in relation to normative ideals and historic precedent. We must begin from a deep understanding of the embodied, everyday experiences that people have had, and continue to have, in relation to rights and self-determination.

Any discussion of self-determination must begin from an acknowledgement that Palestinians have lived with a deficit of rights even before 1948. Their rights to remain on their lands and to determine their lives were violated first by British colonial power at the turn of the twentieth century, and later by the United Nations' partition plan that was imposed upon Palestinians by foreign ruling powers. The *Nakba* was an outcome of Palestinians not being granted a right to self-determination over their own land. Since that time, Palestinians have faced a long line of dispossessions from land, citizenship, and rights, that reflect the reality that Palestinians have had and continue to have little to no control over their individual and collective lives.

In this essay, I argue that questions of self-determination must be framed in relation to the vastly different *lived experiences* of rights that Palestinians (living within and outside of historic Palestine) and Jewish citizens of Israel, as well as Jewish people living across the globe, have had in relation to the Palestinian-Israeli conflict. Self-determination, as I see it, acknowledges that oppressed groups have a right to collective decision-making and action to define and secure a just and peaceful resolution to the conditions of oppression. The question of self-determination for stateless Palestinians, Palestinians living under occupation and in the diaspora, Palestinian citizens of Israel, and Jewish citizens of Israel cannot be considered outside of the settler-colonial context. Moreover, in foregrounding the question of rights, I suggest that a resolution of the current conflict will depend on recognition of the deficit of rights, and of the context of ongoing oppression and injustice to which Palestinians are subjected. This deficit of rights is tied to another fundamental dispossession that Palestinians have faced in the aftermath of the *Nakba*: that of citizenship. Since the *Nakba*, Palestinians have lived with myriad "citizenship gaps" (Brysk & Shafir, 2004) that accrue from conditions of statelessness, exile, dispossession, and a spectrum of denials of basic human, political, civil, cultural, and religious rights. Thus, in considering resolutions to the questions of self-determination and the right to exist, we cannot begin from assumptions of parity between two separate ethno-national populations (see Greenstein, this volume), as Sasley (this volume) assumes. Instead, we must ask how to account for the existing imbalance of power and recognize the need to restore the right of self-determination for an indigenous population who have been denied this right.

Self-Determination Depends on Rights

Rights offer a starting point for thinking about self-determination, which is impossible without access to substantive rights. I focus on the question of rights, the expansion of the conception of rights, and the ways that modern life is challenging the conflation of rights with national citizenship.

The development of modern nation-states and their attendant forms of citizenship has been the core source of political commitments to an expanding set of rights. Citizenship, broadly conceptualized, references not only a person's legal status but also their capacity to exercise a range of rights: civil, political, social, and cultural (Castles & Davidson, 2000; Kymlicka, 1995; Marshall, 1964; Rosaldo, 1994; Yuval-Davis, 2011). In particular, modern forms of democratic citizenship evolved initially to include civil rights, which guarantee individual rights, such as free expression and equality before the law, and political rights, which grant people political power.

In more recent times, states have adopted social rights that offer citizens benefits, such as entitlements to certain standards of education, health care, and welfare necessary to guarantee their capacity to participate fully in their societies. Most recently, *cultural rights*—the right to maintain linguistic, cultural, and group affiliation—have also emerged as key aspects of modern citizenship (Castles & Davidson, 2000; Kymlicka, 1995; Rosaldo, 1994).

Citizenship, with its attendant rights, is a key site that regulates inclusion in and exclusion from the state. The question of who warrants consideration for citizenship has been, and continues to be, hotly contested across modern nation-states (see Bosniak, 2006; Castles & Davidson, 2000; Ngai, 2004; Yuval-Davis, 2011). Citizenship mediates individuals' rights to live, work, and participate in political processes, but it also regulates who is and who is not entitled to the full protections of due process. This distinction between citizen and noncitizen critically shapes individuals' capacities to access rights and exercise authority over their lives.

Moreover, one's ability to access a full range of rights, even for citizens, is regulated by one's position in relation to the imagined nation—the ways that nations conjure ideas of membership (Anderson, 1991). Rights can be constrained, formally or informally, for marginalized citizens. Consider, for example, the case of the United States, in which racially oppressed communities have been unable to equally access many rights—from the right to an equal educational system to the right to vote. This reality in states across the world points to the risk of trusting that any state forged around a majority identity group will protect all of its citizens equally. Such an assumption denies the reality that states are, and have been, diverse and the ugly histories of violence and oppression that rest beneath the development of the modern state system.

Over the past century, we have seen the development of a second tradition of rights intended to transcend nation-based citizenship. Codified in international resolutions and laws, human rights are conceptualized as inherent rights due to *all* individuals and groups regardless of their citizenship status. Written into documents such as the Universal Declaration of Human Rights and the Declaration of the Rights of the Child, this tradition includes wide-ranging ideals for constituting a "good" human life. Included within these conceptualizations of rights are those specific to basic political and civil liberties (such as freedom of movement, of speech, freedom from torture and arbitrary arrest) and social rights (to education and adequate economic well-being), as well as broader ideals such as the right to "freely participate in the cultural life of the community, to enjoy the arts and to share in scientific advancement and its benefits" granted in Article 27 of the UN Declaration of Human Rights (UNGA, 1948).

This human rights tradition instantiates not only the rights of individuals, but also the rights of groups. This is how we arrive at the idea of self-determination, particularly one that acknowledges the effects of colonization on indigenous peoples. The United Nations Declaration on the Granting of Independence to Colonial Countries and Peoples and the Declaration on the Rights of Indigenous Peoples, taken together, affirm the rights of indigenous peoples to be free from subjugation, to seek redress from historic injustices, and to control their collective lives. The idea of self-determination is a recognition of people's collective rights to control political, cultural, social, and economic spheres.

In a world in which states are the primary entities with the power to regulate rights, people's ability to leverage this expansive tradition of human rights remains mostly aspirational (Shafir, 2004). Nevertheless, this aspirational quality is evident in the grounded ways that many people across the world articulate struggles for inclusion and justice. The notion that all people, not just citizens of particular states, have a right to myriad protections animates the discourses and practices of countless movements working against oppression across the globe, including the Palestinian movement. Access to rights is the first step on the path to self-determination.

Self-Determination in the Palestinian-Israeli Context

In thinking about the question of self-determination for Palestinians and Israelis we must begin by assessing each group's access to the rights that make self-determination possible. Since 1948, Jewish citizens of Israel have experienced the full and expansive rights of democratic citizenship, with its attendant guarantees of political, civil, and human rights, as well as that of self-determination in relation to cultural and religious expression. Moreover, the State of Israel has granted the right to full democratic citizenship to Jews living anywhere in the world, who can immigrate to Israel without restriction and become citizens.

In contrast, Palestinians across many different contexts have struggled to access any, let alone a full host of, rights. This denial of rights is most evident for the approximately five million Palestinians who remain, to this day, registered refugees (UNRWA, 2018). The original refugee crisis of this community emerged from the aftermath of World War II, when the British asked the newly established United Nations to decide the fate of Palestine. In 1947, the United Nations passed, by a narrow margin, a plan to partition Palestine into two states: a Jewish one and an Arab one, with Jerusalem to be administered as an international city. Although at the time Jews represented 35 per cent of the population and held only 13 per cent of the land, they were awarded 56 per cent of historic Palestine. The war that broke out in 1948 in response to this partition plan—a plan that was established without consultation or consent of the majority of the inhabitants of the land, who were Palestinian—resulted in the mass expulsion of Palestinians from their historic homes. As a result of the massacre of Palestinian civilians and a specific plan of forced transfer engaged in by Zionist paramilitaries, combined with ordinary people's instincts to flee from war, approximately 750,000 Palestinians (more than half the Palestinian population) left Palestine

(Flapan, 1987; Hirst, 1977; Khalidi, 2006; Makdisi, 2008; Pappe, 2006). Despite the United Nations General Assembly's 1948 approval of Resolution 194, which demanded Palestinians be allowed to return to their homes and to receive compensation for lost property, the newly established Israeli state never allowed them to return or compensated them for their property. For many, particularly those who remain to this day stateless, mainly living in refugee camps in Lebanon, Jordan, Syria, and the West Bank and Gaza, the hope that one day they might return to their ancestral land is no idle dream. It is an aspiration for the restoration of the many rights that they continue to be denied, including a right to self-determination in a land from which they were dispossessed.

The 1967 *Naksa* ("setback" in Arabic) is the second lens through which to view the denial of rights and its impact on the question of self-determination. At the end of a six-day war between Israel and Syria, Egypt, and Jordan, Israel occupied East Jerusalem, the West Bank, and the Gaza Strip—the remaining lands that had been part of the original British Mandate of Palestine—the Sinai Desert from Egypt, and the Golan Heights from Syria. Against international sanctions and law, Israel established long-term military occupation in the West Bank and Gaza, laid claim to East Jerusalem, and in 1981 extended Israeli law over the Golan Heights. To this day, the military occupation entails severe administrative measures that control all aspects of Palestinians' lives, including rights of residence, movement, land use, travel, water, and access to basic goods and services, including life-sustaining medical care. At the same time, the Israeli government rolled out a settlement plan that transferred and continues to transfer increasing numbers of Jewish Israelis to the occupied territories—a move that violates international law's prohibition against the transfer of an occupier's population to the occupied land. In developing an extensive network of illegal settlements, Israel has expropriated Palestinian lands and natural resources, built a network of roads that Palestinians in the occupied territories are prohibited from using, and facilitated the development of an armed settler population. Moreover, the military occupation places extreme restrictions on all aspects of Palestinians' lives, regulating the right of residence, movement, travel, and livelihood; controlling land and water use in the Occupied Palestinian Territories; and subjecting Palestinians to indefinite detention without trial, with little to no recourse to challenge violations of their civil and human rights (Makdisi, 2008).

A third context for thinking about rights and self-determination is the Palestinians who remained inside the "Green Line" (the boundaries of the 1949 armistice negotiated at the end of the war, which effectively defined the borders of the State of Israel through 1967). These Palestinians faced further dispossession of lands, and for many years a denial of the right to citizenship. Although they eventually became citizens of Israel, the struggle for equality as citizens continues to this day. During and even well after the 1948 war, over 400 Palestinian villages inside the Green Line were destroyed; their Palestinian inhabitants were dispossessed of land (Davis, 2011; Khalidi, 2006; Makdisi, 2008). From 1948 to 1966, Palestinians inside the new State of Israel were subject to military law, which was explicitly not applied to Jewish Israelis (Jiryis, 1976). Through a series of administrative measures, many had their land confiscated and were unable to return to their homes. Some Palestinians continue to fight in the courts to return to their confiscated homes and land (Kimmerling & Midgal, 2003), while many Palestinian villages remained "unrecognized," denied basic services, and subject to demolition orders (Makdisi, 2008). To this day, Palestinians in Israel face systematic discrimination and second-class citizenship (Tocci, 2011). In fact, this unequal citizenship was once again highlighted with the law passed in July 2018 by the Knesset, the Israeli Parliament, declaring that the "right to exercise national self-determination in the State of Israel is unique to the Jewish people." Sasley's argument (this volume) seeking to distinguish these Palestinians from Palestinians elsewhere is untenable for two reasons: it occludes the shared colonial history that shapes all Palestinians' collective imaginations, and it denies the fact that Palestinians with Israeli citizenship largely identify as Palestinians engaged in a struggle for self-determination.

Finally, there is the question of rights of self-determination for Palestinians in the diaspora who have obtained citizenship from other states. Many Palestinians, whether born in Palestine or the descendants of those born in Palestine, have sustained affiliative relationships with Palestine—relationships to people, land, memories, and more. The contrast between the Israeli state's guarantee of the rights of Jews living anywhere in the world to immigrate to Israel and be granted citizenship, and the parallel exclusion of Palestinians and their descendants from a land in which they have a recent history of sustained presence makes visible the enormity of such current injustices. Understanding the place of Palestinians in the diaspora, within the broader context of displacement brought about by a settler-colonial dispossession, means that they must be included in the right to self-determination, including the possibility that they may wish to return to their and their recent ancestors' homeland.

Grounded Acts of Self-Determination

Despite the ongoing denial of the right to self-determination that Palestinians have been subjected to since the *Nakba*, they have also determinedly created a collective presence wherever they are, calling for recognition of their right to exist through myriad forms of participation. From grass roots economic collectives to transnational political actions (like the Boycott, Divestment, Sanctions Movement) to building Palestinian heritage museums, keeping alive craft traditions, and developing poetry and music of resistance, Palestinians everywhere have continued to insist on their right to self-determination and justice.

Conclusion

The question of self-determination for Jewish Israelis and Palestinians is embedded within an existing denial of and deficit in Palestinian rights. Subject to exile, occupation, statelessness, and second-class citizenship, Palestinians have been living for seventy years without the capacity to determine the course of their collective lives. Any dialogue about self-determination must begin from a recognition of this reality and must create real pathways for Palestinians across the diaspora to be meaningfully involved in decision-making about their future.

Thus, I am not arguing for particular resolutions to the conflict. Rather, I suggest that any resolution of the current conflict must start, not from an assumption of parity for each party involved, but rather from an acknowledgement of the fact of colonization that creates a deficit in the rights of citizenship (broadly construed) for Palestinians. A resolution to the conflict must account for this deficit. Deficits accrue debt, which suggests that Palestinians need not only the restoration, and guarantee, of fundamental rights, but also reparations for what has been lost (e.g., honoring a right of return and compensation). There is also a need for Israel to repay its debt in the moral arena by acknowledging the *Nakba* and taking responsibility for its subsequent actions, policies, and practices. Only with attention to this debt—created by Israeli settler colonialism—can the conditions be created for substantive self-determination and a right to exist that could create hope for justice and a lasting peace for Palestinians and Israelis.

Thea Renda Abu El-Haj is a professor of education at Barnard College, Columbia University, and is an anthropologist of education. Her research explores questions about belonging, rights, citizenship, and education raised by transnational migration and conflict. Her second book, *Unsettled Belonging: Educating Palestinian American Youth after 9/11* (University of Chicago Press, 2015), won the 2016 American Educational Studies Association Critics Choice Award. She is currently conducting a collaborative ethnographic study of public kindergartens in Beirut, Lebanon, that focuses on questions of conflict and refugee policy. A recent article on this study, "Fifi the Punishing

Cat and Other Civic Lessons in a Lebanese Public Kindergarten," can be found in the *Journal on Education in Emergencies*. Abu El-Haj is principal investigator of a US national interview study exploring the civic identities and civic practices of youth from Muslim immigrant communities, funded by the Spencer Foundation.

References

Anderson, B. (1991 [1983]). *Imagined Communities: Reflections on the Origin and Spread of Nationalism*. New York, NY: Verso Press.

Bosniak, L. (2006). *The Citizen and the Alien: Dilemmas of Contemporary Membership*. Princeton, NJ: Princeton University Press.

Brysk, A., & Shafir, G. (2004). "Introduction: Globalization and the Citizenship Gap." In A. Brysk & G. Shafir (eds), *People Out of Place: Globalization, Human Rights, and the Citizenship Gap* (pp. 3–10). New York, NY: Routledge.

Castles, S., & Davidson, A. (2000). *Citizenship and Migration: Globalization and the Politics of Belonging*. New York, NY: Routledge.

Davis, R.A. (2011). *Palestinian Village Histories: Geographies of the Displaced*. Stanford, CA: Stanford University Press.

Flapan, S. (1987). *The Birth of Israel: Myths and Realities*. New York, NY: Pantheon.

Hirst, D. (1977). *The Gun and the Olive Branch: The Roots of Violence in the Middle East*. London, UK: Faber and Faber.

Jiryis, S. (1976). *The Arabs in Israel*. New York, NY: Monthly Review Press.

Khalidi, R. (2006). *The Iron Cage: The Story of the Palestinian Struggle for Statehood*. Boston, MA: Beacon Press.

Kimmerling, B., & Migdal, J.S. (2003). *The Palestinian People: A History*. Cambridge, MA: Harvard University Press.

Kymlicka, W. (1995). *Multicultural Citizenship: A Liberal Theory of Minority Rights*. New York, NY: Oxford University Press.

Makdisi, S. (2008). *Palestine Inside Out: An Everyday Occupation*. New York, NY: Norton.

Marshall, T.H. (1964). *Class, Citizenship, and Social Development: Essays of T.H. Marshall*. Westport, CT: Greenwood.

Ngai, M. (2004). *Impossible Subjects: Illegal Aliens and the Making of Modern America*. Princeton, NJ: Princeton University Press.

Pappe, I. (2006). *The Ethnic Cleansing of Palestine*. Oxford, UK: One World.

Rosaldo, R. (1994). "Cultural Citizenship and Educational Democracy." *Cultural Anthropology, 9*(3), 402–11. https://doi.org/10.1525/can.1994.9.3.02a00110

Shafir, G. (2004). "Citizenship and Humans Rights in an Era of Globalization." In A. Brysk & G. Shafir (eds), *People Out of Place: Globalization, Human Rights, and the Citizenship Gap* (pp. 11–28). New York, NY: Routledge.

Tocci, N. (2011). *The EU and the Palestinian-Arab Minority in Israel*. Brussels, Belgium: Euro-Mediterranean Human Rights Network. Retrieved May 29, 2018, from https://www.adalah.org/uploads/oldfiles/Public/files/English/International_Advocacy/EUArabMinorityReport.pdf

UNGA (United Nations General Assembly). (1948, December 10). *United Nations Declaration of Human Rights*. Retrieved from http://www.ohchr.org/EN/UDHR/Documents/UDHR_Translations/eng.pdf

UNGA. (1960, December 14). *Declaration on the Granting of Independence to Colonial Countries and Peoples.* Retrieved from https://undocs.org/A/Res/1514(XV)

UNRWA (United Nations Relief and Works Agency). (2018). "Frequently Asked Questions." Retrieved May 29, 2018, from https://www.unrwa.org/who-we-are/frequently -asked-questions

Yuval-Davis, N. (2011). *The Politics of Belonging: Intersectional Contestations.* London, UK: Sage.

three
Settler Colonialism

Many arguments around Israel/Palestine can be whittled down to particular assumptions about Israel, Palestine, and Zionism. For instance, oftentimes those debating the Israeli-Palestinian conflict come from different places regarding whether or not they consider the State of Israel to be a settler colony. In the twenty-first century, it is widely accepted in academic circles that colonialism is an oppressive system, an institutionalized mechanism that harms indigenous communities for the benefit of another group (i.e., colonists). If one considers Israel to exemplify a colonial project similar to others emerging from nineteenth- and twentieth-century Europe, it is difficult to simultaneously defend its establishment. It would also follow that contemporary activists who believe that Israel is a settler-colonial state might call for *decolonizing* it. This might entail pushing for different structural relations between Jews and Palestinians in Israel/Palestine on a massive scale.

Embodying the general discourse of the time, many Zionists emerging from Europe and Russia during the nineteenth and twentieth centuries not only supported colonial projects but self-identified their movement to be a colonial project as well. Two of the most important early Zionists, Theodor Herzl and Ze'ev Jabotinsky, used the terms "colony" and "colonization" a number of times when referring to the Zionist project in the Land of Israel. Similarly, one of the first Zionist organizations charged with settling Ottoman-controlled Palestine was the Jewish Colonization Association. Further, during the first two Zionist Congress annual meetings, organization members established the Jewish Colonial Trust (sometimes called the Jewish Colonial Bank) to help in purchasing land and supporting Jewish settlements in Palestine. This is to say nothing, of course, of the use of these terms by virtually all British individuals involved in Jewish settlement of the land during this period (Cohen, 1959; Jabotinsky, 1937; Wheatcroft, 2013). At the same time, Zionists also saw their project as fundamentally one of national self-liberation—helping Jews escape centuries of anti-Semitism and enabling them to chart their own course of self-determination. In addition, many Zionists prioritized hiring Jewish over non-Jewish workers to this same end.

In the academy, the dominant discourse among contemporary Middle East studies scholars describes Zionist settlement of the Land of Israel as mirroring other colonial projects of the era. For example, as Zachary Lockman (1996) writes, "most of these settlements had come to be organized on the Algerian colonial model preferred by Baron Rothschild and his agents, with European Jewish farmers employing local Arab peasants to cultivate their vineyards, citrus groves, and fields. Zionist historiography has tended to focus on this segment of the growing *yishuv* [body of Jewish residents in pre-Israel Palestine], seeing in these struggling farmers the forerunners of Zionism's settlement and state building project" (pp. 25–26; see also Kimmerling, 1983; Shafir, 1989).

The authors of the two essays in this chapter agree that the settler-colonial model has value. Where they disagree is whether it is the *best* model for understanding the establishment of Israel and the ongoing Israeli-Palestinian relationship. Sam Fleischacker begins his essay, "Interrogating the Limits of the Settler-Colonial Paradigm," by stating that scholars discussing the Israeli-Palestinian conflict most commonly explain this conflict in one of two ways: as "a settler-colonialist paradigm, characterizing Zionism as one of many examples of European attempts to take lands from indigenous peoples, or a clash-of-nationalisms paradigm, describing the struggle between Zionists and Palestinians as a struggle between two nationalist movements claiming ownership over the same territory." After delving into the myriad ways the Zionist movement differs from other colonial projects of the era, arguing that such simplistic understandings distort the Zionist movement altogether (similar, he says, to reducing all forms of anti-Zionism to anti-Semitism), he makes the case for instead approaching this conflict as one in which there is a "clash of nationalisms," two different nationalist movements fighting with one another over the same land.

In contrast, the second essay, As'ad Ghanem and Tariq Khateeb's "Israel in One Century—from a Colonial Project to a Complex Reality," contends that "what started more than a century ago as part of a colonial project has gradually morphed into a state combining colonial and national elements." They assert that it is imperative to understand the foundations of Israel using a colonial lens, exclusively if not partially, if for no other reason than because "the drive for a Jewish entity in Palestine stemmed from colonial aspirations and constituted a colonial phenomenon." In making a case for how Zionism fits into a normative understanding of colonialism, despite also having unique characteristics, they explain how it falls into the type of colonial project in which a settler community is established that imposes forms of control and collective punishment on an indigenous group while also seeking to eliminate it. Although they cede that Jewish Israelis are embedded in a nationalistic conflict as well, Jewish-Israeli nationalism, they say, emerged out of and was produced within a colonial context, which developed over a century.

Whether one favors a settler-colonial lens or a competing-nationalisms lens (or some combination of the two) for examining the case of Israel/Palestine, both essays point us to tools for interpreting the historical and contemporary motivations of various sets of actors, for understanding the structural dynamics between them, and for identifying other relevant cases for comparison.

References

Cohen, I. (1959). *Theodor Herzl: Founder of Political Zionism*. New York, NY: Thomas Yoseloff.

Jabotinsky, Z. (1937, November 26). "The Iron Wall (We and the Arabs)." *Jewish Herald*. Retrieved from http://www.danielpipes.org/3510/the-iron-wall-we-and-the-arabs

Kimmerling, B. (1983). *Zionism and Territory: The Socio-territorial Dimensions of Zionist Politics*. Berkeley, CA: University of California Press, 1983.

Lockman, Z. (1996). *Comrades and Enemies: Arab and Jewish Workers in Palestine, 1906–1948*. Berkeley, CA: University of California Press.

Shafir, G. (1989). *Land, Labor, and the Origins of the Israeli-Palestinian Conflict, 1882–1914*. Cambridge, UK: Cambridge University Press.

Wheatcroft, G. (2013, May–June). "Zionism's Colonial Roots." *National Interest, 125,* 9–15. https://nationalinterest.org/article/zionisms-colonial-roots-8377.

Interrogating the Limits of the Settler-Colonialist Paradigm

SAM FLEISCHACKER

Scholarly explanations for the conflict over Israel/Palestine generally fall into one of two categories: a settler-colonialist paradigm, characterizing Zionism as one of many examples of European attempts to take lands from indigenous peoples, or a clash-of-nationalisms paradigm, describing the struggle between Zionists and Palestinians as a struggle between two nationalist movements claiming ownership over the same territory.

These paradigms provide both a way of explaining the conflict and a normative framework for assessing and resolving it. As modes of explanation, they attempt to make sense of the intentions of leading actors in the conflict as well as the social forces shaping the actors' goals and strategies. As normative frameworks, the settler-colonialist paradigm suggests that nothing less than the full dismantling of Zionism will bring about justice, while the clash-of-nationalisms paradigm views the conflict as a classic tragedy where full justice is impossible and an appropriate solution requires compromise on both sides.

After laying out the core of truth in the settler-colonialist paradigm, I argue that as a whole it distorts the history of Zionism, painting its supporters as deceptive or self-deceptive. To bring out the explanatory and normative limitations of this framework more clearly, I then compare the settler-colonialist paradigm with views that reduce anti-Zionism to anti-Semitism. I also offer a critique of As'ad Ghanem and Tariq Khateeb's argument (this volume). Finally, I describe the alternative clash-of-nationalisms paradigm and its explanatory and normative advantages.

Zionism as Settler Colonialism?

To begin, it is worth noting that when people speak of settler colonialism they usually have in mind a Western project rooted in a particularly Western, virulent form of racism. Maxime Rodinson's description is typical: "The creation of the State of Israel on Palestinian soil is the culmination of a process that fits perfectly into the great European-American movement of expansion in the nineteenth and twentieth centuries, whose aim was to settle new inhabitants among other peoples or to dominate them economically and politically" (quoted in Ram, 1999, p. 56). Similarly, for D.K. Fieldhouse (1981) colonization involves "the creation of permanent and distinctively European communities in other parts of the world" (p. 5).[1]

But attempts to "settle new inhabitants among other peoples or to dominate them economically and politically" are by no means limited to the West. Consider, for instance, the takeover of Taiwan from its native Malay inhabitants by the Chinese, which followed exactly the same pattern as European settler colonialism. Saddam Hussein's Arabization of Iraq, which displaced half a million Kurds, Assyrians, and other minorities, is a similarly clear example of settler colonialism, as is the Moroccan government's attempt to settle its citizens in Western Sahara, so as to wrest control over it from its native Sahrawi inhabitants. The term "settler colonialism" can also be applied to Myanmar's programs for moving Buddhists into areas where the Rohingya live—even before the current crisis—to China's policies in Tibet, and to the Philippine government's settlement of Christians in Mindanao.

These examples are important for three primary reasons. First, some features of European colonization, like the attempt to form "distinctively European" communities, are ill fitted to Zionism, many of whose adherents were interested in reawakening or creating distinctively non-European aspects of Jewish culture (hence the revival of Hebrew, among other things). Second, the effect of calling Zionism a settler-colonial movement is to present Jews as, culturally, similar to Europeans, which distorts both their history and their self-understanding. Third, the elements of settler colonialism in places like Iraq and Myanmar suggest that it cannot be sharply separated from nationalism; it may indeed be an outgrowth of nationalism.

Assessing the Arguments for the Settler-Colonial Paradigm

Let us turn now to the reasons in favor of applying the settler-colonial paradigm. Its advocates usually make three claims. First, Zionism sought and received the support of imperial powers during its history, including the British Empire in its founding period and the United States in later years. Second, Zionists have often displayed the same racist condescension and contempt towards the indigenous inhabitants of Palestine that colonialists have shown towards other native peoples. Third, the socioeconomic structure of the Zionist settlement in Palestine, which exploited Arab labor while simultaneously trying to keep Arabs from having political rights, closely resembles the socioeconomic structure of other colonialist projects.

These claims are of varying import. The first is true only in part, and that part is misleading. Zionism had no imperial sponsor for its first 35 years (the first wave of Jewish immigration, or *aliyah*, is usually dated to 1882), and, for all intents and purposes, it lost support from Great Britain when Britain issued its White Paper restricting Jewish immigration in 1939. Even between 1917 and 1939, the relationship between the Zionist movement and Britain was rocky, since the British were trying to balance their commitment to it with their interest in cultivating relationships with the Arab world. These points illustrate that the Zionist movement was not a project *of* the British Empire, but a separate entity—serving Jews around the world rather than British people—with sometimes convergent, sometimes divergent, interests from the British.[2] This is entirely unlike the relationship between Britain or Spain or France and their respective colonists in Africa, the Americas, Australia, and India.

The second claim—that Zionists have often displayed racism towards Palestinians—is undeniable. As early as 1891, the renowned Zionist Ahad Ha'am complained that "our [Jewish] brethren in the Land of Israel ... behave toward the Arabs with hostility and cruelty, infringe upon their boundaries, hit them without reason, and even brag about it" (Avineri, 1981, p. 123). Ahad Ha'am was unusual among early Zionist leaders for acknowledging this problem. Many of them, while disapproving of the sort of open thuggery that Ahad Ha'am describes, shared the contemptuous attitudes underlying such behavior. Some believed that most Palestinian Arabs actually welcomed the Zionists for the material benefits they brought (Tessler, 2009, p. 134). Others thought that European Jews, as representatives of what they regarded as a higher civilization, had a right to rule over Arabs. Chaim Weizmann, a negotiator of the Balfour Declaration and Israel's first president, declared: "There is a fundamental difference in quality between Jew and native" (Segev, 1999, p. 109). Ze'ev Jabotinsky, the founder of revisionist Zionism, remarked, "we [Jews] come to the Land of Israel in order to push the moral frontiers of Europe up to the Euphrates" (Avineri, 1981, p. 180).

But the fact that many Zionist leaders talked or acted in racist ways is not enough to prove that racism pervaded or defined the movement. In the first place, there were Zionists who pushed back against the Eurocentrism of figures like Weizmann, calling on their fellow Jews to "consolidate our Semitic nationality and not obfuscate it with European culture" (quoted in Tessler, 2009, p. 135). In the second place, pronouncements by leaders do not of themselves define movements. Karl Marx and Friedrich Engels made racist remarks; Adolf Hitler condemned the inequities of capitalism. Neither of these things turns socialism into racism or racism into socialism.

The third claim above—concerning the exploitation of Arab labor—is the strongest reason for favoring the settler-colonialist view. Gershon Shafir (1999, pp. 87, 89) has shown how early Jewish settlements and the World Zionist Organization looked to the French colonization of Algeria and Tunisia and German colonization in Prussia as models in designing their own communities.[3] From these examples, Zionists learned to organize labor and land in ways that exploited or excluded the native population. Shafir goes on to assert that the legacy of these strategies persisted in the social structures of the State of Israel from 1948 onward—both directly, in that the state maintained the Jewish National Fund and Jewish Agency as its means for acquiring land (collectively, and for Jews only), and indirectly, in that a tendency to exploit or exclude Palestinians has characterized Israeli society throughout its history. Shafir makes these points in careful detail; they are hard to gainsay.

Yet some of his points would equally support a nationalist explanation of Zionism. For instance, Shafir (1999) uses the policies of the newly founded nationalist state of Germany, within its own borders, as one of his examples, and at times explicitly throws nationalism and colonialism together.[4] He also acknowledges that there are ways in which Zionism does not fit the settler-colonialist mold, such as the fact that many of the Jews immigrating to Palestine were refugees from European countries, rather than representatives of them (Shafir, 2017, pp. 93–94).

Settler Colonialism's Need for a Metropole

This last fact is indeed important. French settlers in Algeria, German settlers in Namibia, Portuguese settlers in Mozambique, and virtually all other settler colonialists saw themselves as French, German, Portuguese, and so on, and their new communities as extending the power of their home countries. In stark contrast, the Jews from Russia, Poland, Germany, and other countries who came to Palestine from the 1880s through the 1940s did not see themselves as Russian, Polish, or German. They saw themselves instead just as *Jews*, who were excluded and badly treated by the dominant ethnic group in their countries of origin. They had no interest in extending the power of Russia, Poland, or Germany; they sought a Jewish home in Palestine, not a Russian or Polish or German one. Their relationship to their countries of origin was one of alienation, not representation.

An alternative way of making this point is to note, as opponents of the settler-colonialist model often do, that Zionism had no "metropole" as the source of their project or to return to if their project failed. Even in cases where the incoming Jews were not refugees, strictly speaking—such as when they were fleeing poverty and cultural alienation rather than outright persecution—they can hardly be regarded as peripheral representatives of a distant center. No European power regarded them as its emissaries; no European power devoted its resources to their settlements; and they did not swear allegiance to any European government. They may have wanted Great Britain to help them, but they were willing to take such help from anyone. They had no loyalty to Britain and did not care about furthering British interests. Britain was an ally, not a sovereign, for them; nor did they regard any other European nation as their true ruler or home.

But without a metropole, the settler-colonialist paradigm is unsustainable. The absence of a metropole explains why the Jews could not just "go home" if their project failed, and why they regarded their buying up indigenous land as a necessary condition for their hitherto landless group to establish a national home for itself, rather than an addition to the resources of some faraway country. These points are crucial to understanding Zionism, however one wants to judge it.

They also make for a sharp distinction between the establishment of the State of Israel and Israel's settlement project after the Six-Day War in 1967. Israel's decision to settle Gaza and the West Bank after conquering these lands fits the settler-colonial paradigm well. In 1967, Israel was an established state, and when its citizens went out into the territories it had conquered, they acted as settlers moving from a metropole (the State of Israel) to a periphery (the newly conquered lands). Throughout the decades since the 1967 war, these settlers have had a home to return to and they have seen themselves as representing Israel and expanding its power. Israel has also used its power to protect and develop their communities, while oppressing and dispossessing the area's indigenous, Palestinian inhabitants.

Moreover, there has been a debate within the Israeli metropole for decades, much like the debates in Britain when it ruled India and France when it ruled Algeria, over whether the settlers should pull up stakes and come home—a debate that did not take place within the Jewish community that established itself in Palestine before 1948. Relatedly, there is a clear moral case in favor of uprooting the settlements on the West Bank and relocating the settlers to Israel proper.[5] It would have been much harder to justify "sending back" the Jews of 1882–1948 Palestine given that that would have meant rendering them homeless or, in many cases, dead.

Applying the settler-colonial paradigm to Israel's actions in the territories it captured in 1967, therefore, makes both explanatory and moral sense. That is not true of the settler-colonialist model as applied to Zionism before 1948. There the model renders unintelligible how the Jews saw themselves, how they were viewed in their countries of origin, and the political relationship they had to their imperial sponsor.

But a mode of explanation that runs against the grain of how people conceive themselves is driven to claim that those people must be lying to themselves or others about their own identity. It is both implausible and offensive to attribute such deep dishonesty or self-deception to people, however. While the settler-colonial paradigm makes good sense of certain elements of Zionism, therefore, it has both explanatory and moral failings as an account of the movement as a whole.

Anti-Zionism as Anti-Semitism

The shortcomings of the settler-colonialist paradigm become clearer if we compare them with the claim that anti-Zionism is a form of anti-Semitism. (Although this perspective is derided among scholars, it has wide currency in Jewish communities).

According to such a view, Jews have been hated by Christians and Muslims for centuries. The rejection of a Jewish right to self-determination, which is granted unreservedly to every other people, is simply the latest version of this animosity. Advocates of this perspective add that anti-Semitism can be found throughout the rhetoric and practice of anti-Zionists, from the pro-Nazi ravings of Haj Amin al-Husseini, the Grand Mufti of Jerusalem from 1921 to 1937, to the Hamas Charter, which includes passages lifted from the conspiracy theories of the infamous *Protocols of the Elders of Zion*.

Much about this view is obviously wrong. The right to political self-determination has not been granted to every people. The Acehnese, Basques, Catalans, Ibos, Kurds, and Tamils are just a few of the many groups whose call for self-determination has been unfavorably received by most of the world community. Realizing such rights—at least, if that means granting a people its own state—generally comes at a serious cost to other peoples and states. There is therefore no need to cite anti-Semitism when explaining why there has been resistance to the idea of a Jewish state. There is even less need to claim anti-Semitism when explaining why *Palestinians* might reject the idea that the land where they live should be turned over to the Jews.

That said, major Palestinian leaders, including the Grand Mufti and the leaders of Hamas, have often employed openly hateful rhetoric about Jews generally, not just about Zionists, calling for their subordination or extermination. A strand of virulent anti-Semitism has indeed run through anti-Zionism throughout its history. A few examples demonstrate this point:

- In 1913, the prominent Palestinian journal *al-Filastin* published a poem with the lines "Jews, sons of clinking gold, stop your deceit / ...The Jews, the weakest of all peoples and the least of them / Are haggling with us for our land" (Morris, 1999, p. 65).
- In 1919, the Jerusalem notable 'Aref Pasha Dajani said that "in all the countries where [Jews] are at present they are not wanted ... because they always arrive to suck the blood of everybody" (Morris, 1999, p. 91).
- In 1920, Palestinian demonstrators chanted, "We will drink the blood of the Jews!" and "Palestine is our land and the Jews are our dogs," while holding up signs with messages like "Death to the Jews" and

"Shall we give back the country to a people who crucified our Lord Jesus?" (Morris, 1999, pp. 94–95).

- Immediately after the 1947 UN Partition proposal was approved, dozens of local Jews were murdered and homes, stores, and synagogues were destroyed in Bahrain, Egypt, Iraq, Morocco, Syria, and Yemen (Morris, 2008, pp. 70–71; Stillman, 1991, pp. 99–100, 142–46; Yakobson & Rubinstein, 2009, pp. 49–53). In many of these countries, persecution of Jews continued for decades after Israel's creation.
- In the 1970s and 1980s, Palestinian guerilla attacks targeted synagogues, kosher restaurants, and other Jewish communal centers all over the world, despite claims by the movements they represented that their enemy was Israel and Zionism, not Jews and Judaism.

So it is not hard to find language and strategic choices in the history of anti-Zionism that suggest it has been fueled by a hatred of Jews, just as it is not hard to find language and strategic choices in the history of Zionism that suggest it has been fueled by a colonialist mentality. But what do these bits of language and practice show? Can they really tell us what most drove the people who flocked to movements that presented themselves as promoting Jewish or Palestinian self-determination? I submit that the answer is a clear no in both cases. Rashid Khalidi (2006) rightly characterizes the idea "that the Palestinians [have been] motivated by no more than antisemitism in their opposition to Zionism" as "ludicrous" (p. 119). It is bizarre to suppose that Palestinians seeking their own individual and collective rights have been motivated merely by a hatred of Jews. But it is equally bizarre to suppose that Jews fleeing European persecution and trying to set up a polity of their own were motivated merely by a European desire to dominate non-European peoples.

A Pre-Zionist National Jewish Identity

Ghanem and Khateeb (this volume) reject this argument. They grant that a sense of national identity exists today among Jews in Israel, but deny that any "collective national awareness" existed among Jews in nineteenth-century Europe. In making this claim, they say that "there was no serious Jewish national group" before the end of World War I. On one level, this is true. Most Jews, whether in Europe or elsewhere, saw being Jewish as primarily a religious or cultural identity for most of the past two millennia. Only a minority identified themselves as predominantly a national group—a group that needed a state of its own—until well after World War I. But the same can be said of Palestinians, of Arabs more widely, and of Greeks, Italians, Turks, and Malays before the rise of their respective nationalist movements.

As Palestinian historians have acknowledged, it was the emergence of Palestinian nationalism that gave rise to a distinctively Palestinian national identity (Khalidi, 1997; Muslih, 1990). Similarly, it took the emergence of Jewish nationalism—Zionism—to give rise to a Jewish national identity.

But this is true of all nationalisms. As Clifford Geertz (1973) noted regarding nationalism in India, Pakistan, and Indonesia, the idea driving the movements to found these states was precisely that "the nationalists would make the state, and the state would make the nation" (p. 240). There is nothing about the fact that Jews did not see themselves as potential citizens of a Jewish nation-state until the late nineteenth century that impugns the legitimacy of Jewish nationalism any more than similar facts undermine other nationalist movements.

In dismissing a pre-Zionist Jewish national identity while allowing a national identity for other groups, Ghanem and Khateeb (this volume) must mean that Jews, until after World War I, did not even form what Eric Hobsbawm (1992) calls a "proto-national" group—a "people" (chap. 2), a group united by literature and cultural practices and a shared history. That, however, is false. Jews across the world have always had a strong sense that they belonged to a single, worldwide community, united by history, a literature reflecting on that history, and religious practices. They have interacted with one another across vast distances for centuries, often absorbing refugees from other Jewish communities when those communities were persecuted or exiled; their daily liturgy, for over 1,500 years, has called for the gathering of all Jews under Jewish judges and a Jewish king; Jewish poets and philosophers and communal leaders over that same time period have expressed similar yearnings. Even Jews who opposed political Zionism at the turn of the twentieth century, like Samson Raphael Hirsch and Hermann Cohen, insisted emphatically that the Jews are a people: just not a people that should seek its own state.

Some of the factors I have just cited as unifying Jews are religious ones, but Ghanem and Khateeb are wrong to distinguish sharply between religion and nationalism. There are Islamic, Hindu, and Buddhist nationalisms, as well as ethnic nationalisms with strong religious components. Think of the role that Islam plays in most Arab states or of Christian Orthodoxy in Greek and Russian national identities. Moreover, Jews have long been criticized for having a religion rooted in law and ethnic identity. Jews are thus perhaps the *paradigm example* of a proto-nationalist group, a culture or people that was primed for the blandishments of nationalism when that political ideology swept over nineteenth-century Europe.

Accordingly, although Ghanem and Khateeb are right to say that Zionism was shaped by nineteenth-century "European concepts," it was shaped by European conceptions of the *nation*, rather than of empire. Nationalist concepts eventually came to shape political formations all over the world, however, helping to define the self-determination sought by Arab, Chinese, Indian, Malay, and many other peoples. To separate Zionism from other nationalist movements, and turn it into an extension of European colonialism instead, requires precisely the assimilation of Jews to "Europeans," and blindness to how Jews in Europe saw themselves and were seen by others, discussed above.

To see Zionism as aimed at "turn[ing the Jews] into a major military force that would expel the indigenous group [in Palestine]" (Ghanem and Khateeb) is a yet greater distortion of history. To begin with, the idea that anyone saw Jews as a potential "major military force" when Zionism began is preposterous—Jews were in fact often regarded as incapable of military service (Crim, 2014, p. 25). In addition, saying that the point of Zionism was to expel the indigenous population of Palestine would make sense only if we overlook, among other things, the fact that prominent early Zionists, including Theodor Herzl, considered Argentina, Cyprus, and Uganda as alternative homes for a Jewish state: they were looking *precisely* for a place where a Jewish state could be established without infringing on any indigenous population's rights.[6] And other Zionists, right up until the foundation of Israel, sought a binational rather than a specifically Jewish state.

To be sure, more exclusivist elements of the Zionist movement came to dominate it, and the State of Israel has pursued ever more ethnocratic policies over the course of its history. But this is once again best attributed not to a lingering colonialist strain that distinguishes Zionism from other nationalisms, but to intrinsic features of all forms of nationalism. Policies that favor one ethnic or religious group over another, often extending to ethno-religious "cleansing" of one kind or another, have been pursued in Greece, Russia, China, Myanmar, Iraq, Egypt, Algeria, Turkey, the Philippines, and Malaysia, among other places, not just in Israel. That does not excuse the prevalence of "ethno-superiority" in Israel, but it does provide a different, more plausible diagnosis for it than the one Ghanem and Khateeb give—and a warning that something similar is to be expected in any nationalist state, including a future Arab and/or Muslim Palestinian state.

The Pros and Cons of Nationalism

Which brings us, finally, to the alternative paradigm for explaining the Israel/Palestine conflict mentioned at the beginning of this essay: a paradigm that starts from the view that both Zionism and its Palestinian opposition are forms of nationalism. This model has the advantage of fitting the way that both most Zionists and most Palestinians see themselves, removing any attribution of massive deception or self-deception to either group. There is also no need to attribute racist and hateful attitudes to either group as the prime motivator for its political behavior. On the clash-of-nationalisms paradigm, we can see both the pre-1948 Jewish immigrants to Palestine and the Palestinians who already lived there as being primarily concerned with securing political rights for their own peoples, rather than harming anyone else.

This also fits the history of both movements. Zionism has seen itself as a nationalist movement from its beginning, modeling itself on earlier national-ist movements that claimed to revive ancient peoples and build states for them (e.g., Greek, German, and Italian nationalisms), and on contemporane-ous efforts to form or transform a state along nationalist lines (among, e.g., Magyars, Slavs, Poles, and Russians). It drew on figures like Johann Gottlieb von Herder, the main intellectual inspiration of nationalism in Europe, and was accompanied by, and in part arose out of, a revival of Hebrew that paralleled a move to renew indigenous languages among nationalist activists elsewhere.

Similarly, Palestinians opposed to Zionism have for the most part identi-fied themselves as part of a national movement, with institutions bearing names like "the Palestinian National Council" (Tessler, 2009, p. 441). They have also consistently stressed that being Palestinian entails being Arab—that it is a specific ethnic identity, not a civic one open to people of any ethnic group. Both the 1964 and the 1968 versions of the Palestinian National Covenant, and the 2003 Constitution of Palestine, proclaim the Palestinian national movement to be an integral part of Arab nationalism more generally.

Now, nationalism involves a very specific view of politics. Unlike other styles of politics, it maintains that ethno-cultural groups need or deserve some kind of self-rule; it rejects the idea that the mission of states is merely to protect the individual rights treasured by liberals or promote the socio-economic equality stressed by Marxists. It also takes nonpolitical forms in which it promotes a cultural revival alone. Early nationalists in many places were more interested in promoting their people's language or music or litera-ture than in building a state. The basic idea is that human beings are deeply shaped by culture and cannot be characterized in the baldly universalist ways favored by Enlightenment ideologies like liberalism and Marxism. There is something attractive about this idea, and many who do not identify with nationalist movements politically have welcomed its emphasis on culture, and its resistance to Enlightenment universalism. Moreover, the political demands of nationalism have varied widely. Depending on the geopolitical circum-stances of the group that takes it up, it may call for a degree of political autonomy within a larger state, for secession from that larger state, or for the transformation of a liberal or Marxist state into one that represents and promotes a particular culture.

Both Zionism and its Palestinian opposition fit this profile perfectly. They have very much been cultural as well as political movements, giving rise to bodies of literature and film and music as well as political organizations. Zionism has indeed been as much a revival and reworking of what it means to be Jewish as a movement of settlement and state-building. And both movements have been concerned to build states representing and fostering a particular cultural identity, not just individual rights or the well-being of an ethnically undifferentiated proletariat.

Both movements also exemplify the problems with nationalism. Above all, they both display the xenophobic characteristics to which nationalism has been prone. This brings us to another advantage of the clash-of-nationalisms paradigm: it can make sense of the colonialist elements in Zionism and the anti-Semitic elements in anti-Zionism. Nationalist movements have often engaged in colonialist projects; there is nothing about seeking self-rule that bars a nation from seeking to bring other nations under its rule. Indeed, this tendency may be essential to nationalism. A particular territory, hitherto inhabited by many different sorts of people, can function as the state of group X alone only if the political aspirations of other groups are squelched.

In this light, it should be obvious that Israel's movement of Jews into the Galilee and the West Bank is not an abandonment of nationalism, but an extension of it. To call Zionism a nationalist movement is not to exempt it from the charge of having colonialist features, especially after a Jewish state was established. But this is different from saying that it was part of the colonialist expansion of nineteenth-century Europe. We should instead compare Zionism with Arab, Filipino, and other nationalisms in developing countries. All of these movements have similar sources and profiles, and their tendency to colonialist expansion derives from their nationalist structure, not from European influence.

By the same token, viewing Palestinian nationalism as prone to anti-Semitism because nationalist movements in general are prone to xenophobia helps both explain that aspect of the movement and reduce its importance. The xenophobic hatred that has pockmarked the history of Palestinian nationalism is by no means unusual in the history of nationalism—among other things, as we have seen, it has parallels in the history of Zionism—and it should not obscure the fact that the *main* Palestinian goal is a political arrangement that can give dignity to the Palestinian people, not the oppression of any other group.

A Clash of Nationalisms

Finally, nationalisms clash in many places over issues similar to the ones that divide Zionists and Palestinians. Serbs and Croats, Indians and Pakistanis, Greeks and Turks, and many other groups have battled fiercely, often for decades, over which group should dominate territories they both claim. These struggles take various forms. Sometimes two nation-states battle over border areas; sometimes several national groups within a state contend for power; sometimes a secessionist movement seeks a state of its own.

And in practically every clash of nationalist movements, we find the following features:

1. Ardent nationalists on each side tend not to see any justice in the claims of the other side, and to be unwilling to compromise any of their own claims.
2. Both sides engage in historical myth-making, rooting their rights to territory in ancient events, and exaggerating the connection of their contemporary populations to that history—all the while calling out the myths promoted by the other side.
3. Both sides see violence as a legitimate tool, rejecting the liberal emphasis on nonviolent procedures.
4. Each group appeals where it can for help from great powers.

Needless to say, all four of these features mark the struggle between Zionism and Palestinians. The blind confidence of each side that its claims are wholly justified and the other side's wholly wrong; the historical myths; the racism; the constant resort to violence, including violence against civilians; the appeal to powerful outside sponsors (the United States on one side, the Soviet Union and now Iran on the other); the rejection of compromise—all of these exemplify a clash of nationalisms.

Conclusion

On an explanatory level, the clash-of-nationalisms paradigm fits the Israel/ Palestine conflict better than the settler-colonialist paradigm—just as it fits that conflict better than reducing anti-Zionism to anti-Semitism. On a normative level, it allows both sides to see their opponents as people with respectable ideals rather than as hate-filled liars.

It also has normative advantages when it comes to envisaging how the conflict might be resolved. Above all, it keeps all parties to the conflict from expecting a solution to it that they would regard as wholly just. Under the clash-of-nationalisms paradigm, no awakening from the false consciousness of colonialism or anti-Semitism will lead decent people on one side or the other to give up their claims. There is also no use in proposing cosmopolitan ideologies, like liberal democracy or a Marxist state of the proletariat, as the solution to the conflict. A victory by Palestinian nationalism would almost certainly not result in a liberal democratic state in which every individual is treated equally; it would result instead in a state that identified itself as Arab and Muslim, favoring those groups in much the way that Israel favors Jews. On the other hand, Israel is not and never has been the liberal democracy that it boasts of being, and is unlikely to become one any time soon.

Recognizing these points encourages an approach to solving the conflict that emphasizes compromise and slow change. Such a compromise might take the form of a two-state solution along with robust enforcement of minority rights in both states, a single binational state with separate cantons for Jews and Palestinians, or a confederation of some sort between two autonomous regions. Any of these outcomes will require both Jewish and Palestinian nationalists to give up a good deal of what they have struggled for.

And while such a pragmatic, compromising approach would be resisted by some people on both sides, in the end it is both more likely to succeed and more respectful of most people on both sides than one based on the ideologies that lie behind the settler-colonialist paradigm or the attempt to reduce anti-Zionism to anti-Semitism. The clash-of-nationalisms paradigm encourages solutions to the conflict that respect the individual rights as well as the collective aspirations of Jews and Palestinians alike. Even if it lacked the other advantages I have attributed to it, that alone would be reason to uphold it.[7]

Sam Fleischacker is LAS Distinguished Professor of Philosophy, director of Religious Studies, and founder of the Jewish-Muslim Initiative at the University of Illinois in Chicago. He works on moral and political philosophy and the philosophy of religion. He has written eight books, including *A Third Concept of Liberty* (Princeton University Press, 1999), *A Short History of Distributive Justice* (Harvard University Press, 2004), and the forthcoming *Being Me Being You: Adam Smith and Empathy* (University of Chicago, 2019). He has also founded the New Haven chapter and has been active in the Chicago chapter of Americans for Peace Now. He has written on the Israel/Palestine conflict before, especially in "Owning Land vs. Governing a Land: Property, Sovereignty, and Nationalism," *Social Philosophy and Policy* (2014).

Notes

1   The assumption that colonialism is essentially a European project is pervasive in the literature on this subject. See, for instance, Fredrickson (1988, pp. 219–23) and Veracini (2010, pp. 2, 6), though Veracini acknowledges that non-Europeans have also been settlers. Lynn's (2005) work is a welcome exception.

2   The historian and critic of Zionism Susan Pedersen (2002) writes: "Unlike the cases in South West Africa or Tanganyika … Zionist settlers in Palestine were not British nationals or settling at the mandatory power's behest. Although it took place under the protection of the League [of Nations] and the British Empire, and adapted methods common to other settler efforts, Zionism was in conception a nationalist and not an imperialist project" (p. 128).

3   Shafir (1999, pp. 87, 89) argues that in the late nineteenth century Baron de Rothschild enlisted French experts who had worked in North Africa to help him reorganize the *Yishuv*. He does not, however, show any direct connection between WZO and German experts.

4   For instance, Shafir (1999) notes: "It was [the German] state-initiated, non-market-based colonization, motivated by nationalist considerations, which found its way into Zionism" (p. 89).

5   The settlements in Gaza were uprooted in 2005.

6   The slogan "A people without a land for a land without a people" was indeed used by Israel Zangwill, its primary champion, to urge Zionists to turn *away* from Palestine, since a people was already living there (see Garfinkle, 1991).

7   I am grateful to Chaim Gans, Paul Scham, Mira Sucharov, and Aaron Hahn Tapper for comments on earlier drafts of this essay.

References

Avineri, S. (1981). *The Making of Modern Zionism: The Intellectual Origins of the Jewish State.* London, UK: Metropolitan Books.

Crim, B. (2014). *Anti-Semitism in the German Military Community and the Jewish Response, 1914–1938.* Lanham, MD: Lexington Books.

Fieldhouse, D.K. (1981). *Colonialism, 1870–1945.* London, UK: Weidenfeld and Nicolson.

Fredrickson, G.M. (1988). *The Arrogance of Race: Historical Perspectives on Slavery, Racism, and Social Inequality.* Middletown, CT: Wesleyan University Press.

Garfinkle, A.M. (1991). "On the Origin, Meaning, Use and Abuse of a Phrase." *Middle Eastern Studies, 27*(4), 539–50. https://doi.org/10.1080/00263209108700876

Geertz, C. (1973). *The Interpretation of Culture: Selected Essays.* New York, NY: Basic Books.

Hobsbawm, E.J. (1992). *Nations and Nationalism since 1980* (2nd ed.). Cambridge, UK: Cambridge University Press.

Khalidi, R. (1997). *Palestinian Identity: The Construction of Modern National Consciousness.* New York, NY: Columbia University Press.

Khalidi, R. (2006). *The Iron Cage: The Story of the Palestinian Struggle for Statehood.* Boston, MA: Beacon Press.

Lynn, H.G. (2005). "Malthusian Dreams, Colonial Imaginary: The Oriental Development Company and Japanese Emigration to Korea." In C. Elkins & S. Pedersen (eds), *Settler Colonialism in the Twentieth Century: Projects, Practices, Legacies* (pp. 25–40). New York, NY: Routledge.

Morris, B. (1999). *Righteous Victims: A History of the Zionist-Arab Conflict, 1881–1998.* New York, NY: Vintage Books.

Morris, B. (2008). *1948: A History of the First Arab-Israeli War.* New Haven, CT: Yale University Press.

Muslih, M. (1990). *The Origins of Palestinian Nationalism.* New York, NY: Columbia University Press.

Pedersen, S. (2002). "Settler Colonialism at the Bar of the League of Nations." In C. Elkins & S. Pedersen (eds), *Settler Colonialism in the Twentieth Century: Projects, Practices, Legacies* (pp. 113–34). New York, NY: Routledge.

Ram, U. (1999). "The Colonization Perspective in Israeli Sociology." In I. Pappe (ed.), *The Israel/Palestine Question* (pp. 55–80). London, UK: Routledge.

Segev, T. (1999). *One Palestine, Complete: Jews and Arabs under the British Mandate.* New York, NY: Henry Holt.

Shafir, G. (1999). Zionism and Colonialism: A Comparative Approach. In Ilan Pappe (ed.), *The Israel-Palestine Question* (pp. 81–96). London, UK: Routledge.

Shafir, G. (2017). *A Half Century of Occupation: Israel, Palestine, and the World's Most Intractable Conflict.* Oakland, CA: University of California Press.

Stillman, N. (1991). *The Jews of Arab Lands in Modern Times.* Philadelphia, PA: Jewish Publication Society.

Tessler, M. (2009). *A History of the Israeli-Palestinian Conflict* (2nd ed.). Bloomington, IN: Indiana University Press.

Veracini, L. (2010). *Settler Colonialism: A Theoretical Overview.* London, UK: Palgrave Macmillan.

Yakobson, A., & Rubinstein, A. (2009). *Israel and the Family of Nations: The Jewish Nation-State and Human Rights* (R. Morris & R. Avital, trans.). London, UK: Routledge.

Israel in One Century—From a Colonial Project to a Complex Reality

AS'AD GHANEM AND TARIQ KHATEEB

Intense debates underlie how to define Zionism and the State of Israel, including its system of government and society. Many researchers present Israel as a national entity that embodies the right of Jews, as a national group, to self-determination, a formula that is generally accepted in Israel and the West. Such an approach often continues by claiming that those who oppose this national right are anti-Semites. Sam Fleischacker (this volume) rejects this approach because it puts all of the blame for the Israeli–Palestinian conflict on Palestinians and it conflates anti-Semitism and anti-Zionism. On the other hand, Fleischacker also rejects the claim that Israel is the result of settler colonialism, as this puts all of the blame on Jews (and Europe). Instead, Fleischacker adopts a third model to explain the ongoing conflict in Israel/ Palestine, what he labels a "clash of nationalisms."

In this essay, we oppose Fleischacker's view of Zionism and Israel as a national phenomenon, thereby proposing a fourth approach: what started more than a century ago as part of a colonial project has gradually morphed into a state combining colonial and national elements. We argue that it is impossible to understand the foundations of Israel, especially before its establishment in 1948, on the basis of a national paradigm alone because there was no national Jewish movement when the modern Zionist movement was created at the end of the nineteenth century. At that stage, the drive for a Jewish entity in Palestine stemmed from colonial aspirations and constituted a colonial phenomenon. Further, as we show, Israel shares many basic colonial characteristics with other colonial entities. We also argue that the colonial characteristics of Zionism and Israel differ from other colonial realities; this should be taken into account in order to understand the origins of each, before and after 1948. Although we oppose the approach that sees Israel as a "national" entity, rooted in the claim that there exists a single Jewish national group, we also do not accept the view that negates the national character of Israeli Jews, even though this status was formed in a colonial context only after the establishment of the British Mandate of Palestine of 1922.

To explain our argument, we will first unpack the "colonial" framework as a system, and synthesize this with an understanding of a "national" approach to Zionism. This will allow us to explain the phenomenon of Israel appropriately. We claim, in essence, that neither the colonial framework nor the national framework can be used to understand Israel irrespective of the other; the combination of these two approaches is a prerequisite in order to understand the status of Israel.

The Many Meanings of Colonialism

To fully grasp how different forms of colonialism are applicable to the issue at hand, we need to first explore the various ways the term "colonialism" is understood by scholars. For example, René Maunier (1949) proposes the following comprehensive definition of colonialism: "One can speak of colonization when there is, and by the very fact that there is, occupation with domination; when there is, and by the very fact that there is, emigration and legalization for it" (p. 37). Maxime Rodinson (1973) builds on this explanation, and applies it specifically to the case of the Jews in Palestine: "The Jews attracted by Zionism emigrated to Palestine, and then they dominated it. They occupied it, and then adopted legislation to justify this occupation by law" (p. 117). Rodinson rejects the understanding that colonialism has a singular and monolithic structure that limits its substance to features, such as forcible land grabs and exploitation of an indigenous population to enrich the colonial power. He argues that there is no colonialism and imperialism as such, but instead a series of social phenomena that indicates their existence. Despite the disclosure of many similarities between colonialism and imperialism, there are also endless differences.

Veracini (2011) discusses the distinction between "exploitation colonialism," which seeks to exploit the colonizer to work for the benefit of the colonial power, and "settler colonialism," which does not want the colonial power to leave but instead wants it to stay in residence forever. One basic way these two forms of colonialism are distinct is that the latter sees the indigenous population as a hindrance to the establishment of a modern capitalist society, since its goal is not to exploit the local population (only), but to take the land on which they live. This latter form aims to eliminate the indigenous people and their claims to the land altogether. According to Glenn (2015, p. 57), such removals have taken various forms in history, including the isolation of the original population or the elimination of their culture.

In terms of understanding colonialism as applied to Israel/Palestine, Gershon Shafir's (1989) book on the colonial character of the Zionist project in Palestine yields multiple new approaches. For instance, Shafir and Yoav Peled argue that colonialism is the theoretical framework capable of understanding and analyzing the evolution of Israeli society from 1882 through today (Shafir & Peled, 2002). Other researchers consider the colonial character of Israel to be central to understanding that Israeli society is built upon the ruins of the Palestinian indigenous people (Pappe, 2006; Yiftachel, 2006). However, this last model lost traction due to the fact that, since 1974, Palestinian leadership has adopted a "phased solution" that implicitly recognizes the acceptance of the two-state solution, partly based on the claim that the conflict is between two national movements on the same piece of land, which can be divided, in accordance with Fleischacker's argument (this volume). This has diminished the conceptualization of the colonial character of Israel in terms of ideology as well as practical levels. In the framework of these explanations of the colonial project, Nadim Rouhana (2004) notes how important it is to arrange historical facts towards any final political settlement. He explains that, for him, the core of Israel's colonization of Palestine rests in its having "tak[en] at least part of the land from the Palestinians and uproot[ed] its indigenous population" (p. 70). He goes on to note that since the Palestinian national movement's efforts to establish a state beside Israel has reached a dead end, the idea of Palestinian victory over Zionism has taken on different meanings because the conflict has altered in turn. Put another way, reconciliation between Palestinians and Israelis has become a process of decolonization rather than the building of an independent Palestine in the West Bank and Gaza.

According to Honeida Ghanim (2011), the *Nakba*—the Palestinian catastrophe of 1948 in which Palestinians lost their land—was the result of ethnic cleansing carried out by the Zionist forces with the explicit intention to evict the native population in order to establish a new Jewish state in its place, an idea supported by Ilan Pappe (2006), Nur Masalha (1991), and many others. For example, between 1948 and 2013, Israel, in addition to displacing many Palestinians, erased nearly 400 Palestinian villages. During this same time, more than a thousand Jewish localities were built, many of them directly on top of Palestinian villages, and were given biblical names to replace the Palestinian ones. Ghanim (2013, p. 122) notes that in and through this process the indigenous population is being replaced by a colonial population accompanied by a national narrative and a spiritual claim that has created a historical relationship—dating back well over 2,000 years, to a proto-Jewish kingdom—between the colonizer and the land.

Nadra Shalhoub and Suhad Dahir-Nash (2015) address other aspects of the colonial nature of Israel by analysing the meaning of Israel's "*Nakba* law," which authorizes the finance minister to reduce state funding or support to an institution if it holds an activity that commemorates "Israel's Independence Day or the day on which the state was established as a day of mourning" (Adalah, 2018). Their analysis leads to an understanding of what they call the psychological aspect of Jewish privilege, in which Israel attempts to legitimize this privilege by opposing the revival of events commemorating the Palestinian *Nakba*. The dominant Israeli narrative denies this Palestinian tragedy altogether, orienting towards the *Nakba* as if it is a harmful threat, one that would support the demand for the return of the refugees that were expelled from their homes in 1948. According to Shalhoub, this is yet another form of Zionist settler colonialism.

Four Types of Colonialism in Palestine/Israel

One way to understand the emergence of the Zionist movement and its historical development is as a movement associated with European phenomena of the late nineteenth century. This reading is important in understanding the colonial nature of Zionism and the establishment of the State of Israel in the mid-twentieth century. However, this framing of the movement does not account for the myriad ways the colonial project of Zionism developed in different periods of time and different political contexts.

There were at least four different colonial manifestations of Zionism in Palestine both before and after the *Nakba* in 1948, when the majority of Palestinians were expelled from their homeland to the refugee camps:

1. as an arm of the European colonial movement;
2. as an independent European colonial movement;
3. as a form of economic colonization looking for markets in the Arab world to dispose of surplus goods or to import labor forces; and
4. as an internal colonization movement that, from its inception, has extended the interests of the dominant group in the Palestinian space, inside and outside the Green Line, by occupying land and turning Palestinian Arabs into a working class without a coherent independent economy.

None of these forms of colonialism, however, deny the formation of a Jewish national group in Palestine before 1948, when these forms of colonialism first became reality, in the establishment of the State of Israel. In other words, what began as a colonial-settlement project ended a century later in a different form, a gradual process that has continued on through the present day.

Zionism as an Arm of the European Colonial Movement

The claim that Zionism is an arm of European colonial phenomena is based on the idea that the early Zionist movement was an advanced base of European colonialism and imperialism that played a functional role in dividing up the Middle East for the purposes of European powers. As Rodinson (1973) contends, the Zionist movement played on European anti-Semitism and the desire to expel Jews from Europe. At the same time, Zionism was a movement that originated in Europe, and Zionist activists proposed that a Jewish colony would represent European civilization in the "East," arguing that the "Western" world would benefit if they supported the Zionist movement. This cannot be read in isolation from the concept of European supremacy instilled in the hearts of many Europeans, Jews among them: the possibility of occupying every "empty land" outside Europe. In this case, "empty" did not mean empty of people, but rather a cultural void that allows "civilized" cultures to colonize these lands and their inhabitants and to build "incentives of development."

Edward Said (1979) attributes the emergence of the Zionist movement and its nature to the birth of the Jewish bourgeois class integrated in the European countries, which saw impoverished Jewish immigrants from Russia to western Europe as a burden on the countries where they resided and a source of anti-Semitism.

In a slightly different formulation, Abdul Wahab Al-Messiri (2009, p. 17) maintains that Zionism is a "Western" political ideology with a settler-colonial orientation. Al-Messiri goes on to say that the Zionist project aimed at transferring the "Jewish problem" from Europe to Palestine, claiming that their relocation was also intended to turn these people into a major military force that would expel the indigenous group and suppress them. He concludes by saying that the Zionist presence in the Arab region was intended to exert a controlling role over the locals (p. 529).

Zionism as an Independent European Colonial Movement

Fayez Sayegh (1972) asserts that the Zionist movement rejected the solutions adopted by European Jews in their struggle against anti-Semitism in Europe, including integration into European society or moving from one part of Europe to another, favoring instead the establishment of a new Jewish country. In Sayegh's opinion, Zionist ideology was permeated by the national, colonial settlement, and imperialist concepts and movements prevailing at the time, although he emphasizes that the Zionist movement had its own distinct way of interpreting these concepts. As Sayegh stresses, it is wrong to regard the Zionist movement as an arm of the European imperialist movement or of European colonialism in absolute terms. Zionism was not a shadow of the original doctrines or an extension of an external force; it had its own aims, power, and interests and was an altogether separate entity, although it began as an expression of European imperialism and colonialism, and each can to this day still be identified in the policies of the State of Israel. After the establishment of Israel, the state developed two new forms of colonialism, discussed below.

Zionism as a Form of Economic Colonization

According to this framework, Israel represents an economic colonial project looking for markets in the Arab world to export surplus goods or to import cheap labor. This conceptualization was suggested by Jalal Al-Azem (1971), whose analysis indicates that Israel has aspired to transform the markets of the Arab world and its human resources into a tool that provides economic capabilities, simultaneously strengthening its control over the Arab world in general and the Palestinian people in particular.

We suggest that this approach was reinforced after the 1993 Oslo Accords, following Israeli leaders' expressions of their visions for the future, such as that of former president Shimon Peres (1995), who noted in his book *The New Middle East* that during a future era of peace, Arab-majority countries will open their borders with Israel for the promotion of economic relations including the unimpeded movement of goods, the development of a common infrastructure, and the pursuit of economic and security cooperation (Peres, 1995, pp. 19–20, 90–91, 169). In 2008, opposition leader and prime ministerial candidate Benjamin Netanyahu (the current prime minister) charted his way "to achieve peace with the Palestinians" utilizing a similar framework. Netanyahu's model of economic peace, which he presented in his book *Fighting Terrorism* (2001), has two elements: first is the normalization of Palestinian-Israeli economic relations—that is, between the dominated and the dominant—and second is the "price of loss," which relies on free market logic. In the context of the various periods in Israeli history—such as before and after the Oslo Accords—Netanyahu's model appears to refer to the integration of Palestinian workers from the territories occupied in 1967, when the Israeli economy expanded into Palestinian lands and Israel's need for manpower drew thousands of Palestinians into the work force, where the wages they were given were much lower than those of Jewish Israelis (Farsakh, 2005).

Zionism as an Internal Colonial Movement

This argument sees the Judaization of the land of historic Palestine, inside the Green Line and outside it, in the occupied territories since 1967, as an internal colonial project not confined to the post-establishment period of the Jewish state. The goal of infusing and dominating this territory with a Jewish identity is a central force in streams of Zionism and is arguably the core framework upon which the State of Israel is based. In other words, Judaization embodies the intention to impose a new structural and legal framework on the land. In the wake of the *Nakba*, many of the Palestinian

Arab villages in the Galilee region of northern Israel were abandoned. Of the 190 villages in the Galilee, only 66 remained after 1948 (Efrat, 2013). The reduction of the Arab presence in the Galilee led to the beginning of Jewish settlement there, involving intense construction. This is confirmed by Sofer and Finkel (1986), who note, "The Arab population did not constitute an obstacle to settlement in this period, because of their severe decline after the events of 1948, and the trauma they suffered as a result of the Nakba and the imposition of military rule on them" (p. 10).

Since 1948, the state has employed various means to expel many Palestinians in Israel, especially a total denial of the claim of return for the internal refugees who left their homes during the 1948 war but remained inside Israel and became Israeli citizens; most of their land became state property (Abu-Hussein & McKay, 2003). The state has also practiced a policy of discrimination against and repression of Israeli citizens identifying as Palestinian. Palestinians who became citizens after 1948 have been subjected to a system of control benefitting Jewish Israelis at their expense, and have remained second-class citizenry in terms of government benefits and a lack of individual and collective rights (Ghanem, 2001). Israel's policies have effectively been devoted to maintaining the benefits of Jewish Israelis while excluding Palestinians in Israel from status as equal beneficiaries. The policy of land confiscation, for example, is but one tool used to control the Palestinians in Israel in order to prevent their territorial "expansion," a policy that is offset by intensive construction of Jewish localities that are granted large tracts of land for future development and expansion (Yiftachel, 2006).

Jews in Palestine/Israel: Between the Colonial Project and the National Community

There is a long and deep debate in the political literature about how to characterize the Jewish community in general, and in Palestine/Israel particularly. Some consider Jews to be a religious group without any national affiliation; others, in sharp contrast, view them as a national group to which all those who believe in Judaism or are born Jewish according to Jewish tradition belong (let alone whether Jews are a culture, ethnicity, or race, to name but a few other social identity categories). Between the two poles of religious versus national group there are many different opinions. In what follows we present a brief summary of this debate.

Zionism emerged in the context of Eastern European societies as a political movement that called upon all Jews to join together to find a collective solution to their collective status, based on a national ideology, including the right to self-determination for Jews alongside other nations. Here we should distinguish between the advocates of the national movement, a small number of elites who called for the formation of a national group, and the majority, who formed or did not form their perspectives against the same background, what Eric Hobsbawm (1992) calls the phenomenon of "pre-nationalism."

In fact, there is no certainty that, in the nineteenth century, there existed a collective national awareness of Jews across Eastern Europe, to say nothing about Jews living in the Middle East and North Africa, most of whom did not join the Zionist movement in large numbers until after World War II, when mass migration—many of them as refugees—from this region to Palestine began. At the same time, a nationalist ideology emerged that attracted Eastern European Jews, which eventually led to the creation of an activist Jewish group that wanted to apply national identity and the right of self-determination to Jews, even sometimes in terms unrelated to Palestine. For example, Theodor Herzl, often said to be the founder of modern, political Zionism, in 1904 himself proposed the idea of establishing a Jewish homeland in Uganda (Friedman, 1994).

This said, the concept of a nation does not involve a formal and stable membership. Individuals can change their national affiliation at will. This can occur in any national movement. Simply put, there is no scientific evidence of the origin-cohesion of any group. Of course, with regard to Jews who lived in volatile and changing circumstances, dealing with wars and conflicts, some emerged and others disappeared.

An excellent example of this dynamic in Israel today is found among the many Russians who have immigrated to Israel since the collapse of the Soviet Union, most of whom have undergone rapid conversion to Judaism. It is certain that some of those who believed in the Zionist idea were not born as Jews, and many of those born as Jews remain outside the nationalist movement; some are even anti-nationalist.

Most leading scholars on nationalism (Anderson, 1983; Gellner, 1983; Hobsbawm, 1992) envisage nationalist movements as a translation of collective consciousness, formed and influenced within a specific context. One can assert that until the end of World War I, there was no serious Jewish national group, with a collective consciousness, whether in Palestine or beyond. As a result of World War I, the British gained control of the Mandate for Palestine, expressed solidarity with the Zionist idea, called for the establishment of a "Jewish homeland" in Palestine, and facilitated the call by allowing Jewish immigration.

This empowered the *Yishuv* (representatives of the Jewish population in the Mandate territories), whose intellectual and political leaders pushed intensely for the formation of a local national Jewish community. Their objective was clearly supported by British colonial powers, and opposed by the local Palestinian Arab population. It was supported by the revival of the Hebrew language, establishment of settlements and national institutions, purchase of land, control of previously unexploited areas, and above all the creation of a Jewish-Israeli national movement following the creation of the State of Israel, which represented the aspirations of this group to determine their fate, whether in a Jewish or binational state (Ghanem & Bavly, 2015).

In other words—and this is the essence of our argument—a hundred years after the beginning of Jewish immigration to Palestine, against the backdrop of the collapse of the Ottoman Empire and Britain's control of Palestine following World War I, Jews aspired to achieve self-determination in Palestine. It is impossible to understand Israel without acknowledging the development and cohesion of a national consciousness among the Jewish Israeli population, which continues to grow in the light of the continuation of the Palestinian-Israeli conflict and the weakening of anti-Zionism among both religious and secular Jews. Today, the majority of Jewish Israelis accept and support the idea of a national identity and the concept of Jewish self-determination through the existence of a Jewish state.

The Zionist movement emerged in the context of developments in Eastern Europe, but it did not succeed in establishing a cohesive national group, even after British control of Palestine during World War I and the imposition of the Mandate. The Palestinian *Nakba* and its consequences— expulsion of the majority of Palestinians and the establishment of Israel—had the greatest impact on the continuation of the Jewish community's cohesion and provided the conditions for intensifying the collective awareness of "Israeli Jews" and a certain part of the world's Jewry.

In historical Palestine, the conflict is between a Palestinian national movement, which is a reflection of the indigenous group's demand for self-determination, and a continuing colonial project that has gradually developed into a local Jewish Israeli nationalism. It is worth clarifying that each of these movements is fundamentally influenced by the other, as well as by their followers and supporters.

We cannot conclude this discussion without mentioning that the Jewish national group in Israel, including its representatives in the government, has established a system that adopts ethno-superiority, creating what is known as an "ethnocracy" (Yiftachel & Ghanem, 2004). This ethnocratic system employs a national project that imposes control over territory through expansion and settlement, resulting in the further Judaization of this territory (Yiftachel, 2006). The ethnically disputed process of domination takes the following steps: establishing new Jewish localities that aim to increase and expand the majority group in a space, limiting the ability of minority members to live in more than 700 localities, implementing planning policies that guarantee division within the indigenous group, and allowing the majority to control development and resource distribution (Yiftachel & Ghanem, 2004).

Conclusion

Israel is the product of a colonial takeover by European states and Jewish activists. Its nature has changed over time according to political developments, which has led to changes in the Zionist movement, such as its having gradually become a national movement, and which bore many advantages of the colonial-settler movement. We do not accept the idea that what is going on in Palestine/Israel is primarily a national conflict between two national groups as presented by Fleischacker (this volume). Instead, we argue that the settler-colonial model is a better framework for understanding the relationship between Jewish Israelis and Palestinians in Palestine/Israel, a context where this settler-colonial movement morphed into a national movement clashing with an indigenous-Palestinian one.

There are three dynamics that can characterize the relationship between any indigenous community and an incoming settler community, in different places and at different times. The first dynamic is the extermination of the indigenous community and the establishment of a state after control of the space has solidified (e.g., the United States and Australia). The second is the integration of the settler or expatriate community within the indigenous population and the creation of a single society (e.g., societies in South America). The third, which applies to the situation in Israel, includes the establishment of a settler community that imposes forms of control and collective punishment, while seeking the elimination of the indigenous group (in this third case also fall those ready to live alongside the remaining part of the indigenous community, but in a territory that is divided up between the two groups). In this third context, there is a tendency for the settler community to expand and gradually narrow the space of the indigenous-local community, alongside the settler community's use of the local indigenous population's property and labour power to enhance and consolidate its wealth and superiority (Kimmerling, 1982).

This essay argues that Israel currently represents the clear mating of a settler colonial entity with Jewish-Israeli nationalism that was produced in a colonial and conflictual clash with the indigenous Palestinians, and which developed over the course of a century. We believe that this argument merits further investigation at the level of research and exploration as well as at the political level, which appears to have gradually nullified the possibilities of national separation between Israelis and Palestinians. We also hope that this essay stimulates thinking concerning the experiences of transition from a colonial community to a democratic society based on equality and justice, where individuals are treated as equal citizens and national groups have the democratic right to self-determination.

As'ad Ghanem is a lecturer in the School of Political Science, University of Haifa. His theoretical work explores the legal, institutional, and political conditions in ethnic states. He has published fourteen books and numerous articles about ethnic politics in divided societies, including about ethnic divisions and Arab-Jewish relations in Israel. His work also covers issues such as Palestinian political orientations, the political structure of the Palestinian National Movement, and the future of the Israeli-Palestinian conflict. His recent publications include *Towards a Bi-national Homeland for Israelis and Palestinians: In Search of a Doable Solution—A United Democracy* (with Dan Bavly) (Lambert, 2015); *Palestinians in Israel: The Politics of Faith after Oslo* (with Mohanad Mustafa) (Cambridge University Press, 2018); and *Israel in the Post Oslo Era: Prospects for Conflict and Reconciliation with the Palestinians* (with Mohanad Mustafa and Salim Brake) (Routledge, forthcoming 2019).

Tariq Khateeb is a master's candidate in the School of Political Science at the University of Haifa, where he also received his LLB degree. His master's thesis is titled "The Institutional Considerations of Palestinian Political Parties and Their Influence on the Formation of Palestinian Identity." He is also the spokesperson of the National Democratic Assembly Party.

References

Abu-Hussein, H., & McKay, F. (2003). *Access Denied: Palestinian Land Rights in Israel*. London, UK: Zed Books.

Adalah. (2018). "'Nakba Law'—Amendment No. 40 to the Budgets Foundations Law." Retrieved February 27, 2018, from https://www.adalah.org/en/law/view/496

Al-Azem, S.-J. (1971, September). "Israel and the Political Settlement." *Palestinian Affairs, 4,* 87–89. [In Arabic]

Al-Messiri, A.W. (2009). *History of Zionist Thought*. Cairo, Egypt: Dar Al-Shoruq. [In Arabic]

Anderson, B. (1983). *Imagined Communities: Reflections on the Origin and Spread of Nationalism*. London, UK: Verso.

Efrat, E. (2013, December 15). "The Arab Galilee." *Haaretz*. https://www.haaretz.co.il/opinions/.premium-1.2189249 (ratified January 9, 2019)

Farsakh, L. (2005). *Palestinian Labor Migration to Israel: Labour, Land, and Occupation*. London, UK: Routledge.

Friedman, Y. (1994). "Herzl and the Uganda Controversy." *Inyunim B'Takumat Yisrael, 4,* 175–203. [In Hebrew]

Gellner, E. (1983). *Nations and Nationalism*. Oxford, UK: B. Blackwell.

Ghanem, A. (1998). "State Minority in Israel: The Case of the Ethnic State and the Predicament of Its Minority." *Ethnic and Racial Studies, 21*(3), 428–48. https://doi .org/10.1080/014198798329892

Ghanem, A. (2001). "The Palestinians in Israel: Political Orientation and Aspirations." *International Journal of Inter-Cultural Relations, 26*, 135–52.

Ghanem, A. (2010). *Ethnic Politics in Israel: The Margins and the Ashkenazi Center*. New York, NY: Routledge.

Ghanem, A. (2011). "The Expanding Ethnocracy: Judaization of the Public Sphere in the Last Decade." *Israel Studies Review, 26*(1), 21–28. https://doi.org/10.3167/ isr.2011.260106

Ghanem, A., & Bavly, D. (2015). *Towards a Bi-national Homeland for Israelis and Palestinians: In Search of a Doable Solution—A United Democracy*. New York, NY: Lambert.

Ghanem, A., & Khatib, I. (2017). "Israeli National Security as an Extended Paradigm and the Palestinian Minority's Shrinking Citizenship." *Citizenship Studies Journal, 21*(8), 38–56. https://doi.org/10.1080/014198798329892

Ghanem, A., Rouhana, N., & Yiftachel, O. (1998). "Questioning 'Ethnic Democracy': A Response to Sammy Smooha." *Israel Studies, 3*(2), 253–67. https://doi.org/10.2979/ isr.1998.3.2.253

Ghanim, H. (2011). "The Nakba." In N. Rouhana & A. Sabbagh-Khoury (eds), *The Palestinians in Israel: Studies in History, Politics, and Society* (pp. 11–20). Haifa, Israel: Mada al-Carmel. [In Hebrew]

Ghanim, H. (2013). "Erasing and Establishing the Zionist Colonial Project." *Journal of Palestine Studies, 96*(2), 118–39. [In Arabic]

Glenn, E.N. (2015). "Settler Colonialism as Structure: A Framework for Comparative Studies of US Race and Gender Formation." *Sociology of Race and Ethnicity, 1*(1), 52–72. https://doi.org/10.1177/2332649214560440

Hobsbawm, E.J. (1992). *Nations and Nationalism since 1780: Programme, Myth, Reality* (2nd ed.). Cambridge, UK: Cambridge University Press.

Kimmerling, B. (1982). "Change and Continuity in Zionist Territorial Orientations and Politics." *Comparative Politics, 14*(2), 191–210. https://doi.org/10.2307/421586

Masalha, N. (1991). *Expulsion of the Palestinians: The Concept of "Transfer" in Zionist Political Thought, 1882–1948*. Washington, DC: Institute for Palestine Studies.

Maunier, R. (1949). *The Sociology of Colonies: An Introduction to the Study of Race Contact* (E.O. Lorimer, trans. and ed.). London, UK: Routledge, Kegan & Paul.

Netanyahu, B. (2001). *Fighting Terrorism: How Democracies Can Defeat Domestic and International Terrorists*. New York, NY: Farrar, Straus & Giroux.

Pappe, I. (2006). *The Ethnic Cleansing of Palestine*. Oxford, UK: One World.

Peres, S. (1995). *The New Middle East*. Tel Aviv, Israel: Stematzky.

Rodinson, M. (1973). *Israel: A Colonial-Settler State?* (8th ed., D. Thorstad, trans.). New York, NY: Pathfinder.

Rouhana, N. (2004). "Reconciliation in Continuing National Conflicts: Power and Identity in the Israeli-Palestinian Situation." *Journal of Palestinian Studies, 57*(3), 76–62. [In Arabic]

Said, E.W. (1979). *The Question of Palestine*. New York, NY: Times Books.

Sayegh, F. (1972). "Zionism over Seventy-Five Years." *Journal of Palestinian Affairs, 12*, 146–99. [In Arabic]

Shafir, G. (1989). *Land, Labor, and the Origins of the Israeli-Palestinian Conflict, 1882–1914*. Berkeley, CA: University of California Press.

Shafir, G., & Peled, Y. (2002). *Being Israeli: The Dynamics of Multiple Citizenship*. New York, NY: Cambridge University Press.

Shalhoub, N., & Dahir-Nash, S. (2015). "Sexual Desire in the Israeli Settlement Colonization." *Journal of Palestine Studies, 104*, 131–47. [In Arabic]

Sofer, A., & Finkel, R. (1986). *Settlements in the Galilee*. Rehovot (Israel): Center for Research Settlements.

Veracini, L. (2011). "Introducing *Settler Colonial Studies*." *Settler Colonial Studies, 1*(1), 1–12. https://doi.org/10.1080/2201473x.2011.10648799

Yiftachel, O. (2006). *Ethnocracy: Land and Identity Politics in Israel/Palestine*. Philadelphia, PA: University of Pennsylvania Press.

Yiftachel, O., & Ghanem, A. (2004). "Understanding 'Ethnocratic' Regimes: The Politics of Seizing Contested Territories." *Political Geography, 23*(6), 647–76. https://doi.org/10.1016/j.polgeo.2004.04.003

four
International Law

International law has played a key role in the struggle for social justice in Israel/Palestine. Since 1947, various United Nations resolutions have been held up by Israelis, Palestinians, scholars, and activists as lending legal and moral authority to one set of actions or another. Some of the particular issues have related to partition, refugees, Jerusalem, the status of the territories conquered by Israel in the 1967 war, the status of Palestine as an international actor, and the legality of the Israeli settlements. Key examples of such resolutions are United Nations General Assembly (UNGA) Resolution 181 (recommending the partition of Palestine into "Independent Arab and Jewish States"), UNGA Resolution 194 (declaring that "refugees wishing to return to their homes and live at peace with their neighbours should be permitted to do so"), United Nations Security Council (UNSC) Resolution 242 (calling, among other things, for Israeli withdrawal "from territories occupied" in the 1967 war), UNSC Resolutions 476 and 478 (declaring Israel's annexing of East Jerusalem to be in violation of international law), UNGA Resolution 67/19 (granting Palestine nonmember observer state status in the UN), and UNSC Resolution 2334 (declaring that Israel is occupying East Jerusalem, the West Bank, and Gaza; that the Fourth Geneva Convention continues to apply; and that Israeli settlements are in violation of international law).[1]

When it comes to the international community and Israel/Palestine, there is general consensus regarding applicable laws and legal principles, as displayed by the volume of related United Nations Security Council resolutions and the overwhelming number of associated annual votes in the United Nations General Assembly. However, successive Israeli governments have consistently contested this dominant perspective. For this reason and more, international law remains a highly politicized endeavor, especially among the parties and respective activists involved in this conflict.[2] For example, supporters of the BDS (Boycott, Divestment, and Sanctions) movement frequently reference international law as a driving force for their activism, while critics of BDS often challenge these same legal interpretations. (See chapter 8 for a deeper discussion of BDS.)

Political scientists and scholars of other disciplines often complain that international law, owing to limited enforcement mechanisms (contrary to domestic law, where individuals convicted of a crime can be imprisoned), lacks "teeth." Michael Lynk's essay in this chapter acknowledges these limitations, arguing that in the context of Israel/Palestine "the role of international law has been shaped more by power than by justice." Still, he contends, international law can play an important role in bringing political peace to Israelis and Palestinians. Lynk—who, in addition to being a legal scholar, is currently the United Nations "Special Rapporteur for the human rights situation in the Palestinian Territories occupied since 1967"—also assesses the legality of Israel's occupation generally, and Israel's annexation of East Jerusalem and parts of the West Bank and the status of the settlements in particular. In light of the "temporary" condition underlying the laws of occupation, Lynk maintains that given the five decades that have elapsed since 1967, when Israel acquired the territories, Israel's status as the occupying power in this situation can no longer be deemed lawful.

In her essay, Lisa Hajjar draws on international humanitarian law to examine Israel's use of violence towards Palestinians in the West Bank and Gaza. In outlining distinctions between official and unofficial Israeli policies, she assesses an array of types of force that Israel uses—torture, targeted killings, incursions, and aerial bombardment—and examines them in light of legal norms and rules, such as proportionality and discrimination. She also demonstrates how, when justifying a range of actions, Israel has interpreted international law in ways that deviate from the dominant international consensus.

The third essay, by Miriam F. Elman, sets out the position that, regardless of one's opinion on the merits or wisdom of Israel's post-1967 settlement project, Israel isn't an unlawful occupying power. She points out what she sees as an unfair application of international law by the UN when it comes to Israel's hold over East Jerusalem, the West Bank, Gaza, and the Golan Heights. She then goes on to assess Israel's counterterrorism policies, the state's response to Palestinian minors engaged in rock-throwing, the legal status of Gaza, and Israel-Hamas conflicts. She concludes with a discussion of the status of access to religious sites in Jerusalem.

As you read these three essays, take note of the different terminology used by the authors. One example is "Jewish residential communities" versus "Israeli settlements." The "separation barrier" that snakes through the West Bank is also a contested term. In the BDS chapter (chapter 8), Tom Pessah, citing the BDS platform, refers to it as "the Wall"; in her essay in this chapter, Miriam F. Elman calls it the "security fence." The terms that scholars or activists use guide listeners towards drawing particular inferences and, perhaps, conclusions, in this chapter and beyond.

Notes

1 Out of all of the votes and resolutions on this list, only United Nations Security Council resolutions are legally binding.
2 The strength of international law is predicated on the existence of an international community, comprised of an association of individual countries, all of whom accept the authority of this legal system. Whereas advocates of international law assert that it does or at least should shape state behavior, some critique the very notion of international law by noting that a consortium of countries all consenting to operate according to this system of rules, laws, and norms doesn't necessarily exist.

International Law and the Israeli-Palestinian Conflict: Closer to Power than Justice

MICHAEL LYNK

The famously eloquent, acerbic, and elliptical Abba Eban, the former foreign minister of Israel, once quipped that "international law is the law which the wicked do not obey and the righteous do not enforce" (quoted in Von Glahn & Taulbee, 2017, p. 5). Exhibit A for his cynicism might well be the Israeli–Palestinian tragedy. No conflict in the post-1945 world has generated as much diplomatic and scholarly advancement on important principles in public international law (Akram, Dumper, Lynk, & Scobbie, 2011), while at the same time delivering so little to those left vulnerable, scarred, and dispossessed by the conflict. Throughout the contemporary course of the Israeli–Palestinian conflict, there has been a remarkable chasm between the recognized obligations of international law and the *realpolitik* of the conflict. Israel has insisted that international law should play no role in the Oslo peace process, the international mediators—led primarily by the United States and Europe—have shown no great interest in enforcing the rights established by law, and the Palestinians have been much too weak to demand a meaningful place for a rights-based approach. In the Middle East, the role of international law has been shaped more by power than by justice (Allain, 2004).

Yet, in the search for a durable Middle East peace, international law has much to offer. Animated by the universal principles of equality, social and economic rights, dignity, reconciliation, the rule of law, and human security that are meant to govern modern state practice, international law provides a comprehensive touchstone for conflict management and resolution that rises above competing nationalist narratives and ethnic struggles. Indeed, the deliberate exclusion of international law from the various peace processes, both before Oslo and since, has been a substantial reason for the serial failures of the Middle East negotiations. As long as the peace process dynamics are determined by the unequal bargaining power between Israel and the Palestinians, we will continue to witness lopsided proposals and agreements that are unsustainable largely because the recognized rights of those who live there have been excluded (Akram et al., 2011, pp. 1–7).

The potential contributions of international law to a just and viable peace in the Middle East are at least fourfold. First, the rules of international law on occupation, self-determination, and conflict resolution are both clear enough to provide a sturdy framework for negotiations and flexible enough to draw from best practices elsewhere (e.g., the Balkans, Northern Ireland,

South Africa, and Central America) that have employed international legal principles to shape lasting peace agreements. Second, a relatively level playing field between Israel and the Palestine Liberation Organization at the negotiations table would become closer to reality, greatly improving the bargaining dynamics. Third, utilizing international law in peace negotiations would enhance the parties' trust in the rule of law as a creative gateway for living together equitably and productively after the signing of a comprehensive peace agreement. And fourth, there already exists that rarest of diplomatic commodities: a virtual wall-to-wall international consensus on the substantive legal framework for the Israeli-Palestinian conflict.

This broad international consensus on the legal framework of the Israeli-Palestinian conflict comes from seventy years of United Nations resolutions, the indefatigable work of Palestinian and Israeli civil society organizations, and the rich contributions made by legal academics. Indeed, many of the leading tomes on the international law of occupation have been authored by Israeli legal scholars, and they are part of this broad consensus, even as they debate among themselves some of the finer points of the law (Benvenisti, 2004; Dinstein, 2009; Gross, 2017; Kretzmer, 2002). In particular, these Israeli scholars are critical of the defiant position of the Israeli government, which virtually alone in the world denies that the Palestinian territory (the West Bank, East Jerusalem, and Gaza) is occupied, that the settlements violate international law, and that the annexation of Jerusalem is illegal. This persistent legal exceptionalism—that Israel is exempt from the obligations of international law—has been profoundly corrosive not only to the decades-long efforts to equitably resolve the conflict, but also to the respect accorded to international law itself.

The Israeli-Palestinian Conflict and the Framework of International Law

Occupation and the Fourth Geneva Convention

One of the central legal issues of this conflict is Israel's occupation. Much flows from this designation. The laws of occupation are a subset of international humanitarian law, whose foundational instruments are the 1907 Hague Regulations, the Fourth Geneva Convention of 1949, and the 1977 Additional Protocol (ICRC, 1907, 1949a, 1949b, 1977). As part of its purpose to regulate the conduct of war generally, international humanitarian law contains a substantial set of protections for civilian populations, and a corresponding set of duties for the occupying power, within conflict zones and under belligerent occupation. The modern laws of occupation—whose core document is the Fourth Geneva Convention—reflect the universal understanding that conquest and territorial annexation are forbidden, demographic engineering is prohibited, and the rights of protected peoples under belligerent occupation are to be liberally guaranteed and are limited only by the strict requirements of security and military necessity (Clapham, Gaeta, & Sassoli, 2015). Among the leading provisions of the Fourth Geneva Convention are the strictures against the transfer of the occupying power's population into the occupied territory (Article 49[6]); the prohibitions against the destruction of real and personal property (Article 53), individual or mass forcible transfers (Article 49[1]), and collective punishment (Article 33); and the protection of the general right to freedom of movement, the enjoyment of cultural and personal rights, and freedom from discrimination (Article 27). Lisa Hajjar (this volume) lays out in ample detail the consequences endured by the Palestinians—the protected people under the laws of occupation—as a result of Israel's refusal to honor its obligations under international humanitarian law.

Israel captured East Jerusalem, the West Bank, and Gaza, along with the Egyptian Sinai and the Syrian Golan Heights, during the June 1967 Arab-Israeli war. Within a week of the war's conclusion, the United Nations Security Council had called upon Israel to observe the Fourth Geneva Convention (UNSC, 1967a). Over the ensuing fifty years, the Security Council has passed a further twenty-six resolutions declaring that the Fourth Geneva Convention applies or that the Palestinian territory is occupied. In December 2016, UN Security Council Resolution 2334 reaffirmed "the obligation of Israel, the occupying power, to abide scrupulously by its legal obligations and responsibilities under the *Fourth Geneva Convention*" (UNSC, 2016). The United Nations General Assembly (2017a), the International Court of Justice (ICJ, 2004, para. 101), the International Committee of the Red Cross (ICJ, 2004, para. 97), the High Contracting Parties to the Fourth Geneva Convention (UN, 2014), and leading international human rights organizations (Van Esveld, 2010) have all stated that Israel is the occupying power and the Fourth Geneva Convention applies to the Palestinian territory. It is difficult to imagine a more widely endorsed diplomatic and legal proposition respecting a particular international conflict.

No-Annexation and Temporariness

An occupying power is absolutely forbidden from annexing or asserting sovereignty over any part of the occupied territory. On at least nine occasions since 1967, the United Nations Security Council has stated that the legal principle on "the inadmissibility of the acquisition of territory" by war or by force is applicable to the Palestinian and Arab territories occupied by Israel (UNSC, 1967b, 2016). In its 2004 Wall Advisory Opinion, the ICJ (2004, para. 87) endorsed the inadmissibility principle. This strict rule against acquisitive occupiers makes no distinction between an occupation initiated by a war of aggression and one initiated by a defensive war (Korman, 1996, pp. 259–60). In the classic commentary of the renowned German jurist Lassa Oppenheim, "There is not an atom of sovereignty in the authority of the occupying power" (quoted in Gross, 2017, p. 20).

Israel annexed East Jerusalem and parts of the West Bank in 1967 (via a cabinet decision) and in 1980 (via Knesset legislation). Today, there are twelve Israeli settlements in East Jerusalem with 210,000 settlers, who enjoy citizenship, far superior political rights and municipal services, and a much larger land base than the 315,000 Palestinian East Jerusalemites living among and alongside them. Most contemporary Israeli political leaders, including Prime Minister Netanyahu, have stated that Jerusalem will remain united under Israeli sovereignty under any final agreement (Liebermann, 2015). In contrast, the United Nations Security Council (1980) has regularly condemned the Israeli annexation as illegal; in Resolution 476, the council reaffirmed that "all legislative and administrative measures ... taken by Israel, the occupying power, which purport to alter the character and status of the Holy City of Jerusalem have no legal validity and constitute a flagrant violation of the *Fourth Geneva Convention*."

Consistent with the no-annexation rule in international law, an occupation is inherently temporary. It cannot be permanent or even indefinite: this is what distinguishes occupation from conquest (Gross, 2017, pp. 34–35). While the laws of occupation do not specify a specific length of time for the lawful duration of an occupation, the principle that an occupation is a transient and exceptional form of alien rule means that the occupying power is required to return the territory to the sovereign authority—the people under occupation—in as expeditious and reasonable a time period as possible. Israel's 51-year-old occupation is the longest in today's world. The only credible explanation for its extraordinary length is Israel's ambition to assert a sovereign claim over all or most of the West Bank, a forbidden colonial exercise (Shafir, 2017).

Israeli Settlements

The delegates who authored the Fourth Geneva Convention, drafted in the immediate aftermath of World War II, recognized the insidious dangers of demographic engineering to world and regional peace. Consequently, Article 49(6) of the Convention was explicit in its prohibition: "the Occupying

Power shall not deport or transfer parts of its civilian population into the territory it occupies." In the 2004 Wall Advisory Opinion, the ICJ ruled that "the Israeli settlements in the Occupied Palestinian Territory (including East Jerusalem) have been established in breach of international law." In the opinion, the court held that Article 49(6) prohibited not only forcible transfers, "but also any measures taken by the occupying Power in order to organize transfers of parts of its own population into the occupied territory" (ICJ, 2004, para. 120). This definition would include a state-sponsored civilian settlement enterprise—particularly one fueled by public funding and monetary incentives, military security, the confiscation of lands, and state infrastructure—within its absolute prohibition (Sfard, 2018).

Since the adoption of the Fourth Geneva Convention in 1949, international law has raised the level of seriousness respecting the illegality of civilian settlements in occupied territory. In 1977, the Additional Protocol I to the Geneva Conventions was adopted. Article 85(4)(a) enhanced the designation of the prohibition against civilian settlements from a "breach" to a "grave breach" in terms of law. In 1998, the Rome Statute of the International Criminal Court stated that settler implantation had acquired the status of a "war crime," and also clarified the definition of this term. Article 8(2)(b)(viii) of the Statute prohibits the "transfer, directly or indirectly, by the Occupying Power of parts of its own civilian population into the territory it occupies" (ICC, 1998).

By December 2017, there were approximately 240 Israeli settlements and 630,000 settlers in the West Bank and East Jerusalem. At the core of the thickening Israeli settlement enterprise is a discriminatory two-tier system of laws, related to political rights, zoning laws, roads, property, public services, and access to courts, based entirely on ethnicity. The settlements are the engine of the occupation: they serve as the irreducible "acts on the ground" to assert Israeli sovereignty and to forestall Palestinian self-determination. They are also central to the systemic human rights harm caused to the Palestinians, such as the ubiquitous use of collective punishment, the confiscation of land and natural resources under various guises, the presence of scores of checkpoints, settlement violence, the forcible transfer of communities, the death and injuries of civilians without accountability by the military and police, environmental degradation, the de-development of the economy, and the denial of fundamental freedoms (Al-Haq, 2013; B'Tselem, 2017).

The United Nations Security Council, in December 2016, reaffirmed its long-standing position that "the establishment by Israel of settlements in the Palestinian territory occupied since 1967, including East Jerusalem, has no legal validity and constitutes a flagrant violation under international law." It directed Israel to immediately and completely cease all settlement activity. Following its adoption, Prime Minister Netanyahu announced that

Israel would not comply with the Security Council's direction, criticizing it as "delusional" and "part of the swan song of the old world" (quoted in Kershner, 2016).

Self-Determination

The right of all peoples to self-determination is the centerpiece of international human rights law (UN, 1966a, 1966b). Self-determination—the right of a people to freely determine their political status and their path to development—is the gateway through which most other human rights can be fulfilled. Self-determination is primarily realized either through an independent state or an agreement to live within a larger state arrangement with other peoples. While international humanitarian law and the laws of occupation do not formally mention self-determination, the clear legal prohibitions on the authority of an occupying power to annex territory and to unreasonably prolong its occupation for acquisitive purposes are consistent with the right of the protected people under occupation to rule themselves. Alien rule—such as occupation or colonialism—is contrary to the right of self-determination, and it is lawful only in limited and temporary circumstances (see Cassese, 1995).

If occupation is the current legal status of the protected people in the Palestinian territory (Gaza, East Jerusalem, and the West Bank), then self-determination is the ultimate destination. The UN General Assembly (2017b) has adopted resolutions supporting the right of the Palestinians to self-determination on a number of occasions. In the 2004 Wall Advisory Opinion of the ICJ (2004, para. 118), the court recognized both the existence of the Palestinian people and their right to self-determination. Beginning in 2002, the Security Council has called for a two-state solution as the preferred resolution to the Israeli–Palestinian conflict and as the answer to the Palestinian quest for self-determination (UNSC, 2002), anchored on the territorial integrity of all of the Palestinian territory in a democratic state with secure and recognized borders. Israel would enjoy self-determination on the same terms within its pre-1967 borders (UNSC, 2009). However, by December 2016, the Security Council in Resolution 2334 was expressing "grave concern that the continuing Israeli settlement activities are dangerously imperiling the viability of the two-state solution based on the 1967 borders."

The Security Council in Resolution 2334 states that "the status quo is not sustainable," and called for significant steps by the international community to salvage the two-state solution. However, this assumption of the occupation's unsustainability, which has informed the entire Oslo process since 1993, has underestimated the creativity of the current Israeli leadership in imagining political models of permanent rule over the Palestinians without granting them self-determination (Fleisher, 2017; Newman, 2014) or, alternatively, conceding a moth-eaten Palestinian statelet with a flag and UN membership, but little else (Booth & Eglash, 2017).

An Evaluation of the Contrary Arguments

Israel ratified the Fourth Geneva Convention in 1951. However, it has consistently resisted the broad international consensus that the Palestinian territory conquered in 1967 is occupied and that the obligations and protections of the Fourth Geneva Convention apply in full. Rather, Israel has contended that Gaza, East Jerusalem, and the West Bank were acquired in a defensive war, and that Egypt (which governed Gaza as a protectorate for a future Palestinian state between 1948 and 1967) and Jordan (which controlled East Jerusalem and the West Bank between 1948 and 1967) were not the true sovereigns of these territories at the time of the 1967 war. As such, Israel maintains, it has a superior title to claim sovereignty over these territories under international law. This reasoning originates with the "missing reversioner" argument first articulated by Israeli law professor (and later Israeli ambassador to the UN) Yehuda Blum (1968). According to this view, the Palestinian territory is not occupied but "administered" or "disputed," the Fourth Geneva Convention does not apply, East Jerusalem has been liberated and not annexed, the settlements are entirely lawful, Gaza is an alien terrorist entity, and the Palestinians have no substantive claim to self-determination. Miriam F. Elman's essay in this collection broadly adopts this approach.

This analysis is fundamentally unsound for three reasons. First, it is untethered from the modern foundations of international law. Sovereignty is no longer regarded in modern international law as a title to land that may be claimed or awarded over the heads of the indigenous people who reside there or who were recently dispossessed from the area. Rather, sovereignty is the inherent right of the people who live in the territory, regardless of whether they have achieved independence or self-determination (Cassese, 1995). In the Palestinian territory, it would be the Palestinians who are the true "reversioners," notwithstanding who has ruled over them, as they have lived there as the indigenous majority throughout the relevant time period. Regardless of the validity of any title that Jordan may have had over East Jerusalem and the West Bank (Egypt had never claimed title over Gaza) up until 1967, the actual sovereign would always have been the Palestinian people. Israel had no title, no recognized sovereign claim, no population, and no control over Gaza,

East Jerusalem, and the West Bank at the time of the 1967 war. Additionally, Israel was not awarded any of these parts of Mandate Palestine under UN General Assembly Resolution 181, passed in November 1947, which is the primary legal basis for Israel's existence. Accordingly, there was never a "missing" reversioner, à la Yehuda Blum, whose mantle Israel could claim.

Second, such an analysis strips all meaning from international humanitarian law and international human rights law. Occupation as a concept is clearly defined in law: the belligerent control over territory of another High Contracting Party as a result of military operations, regardless of how the conflict arose (ICRC, 1907, arts. 42, 43; 1949b, arts. 2, 6). The purpose of this broad definition is to ensure the liberal application of the protections of the Fourth Geneva Convention to the people under occupation. At the time of the 1967 war, Egypt, Israel, and Jordan were all signatories to the conventions, thus satisfying the necessary precondition. According to the authoritative 2016 commentary of the International Committee of the Red Cross (para. 324), the legal status of occupation does not require the existence of a prior legitimate sovereign over the territory in question. Otherwise, as the ICRC (2016, paras. 324, 327) observes, an invading state would only have to raise doubts about the jurisdictional status of the territory in question to evade its legal responsibilities, leaving the occupied population without protection. Israel has similarly resisted the application of the broad protections of international human rights law to the Occupied Palestinian Territory, a position that the International Court of Justice (2004, paras. 111–13) has expressly rejected. Put simply, international law does not recognize the existence of a human rights or humanitarian black hole, where a state authority can rule a population without regard to universal standards. Otherwise, universality would have no content.

And third, this type of analysis is an affront to the broad international consensus on the legal framework for the Israel-Palestine conflict. The core international legal principle of *pacta sunt servanda*—treaties shall be complied with—means that ratified international agreements, such as the Fourth Geneva Convention, are binding, not optional, on states, and states do not have the general capacity to cherry-pick what they will obey. (States do have the right to declare reservations on treaties, but Israel did not do this for the Geneva Conventions.) Further, Article 25 of the Charter of the United Nations—"The Members of the United Nations agree to accept and carry out the decisions of the Security Council in accordance with the present *Charter*"—places Israel in direct defiance of the more than 40 Security Council resolutions since 1967 on the occupation, Jerusalem, the settlements, and Palestinian self-determination. The legal position of Israel and many of its supporters respecting these issues is best characterized not as the lonely stance of a principled dissenter, but as the thin objections of a serial outlier whose evasions are designed to accomplish by stealth and obstruction what justice and the law plainly forbid.

Conclusion

In September 1967, Theodor Meron, the legal advisor to Israel's Ministry of Foreign Affairs, delivered a legal memo to the Israeli cabinet stating that its recent capture of the Palestinian and Arab territories was subject to the obligations of the Fourth Geneva Convention. In particular, he advised the country's political leadership that the embryonic Israeli settlements were expressly forbidden by the Convention, and they would be seen by the international community as an attempt to colonialize these lands as a prelude to an unlawful annexation. Meron's memo was read by the Israeli cabinet and ignored. His inconvenient advice would lie buried in the Israeli state archives for the next four decades (Gorenberg, 2006).

Meron would go on to become a law professor in New York, a leading scholar on international law and, ultimately, the president of the United Nations International Criminal Court for the former Yugoslavia. In 2017, on the fiftieth anniversary of the Israeli occupation, he wrote an insightful reflection on the widening gap between the demands of international law and the Israeli practices in the Palestinian territory. "Disrespect for international law is, alas, not unusual in the affairs of states," he wrote. "It is rare, however, that disrespect for an international convention would have such a direct impact on the elimination of any realistic prospects for reconciliation, not to mention peace."

Accurately, Theodor Meron noted that Israel is far from the only country in the modern world to challenge or reject the application of the laws of occupation. But this admission neither justifies Israel's defiance of its clearly stated obligations under international law nor endorses Abba Eban's cynicism. As Meron observed, international law and the universal rejection of Israel's occupation is based "on the growing perception that individual Palestinians' human rights, as well as their rights under the *Fourth Geneva Convention*, are being violated and that the colonialization of territories populated by other peoples can no longer be accepted in our time" (Meron, 2017, p. 357).

Michael Lynk is an associate professor at the Faculty of Law at Western University in London, Ontario, Canada. He joined the faculty in 1999, and has taught courses in labor, human rights, disability, constitutional, and administrative law. He is the co-author, with Michael Mac Neil and Peter

Engelmann, of *Trade Union Law in Canada* (Canada Law Book, 2018); the co-editor, with John Craig, of *Globalization and the Future of Labour Law* (Cambridge University Press, 2006); and the co-editor, with Susan Akram, Michael Dumper, and Iain Scobbie, of *International Law and the Middle East Conflict* (Routledge, 2011). In March 2016, the United Nations Human Rights Council appointed Professor Lynk as Special Rapporteur for the human rights situation in the Palestinian Territories occupied since 1967. In this capacity, he delivers regular reports to the UN General Assembly and the Human Rights Council on human rights trends in the Occupied Palestinian Territory.

References

Akram, S., Dumper, M., Lynk, M., & Scobbie, I. (eds). (2011). *International Law and the Israeli-Palestinian Conflict: A Rights-Based Approach.* London, UK: Routledge.

Al-Haq. (2013). *Institutionalized Impunity: Israel's Failure to Combat Settler Violence in the Occupied Palestinian Territory.* Ramallah, West Bank: Al-Haq. Retrieved May 31, 2018, from http://www.alhaq.org/publications/institutionalised-impunity.pdf

Allain, J. (2004). *International Law in the Middle East: Closer to Power than Justice.* Surrey, UK: Ashgate.

Benvenisti, E. (2004). *The International Law of Occupation* (2nd ed.). Princeton, NJ: Princeton University Press.

Blum, Y. (1968). "The Missing Reversioner: Reflections on the Status of Judea and Samaria." *Israel Law Review, 3*(2), 279–301. https://doi.org/10.1017/s00212237 00001436

Booth, W., & Eglash, R. (2017, January 26). "Netanyahu Thinks a 'State-Minus' Is Enough for the Palestinians." *Washington Post.* Retrieved from https://www.washingtonpost .com/world/middle_east/israeli-leader-thinks-a-state-minus-is-enough-for -the-palestinians/2017/01/26/658fa5a6-e3cf-11e6-879b-356663383f1b_story .html?noredirect=on&utm_term =.380a3426f9ba

B'Tselem. (2017). *The Occupation in Its 51st Year.* Jerusalem, Israel: B'Tselem. Retrieved May 31, 2018, from https://www.btselem.org/sites/default/files/publications/51st _year_of_occupation_eng.pdf

Cassese, A. (1995). *Self-Determination of Peoples: A Legal Reappraisal.* Cambridge, UK: Cambridge University Press.

Clapham, A., Gaeta, P., & Sassoli, M. (eds). (2015). *The 1949 Geneva Conventions: A Commentary.* Oxford, UK: Oxford University Press.

Dinstein, Y. (2009). *The International Law of Belligerent Occupation.* Cambridge, UK: Cambridge University Press.

Fleisher, Y. (2017, February 14). "A Settler's View of Israel's Future." *New York Times.* Retrieved from https://www.nytimes.com/2017/02/14/opinion/a-settlers-view -of-israels-future.html

Gorenberg, G. (2006). *The Accidental Empire: Israel and the Birth of the Settlements, 1967– 1977.* New York, NY: Henry Holt.

Gross, A. (2017). *The Writing on the Wall: Rethinking the International Law of Occupation.* Cambridge, UK: Cambridge University Press.

ICC (International Criminal Court). (1998, July 17). *The Rome Statute of the International Criminal Court.* Rome, Italy: ICC. Retrieved from https://www.icc-cpi.int/nr/rdonlyres/ea9aeff7-5752-4f84-be94-0a655eb30e16/0/rome_statute_english.pdf

ICJ (International Court of Justice). (2004, July 9). *Advisory Opinion concerning Legal Consequences of the Construction of a Wall in the Occupied Palestinian Territory.* International Court of Justice Reports. Retrieved from https://www.icj-cij.org/en/case/131

ICRC (International Committee of the Red Cross). (1907, October 18). *Hague Convention (IV) respecting the Laws and Customs of War on Land and Its Annex: Regulations concerning the Laws and Customs of War on Land.* ICRC, 187 CTS 227. https://ihl-databases.icrc.org/ihl/INTRO/195

ICRC. (1949a). *The Geneva Conventions of August 12, 1949.* Geneva, Switzerland: ICRC. Retrieved from https://www.icrc.org/en/doc/assets/files/publications/icrc-002-0173.pdf

ICRC. (1949b, August 12). *Geneva Convention relative to the Protection of Civilian Persons in Time of War (Fourth Geneva Convention).* ICRC, 75 UNTS 287. https://ihl-databases.icrc.org/applic/ihl/ihl.nsf/Treaty.xsp?documentId=AE2D398352C5B028C12563CD002D6B5C&action=openDocument.

ICRC. (1977, June 8). *Protocol Additional to the Geneva Conventions of 12 August 1949, and relating to the Protection of Victims of International Armed Conflicts (Protocol I).* ICRC, 1125 UNTS 3.

ICRC. (2016). *Commentary on the First Geneva Convention.* Geneva, Switzerland: ICRC. Retrieved from https://ihl-databases.icrc.org/ihl/full/GCI-commentary

Kershner, I. (2016, December 24). "Netanyahu Promises Retribution for 'Biased' UN Resolution." *New York Times.* Retrieved from https://www.nytimes.com/2016/12/24/world/middleeast/israel-benjamin-netanyahu-united-nations.html

Korman, S. (1996). *The Right of Conquest: The Acquisition of Territory by Force in International Law and Practice.* Oxford, UK: Clarendon Press.

Kretzmer, D. (2002). *The Occupation of Justice: The Supreme Court of Israel and the Occupied Territories.* Albany, NY: State University of New York Press.

Liebermann, O. (2015, May 17). "Benjamin Netanyahu: Jerusalem Will Remain United City." *CNN.* Retrieved from http://www.cnn.com/2015/05/17/middleeast/israel-netanyahu-united-jerusalem

Meron, T. (2017). "The West Bank and International Humanitarian Law on the Eve of the Fiftieth Anniversary of the Six-Day War." *American Journal of International Law, 111*(2), 357–75. https://doi.org/10.1017/ajil.2017.10

Newman, M. (2014, October 15). "Ya'alon: Palestinians Will Have Autonomy, Not Statehood." *Times of Israel.* Retrieved from https://www.timesofisrael.com/yaalon-palestinians-will-have-autonomy-not-statehood/

Sfard, M. (2018). *The Wall and the Gate: Israel, Palestine, and the Legal Battle for Human Rights.* New York, NY: Henry Holt.

Shafir, G. (2017). *A Half Century of Occupation.* Oakland, CA: University of California Press.

UN (United Nations). (1966a, December 19). *International Covenant on Civil and Political Rights.* Retrieved from https://treaties.un.org/doc/publication/unts/volume%20999/volume-999-i-14668-english.pdf

UN. (1966b. December 16). *International Covenant on Economic, Social, and Cultural Rights.* Retrieved from http://www.ohchr.org/Documents/ProfessionalInterest/cescr.pdf

UN. (2014, December 17). "Conference of High Contracting Parties to the Fourth Geneva Convention Declaration." United Nations Information System on the Question of Palestine. Retrieved from https://unispal.un.org/DPA/DPR/unispal.nsf/0/E7B8432A312475D385257DB100568AE8

UNGA (United Nations General Assembly). (1947, November 29). *Resolution 181 (II)*. GAOR 2nd Session 131. https://unispal.un.org/DPA/DPR/unispal.nsf/0/7F0AF2BD897689B785256C330061D253

UNGA. (2017a, December 20). *Resolution 72/160*. http://www.un.org/en/ga/search/view_doc.asp?symbol=A/RES/72/160

UNGA. (2017b, December 19). *Resolution A/Res/72/160*. http://www.un.org/en/ga/search/view_doc.asp?symbol=A/RES/72/160

UNSC (United Nations Security Council). (1967a, June 14). *Resolution 237*. https://unispal.un.org/DPA/DPR/unispal.nsf/0/E02B4F9D23B2EFF3852560C3005CB95A

UNSC. (1967b, November 22). *Resolution 242*.

UNSC. (1980, June 30). *Resolution 476*. https://unispal.un.org/DPA/DPR/unispal.nsf/0/6DE6DA8A650B4C3B852560DF00663826

UNSC. (2002, March 12). *Resolution 1397*. https://unispal.un.org/DPA/DPR/unispal.nsf/0/4721362DD7BA3DEA85256B7B00536C7F

UNSC. (2009, January 8). *Resolution 1860*. https://unispal.un.org/DPA/DPR/unispal.nsf/0/96514396E8389A2C852575390051D574

UNSC. (2016, December 23). *Resolution 2334*. www.un.org/webcast/pdfs/SRES2334-2016.pdf

Van Esveld, B. (2010, December 19). "Separate and Unequal: Israel's Discriminatory Treatment of Palestinians in the Occupied Palestinian Territories." *Human Rights Watch*. Retrieved from https://www.hrw.org/report/2010/12/19/separate-and-unequal/israels-discriminatory-treatment-palestinians-occupied

Von Glahn, G., & Taulbee, J. (2017). *Law among Nations: An Introduction to Public International Law* (11th ed.). New York, NY: Routledge.

International Law and Fifty Years of Occupation

LISA HAJJAR

The Israeli government's approach to the occupation of Gaza and the West Bank, including East Jerusalem, for more than fifty years has generated evolving official interpretations of international humanitarian law (IHL) and human rights law. Israeli official interpretations have been undertaken to assert that the territories are not technically "occupied" and to "legalize" policies that violate international law, such as settlement of citizens and the permanent control of captured territory. These interpretations, while intellectually sophisticated, deviate significantly from the international consensus that Israel is occupying these territories.

This essay focuses on forms of state violence directed towards Palestinians. My aim is to explain how officials have interpreted the state's rights to perpetrate contralegal violence, and the consequences of attempts to legitimize policies that patently violate bedrock rules of IHL. Michael Lynk (this volume) summarizes the IHL rules and requirements of occupation and notes the strong and enduring international consensus that they enjoy; his contribution can be read as an example of the international law "ideal." In contrast to both my essay and Lynk's, Miriam F. Elman (this volume) articulates a version of the Israeli government's position in which Israeli policies in the West Bank and Gaza are legitimate and legal. Her contribution can be read as an example of Israeli *realpolitik* burnished with a critique of international law–based criticisms of the kind that Lynk highlights.

Israel's Original Interpretation of the State's Rights and Duties

Following the conquest of the West Bank, East Jerusalem, and Gaza in the 1967 war, Israeli officials charted an original course to assert the state's rights and duties in these territories. Rather than simply *ignoring* constraining international laws, officials *reinterpreted* the Fourth Geneva Convention (GCIV), the main body of IHL that pertains to militarily occupied territories and their civilian population. Israeli officials asserted that the West Bank and Gaza were not "occupied" in 1967 because the displaced rulers, Jordan and Egypt, were not sovereign *there*. According to this interpretation, the status of the territories was *sui generis,* and therefore Israel, as the "administrator" (rather than occupant), was not bound by GCIV in these areas and stateless Palestinians were not the beneficiaries of the law. Although this interpretation never obtained international credibility, as Lynk (this volume) explains, it became the cornerstone of Israel's doctrine on the state's rights in the West Bank and Gaza.

Israel also conflated Palestinian nationalism and aspirations for statehood with terrorism. Not only were Palestinian acts or threats of violence criminalized, but so too were nonviolent activities, including membership in nationalist organizations. This conflation of nationalism and terrorism, combined with Israel's maximalist interpretations of its right to security and land, fueled subsequent developments in the state's interpretive project.

Many states violate and deny people's rights, but few have gone to such lengths to frame such policies as legal, just, and necessary. As Elman (this volume) argues, Israeli officials sought to justify the exclusion of IHL in this context, arguing that the government has the right to interpret its obligations independently and asserting this interpretation to be legally viable even if it is rejected by international opinion.

In an effort to promote the perception that Israel's administration was benign, in 1968 the Israeli attorney general granted Palestinians from the West Bank and Gaza the option to petition the High Court of Justice (HCJ) to challenge the legality of administrative and military policies. Over the decades since, Palestinians have filed thousands of petitions. However, the cumulative outcome of this litigation has not been favorable to them. Rather, with rare exceptions, HCJ decisions have supported Israeli state practices that adversely affect Palestinians and, in so doing, have reinforced the state's interpretative premises underlying them (Kretzmer, 2002; Sultany, 2007).

Israel's interpretative project was particularly evident in relation to torture. From the start of the occupation through 1987, allegations that Palestinians were routinely subjected to torture and ill treatment were consistently denied by Israeli officials as fabrications of "enemies of the state." In 1987, for reasons unconnected to such allegations, an official commission of inquiry was established to investigate possible illegal activities by the General Security Service, the agency with primary responsibility for "internal" security. The Landau Commission confirmed that GSS agents *had* used violent interrogation methods routinely since at least 1971, and that they had routinely lied when confessions were challenged in military courts on the grounds that they had been coerced. Rather than condemn these practices, the Landau Commission adopted the GSS's own position that coercive interrogation tactics were necessary to combat "hostile terrorist activity," which was construed to encompass all activities related to Palestinian nationalism.

The Landau Commission recommended that these practices, euphemized as "moderate physical pressure," be "legalized" in order to end the problem of perjury. In November 1987, the government adopted these recommendations, making Israel the first state in the world to *publicly* justify practices that constitute torture under international law. This sparked intense domestic and international debate and led to protracted litigation in Israeli courts (Hajjar, 2005). In 1999, the HCJ issued a decision prohibiting the *routine* use of "moderate physical pressure," but left open the possibility of using it in exceptional circumstances.

The "legalization" of torture coincided with the start of the first Palestinian Intifada (mass uprising) in December 1987. The Israeli military intensified arrests and prosecutions to squelch protests, and the numbers of Palestinians who were interrogated and subjected to torture and ill treatment skyrocketed. Another illegal practice during the first Intifada, albeit one that was not officially acknowledged, was targeted killing (Ron, 1993). These operations were conducted by undercover units who perfidiously disguised themselves as Palestinians to approach and execute their targets, or snipers who killed from afar. At that time, when the territories were indisputably under full control of the Israeli military and Palestinians were being arrested and prosecuted or administratively detained in unprecedented numbers (Israel had the highest per capita incarceration rate in the world during this time), the killing of Palestinian suspects clearly constituted extrajudicial executions (Alston, 2010).

To evade war crimes allegations, Israeli officials staunchly denied a targeted killing policy. For example, in 1992, in response to a report by the Israeli human rights organization B'Tselem, an Israeli government spokesperson said, "There is no policy, and there never will be a policy or a reality, of willful killings of suspects.... The principle of the sanctity of life is a fundamental principle of the IDF [Israel Defense Forces]" (quoted in Yashuvi, 1992, p. 90). After 1993, there was an uptick of targeted killings following the introduction of suicide bombings by Palestinian Islamists (Niva, 2003).

After Oslo

The Israeli legal interpretation project took a new direction during the mid-1990s in response to political changes resulting from the Israeli-Palestinian negotiations. While the 1993 Oslo Accords did not end the occupation, they ushered in an Israeli military redeployment from Palestinian population centers ("Area A") and the establishment of the Palestinian Authority (PA), a nonsovereign entity tasked with administering daily life and serving as a security-providing proxy for Israel. These changes prompted Israeli officials to assert that areas under the semi-autonomous control of the PA had become differently "foreign." This became highly significant following the collapse of negotiations in July 2000 and the start of a second Intifada in September.

In contrast to the first Intifada, which was described as a breakdown of "law and order," Israel characterized the spread of Palestinian protests at the start of the second Intifada as acts of aggression. The military's rules of engagement were loosened, and heavy weapons were deployed against unarmed Palestinian protestors. Israeli officials justified this war model by asserting that the law enforcement model (i.e., policing and riot control tactics) was no longer viable because the military was "out" of Palestinian areas, and because (some) Palestinians possessed (small) arms (i.e., police and security agents) and thus constituted a foreign "armed adversary." Israeli officials described the second Intifada as an "armed conflict short of war," and asserted a self-defense right to attack an "enemy entity," while denying that these same enemies had any right to use force, even in self-defense (Maoz, 2005).

Under international consensus-based interpretations of IHL, massive use of military force by an occupying state against occupied territories—whose civilian population are "protected persons"—is illegal. By the same measure, indiscriminate violence and the targeting of civilians by militants from an occupied population is also illegal.

The phase of denying targeted killing ended on 9 November 2000, six weeks into the second Intifada, with the killing of a suspected militant and two female "bystanders." For the first time, an Israeli military spokesman acknowledged responsibility and justified the extrajudicial execution (Ben-Naftali & Michaeli, 2003, pp. 238–39). As with its pioneering legacy of "legalizing" torture in 1987, Israel was the first state in the world to publicly proclaim the legality of "preemptive targeted killing." Officials asserted the lawfulness of this practice on the following bases: (1) Palestinians were to blame for the hostilities, which constituted a war of terror against Israel; (2) the laws of war permit states to kill their enemies; (3) targeted individuals were "ticking bombs" who had to be killed because they could not be arrested; and (4) killing terrorists by means of assassination is a legitimate form of national defense (Guiora, 2004). The deaths of untargeted civilians were termed, in accordance with the discourse of war, "collateral damage."

The most notorious targeted killing operation occurred on 22 July 2002, when an F-16 launched a one-ton bomb to assassinate Salah Shehadeh, a Hamas leader. The bomb destroyed the building where Shehadeh lived and eight nearby buildings, and partially destroyed nine others in the densely populated Gaza City neighborhood of al-Daraj. In addition to Shehadeh and his guard, 14 Palestinians, including 8 children, were killed, and more than 150 people were injured. In this instance, the Israeli military responded to public outcry about the size of the bomb, the targeting of a residential neighborhood, and the high casualty rate by conducting an official investigation. The findings justified targeting Shehadeh as a perpetrator of terrorist violence while conceding that there were "shortcomings in the information available" regarding the degree to which "innocent civilians" were in the vicinity of Shehadeh's "operational hideout" (Israel Ministry of Foreign Affairs, 2002).

In 2005, Israel unilaterally withdrew ground troops from Gaza, asserting that this area was "no longer occupied." This interpretative "de-occupation" was another iteration of Israel's position on the legal status of the Palestinian territories, and an essential element in trying to legitimize them as sites of warfare. However, this claim never gained international support because the Palestinian territories *remain* occupied: Israel has retained "effective control" over Gaza (Darcy & Reynolds, 2010). Following the 2006 Palestinian legislative elections that brought Hamas to power, the siege of Gaza intensified.

The Israeli interpretive project in the twenty-first century—including the "legalization" of targeted killing—is perhaps best explained by Daniel Reisner (quoted in Feldman & Blau, 2009), who headed the International Law Division (ILD) of the Military Advocate General's unit until 2005, in the following way:

> We defended policy that is on the edge.... In that sense, ILD is a body that restrains action, but does not stop it....What we are seeing now is a revision of international law.... If you do something for long enough, the world will accept it. The whole of international law is now based on the notion that an act that is forbidden today becomes permissible if executed by enough countries.... International law progresses through violations.We invented the targeted assassination thesis and we had to push it. At first there were protrusions that made it hard to insert easily into the legal molds. Eight years later it is in the center of the bounds of legitimacy.

Between September 2000 and August 2014, the Israeli military killed approximately 440 Palestinians during targeted killing operations, of whom 278 were the targets. (This statistic excludes thousands of Palestinians killed by other means.)

Waging War on Occupied Territories

Even if one were to accept the Israeli rationale that the Palestinian territories are "no longer occupied" and that the second Intifada constituted an "armed conflict short of war," the nature of Israeli military assaults since 2000 has violated many of the basic rules and norms about what is legal in the context of armed conflict. These rules and norms include:

1. *civilian immunity*: prohibiting the deliberate targeting of civilians;
2. *distinction*: the obligations on combatants both to distinguish themselves by wearing visible insignia and carrying arms openly and to distinguish between enemy combatants and civilians;
3. *proportionality*: the injunction to limit the use of force such that it is proportional to the military value of the target;
4. *necessity*: the imperative to restrict targets or tactics to those necessary to achieve *legitimate* military goals; and
5. *humane treatment*: of prisoners.

In late March 2002, Israel launched a massive military campaign in the West Bank in retaliation for a deadly Hamas suicide bombing in a Netanya hotel. "Operation Defensive Shield" signaled a change in Israel's strategies of violence. The new strategy, termed "mowing the grass," was devised to inflict punishing levels of violence and destruction on the Palestinian population with the aim of both debilitating present capacities and deterring future violence against Israel and its citizens (Inbar & Shamir, 2014). During Operation Defensive Shield, Israeli military forces reentered many parts of Area A, laying waste to much of the infrastructure of the Palestinian Authority.

The battle of Jenin, which began on 2 April 2002, was Israel's largest military operation since its 1982 invasion of Lebanon. On 9 April, 13 Israeli reservists were killed in an ambush. This generated intense political pressure to take the Jenin refugee camp quickly, with no additional Israeli casualties. Consequently, instead of soldiers being sent into buildings to capture or kill Palestinian fighters, some buildings were shelled first and some Palestinians were commandeered to act as "human shields" to protect soldiers (Stein, 2002). To finish the Jenin operation, the Israeli military deployed armored bulldozers that flattened everything in their path.

Another example of the desire to avoid soldier casualties was the strategic shift towards greater violence projected from the air or from a distance. Following a 2005 HCJ ruling that prohibited the use of human shields, Israel reinterpreted the concept to assert that Palestinian civilians in targeted areas were *de facto* human shields being used by the enemy. This put the blame for civilian casualties caused by Israeli strikes onto the Palestinian organizations that were being targeted. Moreover, the decision to use aerial technology—whether planes or drones—to bomb individuals rather than manned capture operations illustrates the strategic prioritization of the safety of one's own troops, which runs contrary to the IHL principle of civilian immunity, and fabricates from whole cloth the "civilianization" of war-waging combatants.

Between 27 December 2008 and 18 January 2009, Israel waged full-scale war in Gaza. The backdrop to "Operation Cast Lead" was Israel's post-2006 claims that Gaza was a terrorist-controlled, hostile entity populated by terrorist sympathizers and civilians used by Hamas as human shields. As Neve Gordon and Nicola Perugini (2016) explain, "The post-hoc framing is crucial to this process [of legitimizing bombing that kills large numbers of civilians] since it allows Israel to claim that violence was used in accordance with international law and is, as a consequence, ethical" (p. 179).

In April 2009, the United Nations Human Rights Council authorized an international fact-finding mission to investigate Operation Cast Lead. The mission, headed by South African jurist Richard Goldstone, found that both the Israeli military and Palestinian militants had committed war crimes. According to the Goldstone Report, Israel targeted "people of Gaza as a whole," not distinguishing between civilians and combatants. The report also found that the Israeli targeting of Palestinian civilian infrastructure was deliberate, systematic, and part of a larger strategy. While this report stands as one record of Operation Cast Lead, Elman (this volume) correctly notes that Goldstone later sought to distance himself from the commission's conclusions. In November 2012, Israel waged another war on Gaza. "Operation Pillar of Defense," which started with a targeted killing operation, was an entirely aerial bombing campaign that lasted eight days.

"Operation Protective Edge," a 50-day onslaught in the summer of 2014, was Israel's most violent episode to date. In terms of the overarching objective, Israel was "mowing the grass" to destroy not only present Hamas capacities but also the possibility of future recuperations. The campaign included more than 6,000 air attacks, and the firing of approximately 50,000 artillery and tank shells. The weapons used included armed drones, US-made Apache helicopters firing Hellfire missiles, and F-16s carrying 2,000-pound bombs (Khalidi, 2014, p. 5). The targets included a vast array of Gaza's infrastructure, including desalination plants, electrical grids, hospitals, schools, and universities, as well as every structure identified with the Hamas-led government. Towards the end, Israel bombed and flattened several of Gaza's few high-rise apartment buildings and shopping centers.

There was also evidence of blatant disregard for the lives and safety of Gazans who were trapped in densely populated areas with no means of escape. By the end of this war, more than 2,100 Palestinians had been killed and more than 11,000 had been injured, the vast majority of whom were civilians (Institute for Middle East Understanding, 2014).

Conclusion

Israeli officials have reinterpreted international law to project the legality of state policies in the Occupied Palestinian Territories. These attempts deviate from and defy international consensus about what is lawful in the context of occupation and the conduct of armed conflict (Kutz, 2014). Israel's assertion of its right to use massive military force in Gaza and the West Bank hinges on the proposition that these areas are no longer occupied. This "Israeli model" of extreme violence has become internationalized as other governments, including the United States, have adopted similar legal rationales for their own counterterrorism wars waged throughout the Middle East.

Lisa Hajjar is a professor of sociology at the University of California, Santa Barbara. Her work focuses mainly on issues relating to international humanitarian and human rights laws in the context of political and armed conflicts, including military courts and occupations, torture, and targeted killing. Her publications include *Courting Conflict: The Israeli Military Court System in the West Bank and Gaza* (University of California Press, 2005) and *Torture: A Sociology of Violence and Human Rights* (Routledge, 2013). She is currently working on a book titled *The War in Court: The Legal Campaign against US Torture in the "War on Terror."*

References

Alston, P. (2010, May 28). *Report to the Special Rapporteur on Extrajudicial, Summary, or Arbitrary Executions: A Study of Targeted Killing.* UN Human Rights Council. Retrieved from http://www2.ohchr.org/english/bodies/hrcouncil/docs/14session/A.HRC.14 .24.Add6.pdf

Ben-Naftali, O., & Michaeli, K.R. (2003). "'We Must Not Make a Scarecrow of the Law': A Legal Analysis of the Israeli Policy of Targeted Killing." *Cornell International Law Journal, 36*(2), 238–39. http://scholarship.law.cornell.edu/cilj/vol36/iss2/2

Darcy, S., & Reynolds, J. (2010). "An Enduring Occupation: The Status of the Gaza Strip from the Perspective of International Humanitarian Law." *Journal of Conflict and Security Law, 15*(2), 211–43. https://doi.org/10.1093/jcsl/krq011

Feldman, Y., & Blau, U. (2009, January 29). "Consent and Advise." *Haaretz.* Retrieved from https://www.haaretz.com/1.5069101

Gordon, N., & Perugini, N. (2016). "The Politics of Human Shielding: On the Resignification of Space and the Constitution of Civilians as Shields in Liberal Wars." *Environment and Planning D: Society and Space, 34*(1), 168–87. https://doi .org/10.1177/0263775815607478

Guiora, A. (2004). "Terrorism on Trial: Targeted Killing as Active Self Defense." *Case Western Reserve Journal of International Law, 36*(2), 319–34. https://scholarlycommons.law .case.edu/jil/vol36/iss2/1

Hajjar, L. (2005). *Courting Conflict: The Israeli Military Court System in the West Bank and Gaza.* Berkeley, CA: University of California Press.

Inbar, E., & Shamir, E. (2014). "'Mowing the Grass': Israel's Strategy for Protracted Intractable Conflict." *Journal of Strategic Studies, 37*(1), 65–90. https://doi.org/10.1080/01402390.2013.830972

Institute for Middle East Understanding. (2014, September 10). "50 Days of Death and Destruction: Israel's 'Operation Protective Edge.'" Retrieved from https://imeu.org/article/50-days-of-death-destruction-israels-operation-protective-edge

Israel Ministry of Foreign Affairs. (2002, August 2). *Findings of the Inquiry into the Death of Salah Shehadeh.* Retrieved from http://www.mfa.gov.il/mfa/pressroom/2002/pages/findings%20of%20the%20inquiry%20into%20the%20death%20of%20salah%20sh.aspx

Khalidi, R. (2014). "From the Editor: The Dahiya Doctrine, Proportionality, and War Crimes." *Journal of Palestine Studies, 44*(1), 5–13. https://doi.org/10.1525/jps.2014.44.1.5

Kretzmer, D. (2002). *The Occupation of Justice: The Supreme Court of Israel and the Occupied Territories.* Albany, NY: SUNY Press.

Kutz, C. (2014). "How Norms Die: Torture and Assassination in American Security Policy." *Ethics and International Affairs, 28*(4), 425–49. https://doi.org/10.1017/s0892679414000598

Maoz, A. (2005). "War and Peace: An Israeli Perspective." *Constitutional Forum, 24*(2), 35–76. http://dx.doi.org/10.21991/C90D4M

Niva, S. (2003). "Bombings, Provocations, and the Cycle of Violence." *Peace Review, 15*(1), 33–38. https://doi.org/10.1080/1040265032000059715

Ron, J. (1993). *A License to Kill: Israeli Undercover Operations against "Wanted" and Masked Palestinians.* New York, NY: Human Rights Watch.

Stein, Y. (2002, November 11). "Human Shields: Use of Palestinian Civilians as Human Shields in Violation of High Court of Justice Order." *B'Tselem.* Retrieved from https://www.btselem.org/download/200211_human_shield_eng.pdf

Sultany, N. (2007). "The Legacy of Justice Aharon Barak: A Critical Review." *Harvard International Law Journal Online, 48* (April 30), 83–92. Retrieved from http://www.harvardilj.org/wp-content/uploads/2011/05/HILJ-Online_48_Sultany.pdf

Yashuvi, N. (1992, May). *Activity of the Undercover Units in the Occupied Territories. B'Tselem.* Retrieved from https://www.btselem.org/publications/summaries/199205_undercover_units

Israel's Compliance with the Rule of Law: Settlements, Security, Defense Operations, and Religious Freedom

MIRIAM F. ELMAN

Many people firmly hold to the view that Israel has "stolen territory" that rightfully belongs to the Palestinian people, that Jewish residential communities in the West Bank[1] are illegal, and that the Israel Defense Forces are guilty of war crimes and violations of the laws of armed conflict. In this essay, I argue that these positions are often a function of flawed international legal opinions and a mischaracterization of both Israeli policy and the Israeli-Palestinian conflict itself.

Israel is frequently singled out in discussions focused on the application of international law. There's been a selective use of the law whereby Israel—and Israel alone—is held to standards that are not expected of, or enforced on, any other country.[2] This discriminatory application of what should be neutral legal principles bolsters a false narrative that blames Israel for the absence of peace. Additionally, it sustains a global campaign to demonize and delegitimize the Jewish state; to wage economic, cultural, academic, and legal warfare against Israel; and to increasingly cast doubt on the Jewish people's right to self-determination.

The misapplication and uneven adoption of international law also makes it easier for Palestinian leaders to reject face-to-face negotiations with their Israeli counterparts. Instead of negotiating, Israel's would-be partner for peace—the Palestinian Authority—is incentivized to pursue an international campaign for statehood through a global forum, using international organizations and courts as arenas for engaging in "lawfare" against Israeli officials, businesses, and citizens (Kittrie, 2016; Sher & Aviram, 2014).[3]

The Legality of Israel's Settlements in the West Bank

The claim that Israel's civilian housing communities in the West Bank are not merely an obstacle to peace but an egregious violation of international law has sustained a campaign of incitement and lawfare against Israel based on myths that Israel is an international outlaw and that Jewish settlers have no legal right to live in the West Bank. Whatever one's opinion on the wisdom of Israel's post-1967 settlement policies, the reality is that Israel is not an unlawful occupying power—certainly not according to any binding international laws (Baker, 2017). Describing Jewish settlements as illegal or "colonial" ignores both historical complexities and unique legal circumstances.

Israel's legal claim is derived from the fact that, during the San Remo Conference in April 1920, the Allied Powers recognized Palestine as reconstituting a national home for the Jewish people. Held following the conclusion of World War I, the international meeting determined the boundaries of the territories captured by the victorious Allies during the war. Accordingly, the San Remo Resolution became the basis for the future administration of the territory that was deemed a "national home for the Jewish people," as envisioned in Great Britain's Balfour Declaration (Gold, 2017; Kramer, 2017; Rostow, 2017). In July 1922, the League of Nations established the Mandate for Palestine, incorporating the San Remo Resolution into its preamble and thus confirming Jewish historical and national rights. This Mandate echoed the content of the Balfour Declaration, turning a statement about intended British policy into binding international law.

The word "settlement" first appears in Article 6 of the Mandate: "close *settlement* by Jews on the land" was to be allowed and even encouraged. Yet, Jewish rights to settlement of this land outlasted the British withdrawal that took place in 1948. Article 80 of the United Nations Charter preserved the Jews' right to live in the West Bank (and also in East Jerusalem and Gaza) by recognizing the continued validity of "existing international instruments," including those adopted by the League of Nations.

From the perspective of international law, it is the League of Nations' Mandate borders that are binding. That is, the 1949 armistice line (often called the Green Line) is neither a political nor a territorial boundary and has no legal force under international law, as it did not correspond to any prior administrative border. In this regard, the Fourth Geneva Convention's Article 49(6), passed in 1949, has also been grossly misinterpreted over the years to prohibit a post-1967 Jewish Israeli presence in the West Bank. As Eli E. Hertz (2017) recently remarked:

> Critics and enemies of Israel, including members of the UN and organs such as the International Court of Justice (ICJ) have come to use the Geneva Convention as a weapon against Israel, even when statements by authoritative analysts, scholars and drafters of the document contradict everything said by those who distort history for politically motivated reasons.

In fact, Article 49(6) was explicitly meant to prevent the kinds of deplorable *forcible* deportations and mass transfers of peoples perpetrated by Nazi Germany during World War II. It does not say that civilians cannot voluntarily move to an occupied territory, as has been the case in the West Bank, Gaza, and East Jerusalem. Nor does it require occupying powers to make it difficult or burdensome for its citizens to reside there. That is, the statute was not meant to create a "no-go zone" for the occupying power's nationals, who may wish to migrate into the occupied territory.

The analysis underlying Michael Lynk's claim (this volume), that settlements violate international law, rests entirely on accepting the premise that the West Bank and East Jerusalem are "Palestinian lands." Yet at no point in history were these areas ever under Palestinian sovereignty. Furthermore, the "legal questionability of pre-1967 Jordanian sovereignty" gives added relevance to the competing claim that the concept of belligerent occupation is inapplicable to Israel's unique situation in which there was no "ousted sovereign" (Baker, 2017). Jordan's illegal occupation of the West Bank from 1949 to 1967 suggests that it is actually Israel that has a stronger claim of sovereignty over this territory, by virtue of its having retaken the area in a war of self-defense from an unlawful Jordanian presence.

Jordan's claim to sovereignty in the West Bank before 1967 was not accepted by the international community, with the exception of the United Kingdom and Pakistan. (The United Kingdom did, however, reject Jordan's claim to East Jerusalem.) Moreover, Jordan evicted all Jewish residents from the areas under its control, destroyed the Jewish areas of the Old City, including dozens of ancient synagogues and cemeteries, and prevented Jews from accessing the Western Wall and other holy sites during its 19-year rule—all illegal acts and violations of the terms of the 1949 armistice agreement.

In the immediate aftermath of the 1967 war, which brought the West Bank, East Jerusalem, and other areas under Israeli control, Israeli leaders believed that negotiations within an international framework would determine Israel's eastern border; most harbored no illusions that sheer physical control alone would secure permanent Israeli sovereignty there (Eiran, 2014, p. 220). But the West Bank's post-1967 legal vacuum was exacerbated by Jordan's annexation of the West Bank and East Jerusalem and its refusal to engage in peace talks about the future of these territories (Jordan eventually renounced its claim to the West Bank in the late 1980s). It is also important to note that Israeli civilian communities in the West Bank and East Jerusalem are not uniform. Concluding that all Israeli settlements are unlawful, as Lynk (this volume) does, is today a mainstream viewpoint, but it overlooks the fact that many of them are reconstituted Jewish communities that existed well before the creation of the State of Israel. That is, they were Jewish communities that had been destroyed and, in some instances (e.g., Hebron in 1929 and Kfar Etzion in 1948), their inhabitants slaughtered. Nor were these communities intended to displace Palestinian Arab inhabitants—Israel's Supreme Court has repeatedly precluded requisitioning Palestinian privately held land for Israeli civilian housing (Sher & Ofek, 2013).

Under the 1993 Oslo Accords, the Palestinian Authority (PA) stipulated that Israel's settlements would be an issue to be resolved during permanent status talks, to be held at a later time, thus essentially acknowledging the so-called disputed character of these territories and accepting that Israel's continued settlement-building would have no impact on the final status of the area (Strawson, 2002). Since the mid-1990s, Israel has repeatedly indicated that it's willing to trade away most of this land as part of a negotiated political agreement with the PA (Safian, 2011). Until that day comes, nothing makes it unlawful for Israeli citizens to voluntarily settle in a territory with no other formerly recognized legal sovereign. It should be noted, however, that today the majority of Israeli society continues to express a preference for dividing the land, despite the Palestinian leadership's, and much of the Palestinian public's, deep opposition to this outcome (Polisar, 2017).[4]

Hypocrisy: Hijacking the Laws of Occupation

While there are over a dozen ongoing conflict and occupation situations across the world (e.g., Crimea, East Timor, Northern Cyprus, and Western Sahara), these situations—which involve the extensive transfer of people into occupied territory and the displacement of local populations—are rarely seen as examples of "occupation" by the international community. Unlike Israel's situation, the respective parties involved are rarely censured, much less subjected to sanctions or to global boycott-and-divestment campaigns. As noted by Alan Baker (2017), former Canadian ambassador to Israel:

> The international community does not appear to be very bothered with these occupation situations...., It is rare to find resolutions or agenda items in the highly politicized and partisan UN Human Rights Council that deal with such situations of occupation and transfer of people to establish settlement in the territory they are occupying.... This singling out of Israel for special international scrutiny and criticism is indicative of a distinct double standard, so much so that one cannot but conclude that the laws of occupations have indeed been "hijacked" for one political purpose—to single out Israel only.

A recent example of this hypocrisy is the ongoing effort by the UN Human Rights Council (UNHRC) to create a database of international companies that engage in business with Israeli individuals and entities located in East Jerusalem, the Golan Heights, and the West Bank. A March 2017 UNHRC resolution urges member states to offer guidance to businesses regarding their risk for liability in such situations, as they are understood to thereafter be involved in "gross human rights abuses" and "settlement-related activities." In fact, such business activities are not in breach of any international law and, as critics have rightly argued, establishing such a blacklist is merely "just a backdoor way of reviving the Arab League boycott of Israel" (Cohen, 2017).

The UNHRC has not voiced human rights concerns about firms and companies that operate in occupied territory anywhere else in the world. International businesses play a critical role in supporting settlement enterprises around the globe, but only those with business ties to Israeli communities are to be targeted based on the parameters in this resolution. Some critics have warned that this discriminatory move, in which a unique set of legal rules is being created for Israel alone, will undermine the credibility of the UNHRC and that it represents an illegal usurpation of the UN Security Council's power to levy sanctions and implement enforcement mechanisms (NGO Monitor, 2017; Savage 2017).[5] This is an important critique because a system of law, including the laws of occupation, can only be distinguished from an arbitrary system of control if similar situations are handled in the same manner. If legal principles are applied only when it suits a specific country's detractors, in this case Israel's, then the law ceases to have credibility.

Israel's Counterterror and Military Operations: Compliance with the Rule of Law

Palestinians suffer hardships at the hands of the Hamas regime in Gaza and from the Palestinian Authority in the West Bank (Menenberg, 2014; Rumley, 2016). But Palestinians have also engaged in terrorism and violence, acts that have necessitated Israeli countermeasures. In their essays in this volume, neither Lynk nor Lisa Hajjar holds Palestinian governments accountable for failing to adhere to international law, including legal instruments to which they themselves are signatory. Lynk writes at great length about Israel's legal obligations in the West Bank. However, he does not delineate a single legal duty or responsibility for the Palestinian Authority, perhaps because the PA, like Palestinians generally, is deemed to be "much too weak."[6] Similarly robbing Palestinians of their moral and legal agency, as well as their capacity to make decisions, Hajjar claims that it is Israel that repeatedly "waged full-scale war" in Gaza, as if the Hamas government there is not "patently violat[ing] bedrock rules of international humanitarian law," a claim that she levels at Israel alone.

Countering Violence in the West Bank

In addressing allegations that Israeli counterterror operations in the West Bank violate international law and norms regarding the use of force, it is important to understand the legal documents related to the Oslo negotiations, especially the agreement signed between Israel and the PLO in September 1995 known as the Oslo II Accord. Israel, the PA (established in 1994), the United States, and other members of the international community continue to regard the legal distinctions and jurisdictions established in this document as binding—to be supplanted only by a final status agreement (Frisch, 2016).

In his essay in this volume, Lynk suggests that there was a "deliberate exclusion" of international law from the Oslo peace process. On the contrary, the Oslo Accords possess legal force as a structure conferring rights and obligations on all signatory parties (Watson, 2000). Accordingly, in Area A, comprising some 18 per cent of the landmass in the West Bank, including all major urban centers, the PA was to have exclusive political and security jurisdiction. In Area B, comprising approximately 22 per cent of the West Bank, the PA and Israel were to share jurisdiction. More specifically, the PA was to have political, administrative and police jurisdiction over the Palestinian Arab inhabitants there, who were to be subject to the same laws and tax requirements and benefit from the same public services that the PA provided in Area A; whereas Israel was to have jurisdiction over Jewish Israeli residents and exclusive security authority. Lastly, Israel was to have exclusive jurisdiction over Area C, which comprises much of the geographic area of the West Bank (60 per cent), but is sparsely populated.[7]

From 1996 to 2002, the Israel Defense Forces (IDF) withdrew from the major urban areas of the West Bank, thereby enabling the PA to achieve effective control. However, the PA was unable, and arguably unwilling, to prevent Hamas and other Islamist groups from establishing safe havens in Palestinian Arab towns, including Bethlehem, Jenin, Nablus, and Tulkarm. As a result, over 1,000 Israelis were killed in indiscriminate terror attacks during the period of the second Intifada (2000–2006).

But it was only after Iran sent a massive shipment of arms to the PA—exposed through a joint Israeli and US intelligence operation and the takeover of the ship *Karin A* in February 2002—that Israel decided to "switch gears from a policy of essentially absorbing casualties to a major frontal assault" (Frisch, 2016). The following month, a Hamas operative from the West Bank city of Tulkarem carried out a suicide bombing attack during a Passover Seder held at the Park Hotel in Netanya, killing 33 Israelis. It provided further resolve for "Operation Defensive Shield," in which Israel changed the status of Area A to the status of Area B, with the IDF becoming responsible for security there.

The efficacy of this change has been reflected in the reduction of mass-casualty terror attacks that occurred during the second Intifada. IDF and Shin Bet (Israel Security Service) incursions into Area A to make preventive arrests is considered by security experts to be among the "most effective means by far in reducing terrorism," resulting in a decline of large-scale terror attacks even before Israel began constructing a security fence, designed to prevent the infiltration of terrorists from the West Bank into Israel. The number of arrests increased following the 2015–16 wave of violence, characterized by hundreds of stabbings, shootings, vehicular rammings, firebombing, and stone-throwing attacks.

The Engagement of Palestinian Minors in Violence

The PA has claimed that Palestine is ready for statehood, and has responded to the United Nations General Assembly's (UNGA) formal recognition of its "nonmember observer state" status by formally agreeing to a range of international legal instruments, including conventions prohibiting the involvement of children in armed conflict. However, in many instances, Palestinian children who have perpetrated acts of violence and terrorism were encouraged to do so by PA officials (Goodman & Kuperwasser, 2016). The PA's ongoing incitement of Palestinian youth is a flagrant violation of its legal obligations pertaining to the rights of the child (Human Rights Voices, 2017).

Rock-throwing remains among the primary ways in which Palestinian minors engage in politically motivated violence. As Jeremy Pressman (2017) notes, throwing stones is an iconic mode of Palestinian protest, initially emerging as a regular feature of demonstrations during the first Intifada during 1987–92. Pressman documents that, despite its frequent portrayal as a nonviolent rite of passage, rock-throwing has been deadly, resulting in civilian deaths, scores of injuries, and significant damage to property.

According to experts familiar with such cases, rock-throwing is mostly perpetrated by unorganized and leaderless Palestinian youth, making it difficult for Israel's security and intelligence forces to prevent such attacks. In September 2015, as a measure to address this threat, Israel eased open-fire restrictions against violent perpetrators involved in rock-throwing. Prior to these new rules of engagement, Israel's courts had typically not sentenced rock-throwing minors to lengthy incarcerations, resulting in what had been criticized as a "revolving door" for repeat offenders. Israel has now made prison sentences for such violent offenses more stringent.

According to international law, Israel, like all countries, has a legal right and obligation to defend its citizens against violence, in this case perpetrated by Palestinians based in the West Bank. Recently, there is reportedly a "growing motivation" by Hamas to finance, orchestrate, and carry out terror attacks via West Bank–based cells. Of late, the Shin Bet announced in 2017 that it thwarted more than 400 terror attacks, including 13 planned suicide attacks, 8 kidnappings, and over 1,000 lone-wolf attacks. During this same year, 54 attacks were successfully carried out, compared to 108 in 2016. Some maintain that Israel's presence in the West Bank renders the PA Israel's "security-providing proxy," as Hajjar (this volume) notes. But the reality is that IDF operations, preventive arrests, and cooperation between Israeli and PA security forces in the West Bank not only help to reduce attacks on Israelis, but also prevent Hamas from toppling the PA (Gerecht, 2017).

Minimizing Civilian Harm during Operation Protective Edge

Contrary to Lynk and Hajjar's assertions in their essays in these pages, Israel is not currently "occupying" Gaza according to international law, even with the Gaza blockade in place (Bell & Shefi, 2010; Sher & Wolf, 2016). Since the Israeli military and some 8,000 of its civilians left Gaza in 2005, Israel has not met the conditions of "belligerent occupier." Rather, since 2007 Hamas has been the governing authority in Gaza, responsible for the local Palestinian population, having wrested power in a violent coup in which scores of its political rivals from the PA were murdered in extrajudicial killings. Today Gaza functions as an independent terror state. As has been documented, Hamas governs Gaza with an iron fist, denying basic civil liberties to Palestinians while routinely depriving them of humanitarian aid, which it diverts to build its terror infrastructure (Israel Ministry of Foreign Affairs, 2016).

Hajjar argues that over the past decade, Israel has repeatedly "waged full-scale war" on Gaza in a manner that has "violated many of the basic rules and norms about what is legal in the context of armed conflict." She draws on the Goldstone Report, based on the findings of a UNHRC-commissioned investigation of "Operation Cast Lead," Israel's three-week military operation against Hamas carried out in 2008–2009. Yet, according to many, this report has been discredited because its own lead author subsequently issued a statement expressing regret, recanting its main findings (Bronner & Kershner, 2011; Goldstone, 2011).

With regard to the 2014 military operation against Hamas's terror infrastructure—including the effort to dismantle its elaborate system of illegal tunnels leading into Israeli civilian residential spaces—Hajjar's claim that Israel engaged in "blatant disregard for the lives and safety of Gazans who were trapped in densely populated areas with no means of escape" has been roundly refuted in multiple third-party investigations (Elman, 2015; Wittes, 2015). Conducted by high-level international military and defense experts and experts on war crimes, these reports explain that the IDF acted in an exemplary fashion during the 50 days of conflict. While mistakes did happen, as occur in every war, each report concluded that charges of war crimes against Israel were inaccurate, and that the primary responsibility for both the initiation of hostilities and the toll of civilian casualties rested with Hamas.

In particular, these investigations pointed to Israel's system of warning civilians to evacuate targeted facilities (e.g., "knocks on the roof," SMS messages, leaflet drops, radio broadcasts, and communication via United Nations staff in Gaza). The system was designed to give Palestinian civilians a chance to get to safety, and to make sure that each individual targeting decision complied with the legal principles of distinction and proportionality in order to minimize civilian harm. The IDF utilized strict procedures for confirming the validity of a military target; in fact, there were many cases in which it declined to attack due to the detected presence of civilians. Thus, while Hajjar claims that Israel has "the strategic prioritization of the safety of [its] own troops," the reality is that in a number of instances Israel aborted missions in order to spare Palestinian civilian life (Reuters, 2014). In doing so, Israel undermined the effectiveness of its own IDF operations by pausing military action and enabling Hamas to regroup, thereby imposing additional risks on its troops. As Benjamin Wittes (2015) notes, "the Israeli targeting procedures in question are unquestionably impressive.... No other military, including [the US military], takes such measures as a matter of routine."

I also disagree with Hajjar's assertions that Hamas does not use human shields and that Israel has fabricated this claim in order to "put the blame for civilian casualties caused by Israeli strikes onto the Palestinian organizations." In fact, Hamas's own war manual recognizes the benefits of fighting among civilians in a dense urban conflict zone, both hiding among and launching attacks from what international law recognizes to be protected civilian facilities (Bob, 2014). The laws of armed conflict require combatant forces to ensure that civilians are evacuated from combat areas. But in many documented cases, Hamas directed civilians to remain in places where they expected to be on the receiving end of Israeli air strikes (UN Watch, 2015). Unlike Hamas, which reserves its bunkers and shelters for its rockets and fighters rather than for noncombatant civilians, Israel protects its citizens by investing in a state-of-the-art civilian defense system. As Wittes remarks, "it's a little perverse to argue that strong civilian defense renders otherwise appropriate offensive operations disproportionate because one side isn't losing enough people."

Contrary to Hajjar's claims that the IDF lacked restraint and even deliberately targeted innocent civilians in 2014, the Israel-Hamas hostilities at that time were not a case of Israel launching an unprovoked attack, as this was not a war that Israel wanted. The chain of events that led to this particular conflict began with the kidnapping and brutal murder of three Israeli teens in the West Bank by a Hamas cell. Hamas then escalated by indiscriminately firing thousands of rockets from Gaza on Israeli towns and cities. Missiles were deliberately fired at Israel's main airport, disrupting and threatening all international air traffic. During this period, which lasted for weeks, Israel exercised restraint as its citizens were continually targeted by rockets. Hamas also tried to use tunnels connecting Gaza to Israel in order to murder and kidnap Israeli civilians. Once the war began, supplies provided by Israel to the civilian population were commandeered by Hamas for its own military use. Hamas also murdered more than 20 alleged informants during the hostilities and tortured dozens more (Amnesty International, 2015). It prolonged the hostilities by repeatedly rejecting ceasefires, or accepting them only to violate their terms immediately thereafter. During one such UN-brokered ceasefire, two IDF soldiers were murdered; their bodies are today still being held illegally by Hamas.

The Uneven Application of Religious Freedom Rights

According to the PA's obligations under the Oslo Accords, Israeli citizens have the right to enter and pass through Area A of the West Bank unharmed, provided they are not involved in any illegal activities (in which case the PA has the authority to temporarily apprehend them before transferring them to Israeli authorities). Yet the PA has never lived up to these legal obligations. Soon after the accords were signed in the 1990s, Israeli citizens were denied the right to freely pass through Area A. When residents from the West Bank settlements of Beit El and Ofra endangered their lives in attempting to exercise this right, Israel barred all of its citizens from entering Area A without explicit IDF permission.

Today, Jews can only visit Jewish religious and historical sites in Area A if they are accompanied by armed Israeli military escorts. Visits must be coordinated with the IDF and occur infrequently, typically in the middle of the night due to the threat of violence from local Palestinian residents. Jewish historical sites in Palestinian-controlled areas, including Joseph's Tomb in Nablus, a very important sacred ossuary that many Jews consider to be one of the five holiest sites in Judaism, have repeatedly come under attack. The Oslo Accords designated Joseph's Tomb to remain under Israeli control. But in a move that was meant to be only temporary, Israel pulled out of the area in October 2000, at the beginning of the second Intifada, after an IDF unit stationed there came under heavy fire from Palestinian gunmen. The decision of then Israeli prime minister Ehud Barak to leave the outpost was widely criticized after much of the tomb was damaged by violent mobs who used pickaxes to wreck the structure, thereafter setting it on fire. The tomb was torched again by Palestinians in 2015. In some cases, PA officials have also been complicit in condoning the desecration of this holy site, even supporting attacks on Jewish worshippers who make pilgrimages there.

Consistent with the universal human right to freedom of religion and belief, through the passage of the Protection of Holy Places Law, in June 1967, Israel has sought to assure access to, and the safety of, sacred sites. Marshall J. Breger and Thomas A. Idinopulos (1998) note in their seminal study:

> Israel defended its 1967 extension of jurisdiction [in east Jerusalem] as a measure undertaken (in part) to protect the holy places. In a 1967 letter to the UN Secretary General, Abba Eban argued that "the measures adopted relate to the integration of Jerusalem in the administrative and municipal spheres, and furnish the legal basis for the protection of the holy places of Jerusalem." (p. 23)

Breger and Idinopulos describe Israel's conduct regarding the holy places as "exemplary," noting that pilgrims, even from countries without formal relations with Israel, have been able to freely visit holy sites in Jerusalem's Old City. But in a separate arrangement also arrived at in June 1967, and further delineated in the 1994 Israel-Jordan peace treaty, the *waqf* (an Islamic Trust administered by Jordan, and since 1994 in conjunction with the PA) was given day-to-day autonomy over the Temple Mount (Haram al-Sharif).

Known as the "status quo arrangement," this denies religious freedom to non-Muslims, including the right to pray, on the Temple Mount, Judaism's holiest site. In principle, Israeli court rulings dating back to the early 1970s recognized religious freedom rights for all citizens (Breger & Idinopulos, 1998, pp. 42–52). However, these rights are contingent on executive (i.e., government and police) decisions regarding the need to maintain public order. This means that, in practice, the deference to public order has amounted to a veto. Continually citing a potential threat of violence, Israel has generally prohibited any kind of worship on the Temple Mount for its Jewish citizens. Via a series of bizarre and draconian restrictions, Jews have been thrown off the site, and even arrested and barred from reentering for significant lengths of time by the Israeli authorities, because they whispered a psalm, drank water, read from a prayer book, or even uttered the word "Temple Mount" in Hebrew (Ben Zion, 2017; Harkov, 2015).

Devout Jewish Israelis and civil society organizations have long petitioned the courts for the right of religious expression on the Temple Mount. While some lower courts have begun to rule in their favor on the grounds of religious freedom, Israeli Supreme Court rulings still continue to defer to the state's interest in maintaining public order. However, in recent years Israeli public opinion has begun to shift on this matter, becoming more supportive of Jewish petitioners (Borschel-Dan, 2016). This swing can be attributed to changes in mainstream rabbinic rulings regarding visitation to the holy site and the fear that the Temple Mount would be transferred to Palestinian Arab control *de jure* during the Oslo peace process (Inbari, 2007). But these claims are also resonating with Jewish Israelis because they're increasingly viewed within the context of the larger Palestinian-led campaign to deny authentic Jewish religious and historical connections to Jerusalem and other holy sites in the West Bank, as manifested in recent heavily criticized UNESCO resolutions (Elman, 2016).[8]

Conclusion

In a recent editorial for the Israeli newspaper *Haaretz*, Israeli legal scholar Ruth Gavison argues that Israel's critics have wrongly turned the debate about the future of the West Bank and East Jerusalem into a battle over legal and human rights. While appreciating the temptation to "phrase things this way," namely, to assert that the "occupation is illegal," thus implying that Israel must end it immediately and unconditionally, Gavison (2017) nonetheless explains why this formulation is "mistaken and dangerous":

> It does not advance the end of the occupation but actually deepens the deadlock. It makes us cast our hopes on a debate disconnected from crucial political, social, cultural, and religious processes in Israeli and Palestinian society.... Adherence to the legalistic and human rights discourse only convinces Israel's Jews that they have no one to talk to and nothing to talk about because this isn't a genuine invitation to negotiations but a demand from Israel for action where the outline of the results is known in advance—and is unacceptable.

In this essay, I have suggested that in the study of the Israeli-Palestinian conflict there is an urgent need for more historically and contextually accurate interpretations, and unbiased applications, of international legal principles and norms. But as Gavison (2017) argues, the conflict's resolution is not only a matter of identifying the right solution based on the language of the law, precisely because "Palestinians have no 'right' to end the occupation—which was the result of a defensive war—and Israel has no obligation to end it without a peace agreement." In sum, the challenges ahead are essentially not legal ones.

Miriam F. Elman is an associate professor of political science and the Inaugural Robert D. McClure Professor of Teaching Excellence at the Maxwell School of Citizenship and Public Affairs, Syracuse University, where she serves as research director in the Program for the Advancement of Research on Conflict and Collaboration. An award-winning scholar and teacher, Elman is editor or co-editor of five books and the author or co-author of over sixty-five journal articles and book chapters covering topics that include international relations theory, democratization, conflict resolution, the nexus between religion and politics, and war and peace in the Middle East. Most recently, Elman is the co-editor of *Democracy and Conflict Resolution: The Dilemmas of Israel's Peacemaking* (2014) and *Jerusalem: Conflict and Cooperation in a Contested City* (2014), both published by Syracuse University Press. She is currently working on a project entitled *Word Crimes: Reclaiming the Language of the Israeli-Palestinian Conflict*.

Notes

1 For much of recorded history, the area was termed Judea and Samaria. Common parlance shifted only with Jordan's illegal annexation of the territory in 1950 (Philologos, 2006).

2 For example, the UN's 45-member Commission on the Status of Women, meeting in its March 2018 annual session, singled out Israel as the only country in the world to be subjected to a condemnatory resolution on women's rights.

3 "Lawfare" refers to the abuse and exploitation of legal procedures and the courts by the Palestinian Authority and Palestinian NGOs in order to advance Palestinian political agendas while bypassing the framework of bilateral negotiations with Israel.

4 In his essay (this volume), Lynk maintains that Israel has "forestall[ed] Palestinian self-determination" by failing to vacate the West Bank in an "expeditious and reasonable" time period. However, this claim ignores Israel's many peace overtures, which have been continually rebuffed by Palestinian leaders (see, for example, Herzog, 2017).

5 The UNHRC has long displayed a bias against Israel. From 2006 to 2016 it adopted 68 resolutions related to Israel compared to 67 dealing with the rest of the world combined. For more on bias against Israel at the United Nations see, for example, Becker, Hillman, Potrafke, & Schwemmer (2014).

6 Also troubling is some of the information that Lynk relies on in order to reach his conclusion that Israel is guilty of causing "systemic human rights harm" to Palestinians. For example, he draws from the reports compiled by Al-Haq, an organization whose leadership has ties to the

Popular Front for the Liberation of Palestine (PFLP), a US-designated terror organization (NGO Monitor, 2018).

7 While Lynk condemns a "thickening Israeli settlement enterprise," settlements have been limited to areas of the West Bank that are likely to revert to Israel in any final agreement (Makovsky, 2017; Rubin, 2016).

8 For more on this campaign to denigrate Jewish attachments to Jerusalem, and how it has become a catalyst for Palestinian violence, see Reiter (2008) and Shragai (2016). Contrary to Lynk's assertion, there is no "wall-to-wall international consensus" that Israel's "annexation of Jerusalem" is unlawful or that the ancient Jewish Quarter, the Western Wall/Kotel, or the Temple Mount, Judaism's holiest site, are "occupied Palestinian territory."

References

Amnesty International. (2015, May 27). "Gaza: Palestinians Tortured, Summarily Killed during 2014 Conflict." Retrieved from https://www.amnesty.org/en/latest/news/2015/05/gaza-palestinians-tortured-summarily-killed-by-hamas-forces-during-2014-conflict/

Baker, A. (2017, September 3). "Hijacking the Laws of Occupation." *Jerusalem Center for Public Affairs*, no. 613. Retrieved from http://jcpa.org/article/hijacking-laws-occupation/

Becker, R.N., Hillman, A.L., Potrafke, N., & Schwemmer, A.H. (2014). "The Preoccupation of the United Nations with Israel: Evidence and Theory." *Review of International Organizations*, 10(4), 413–37. https://doi.org/10.1007/s11558-014-9207-3

Bell, A., & Sheffi, D. (2010). "The Mythical Post-2005 Israeli Occupation of the Gaza Strip." *Israel Affairs*, 16(2), 268–96. https://doi.org/10.1080/13537121003643912

Ben Zion, I. (2017, January 3). "Islamic Guards Try to Boot Guide for Saying 'Temple Mount' on Temple Mount." *Times of Israel*. Retrieved from https://www.timesofisrael.com/islamic-guards-try-to-boot-guide-for-saying-temple-mount-on-temple-mount/

Bob, Y.J. (2014, August 5). "Will Captured Hamas Manual on Using Human Shields Help Israel Block War Crimes Trials?" *Jerusalem Post*. Retrieved from https://www.jpost.com/Operation-Protective-Edge/Will-captured-Hamas-manual-on-using-human-shields-help-Israel-block-war-crimes-trials-370154

Borschel-Dan, A. (2016, April 28). "As Support Widens for Jewish Prayer on Temple Mount, Should We Fear Apocalyptic Consequences?" *Times of Israel*. Retrieved from https://www.timesofisrael.com/as-support-widens-for-jewish-prayer-on-temple-mount-should-we-fear-apocalyptic-consequences/

Breger, M.J., & Idinopulos, T.A. (1998). *Jerusalem's Holy Places and the Peace Process*. Policy paper no. 46. Washington, DC: Washington Institute for Near East Policy.

Bronner, E., & Kershner, I. (2011, April 2). "Richard Goldstone Regrets Saying Israel Purposely Killed Gazans." *New York Times*. Retrieved from https://www.nytimes.com/2011/04/03/world/middleeast/03goldstone.html

Cohen, B. (2017, October 31). "UN Settlements 'Blacklist' of Israeli and International Companies Will Have Scant Legal Impact, Expert Says." *Algemeiner*. Retrieved from

https://www.algemeiner.com/2017/10/31/un-settlements-blacklist-of-israeli
-and-international-companies-will-have-scant-legal-impact-expert-says/

Eiran, E. (2014). "State Elite Perceptions and the Launch of the Israeli Settlement Project
in the West Bank: The International-Domestic Nexus." In M.F. Elman, O. Haklai, &
H. Spruyt (eds), *Democracy and Conflict Resolution: The Dilemmas of Israel's Peacemaking*
(pp. 209–22). Syracuse, NY: Syracuse University Press.

Elman, M.F. (2015, March 24). "The Truths of the Gaza War Revealed." *Legal Insurrection*.
Retrieved from https://legalinsurrection.com/2015/03/the-truths-of-the-gaza
-war-revealed/

Elman, M.F. (2016, October 14). "UNESCO Attempts to Erase Jewish Connection
to Temple Mount." *Legal Insurrection*. Retrieved from https://legalinsurrection
.com/2016/10/unesco-attempts-to-erase-jewish-connection-to-temple-mount/

Frisch, H. (2016, April 23). "Knowing Your ABC: A Primer to Understanding the Different Areas of Judea and Samaria." *Jerusalem Post*. Retrieved from https://www.jpost
.com/Magazine/Knowing-your-ABC-448963

Gavison, R. (2017, June 30). "The Occupation Is a Political Matter, Not a Legal
One." *Haaretz*. Retrieved from https://www.haaretz.com/opinion/premium-the
-occupation-is-not-a-legal-matter-1.5490721

Gerecht, R.M. (2017, January 6). "Protecting Palestine: Israel's Unacknowledged Role
on the West Bank." *Weekly Standard*. Retrieved from https://www.weeklystandard
.com/reuel-marc-gerecht/protecting-palestine

Gold, D. (2017, October 31). "The Historical Significance of the Balfour Declaration."
Jerusalem Center for Public Affairs. Retrieved from http://jcpa.org/article/historical
-significance-balfour-declaration/

Goldstone, R. (2011, April 1). "Reconsidering the Goldstone Report on Israel and War
Crimes." *Washington Post*. Retrieved from https://www.washingtonpost.com/opinions/
reconsidering-the-goldstone-report-on-israel-and-war-crimes/2011/04/01/
AFg111JC_story.html?noredirect=on&utm_term=.abde8483cb9d

Goodman, H., & Kuperwasser, Y. (eds). (2016). *The Knife and the Message: The Roots of the
New Palestinian Uprising*. Jerusalem Center for Public Affairs. Retrieved from http://
jcpa.org/the-knife-and-the-message-the-roots-of-the-new-palestinian-uprising/

Harkov, L. (2015, September 8). "Reporter's Notebook: By the Temple Mount, We Sat
and Wept." *Jerusalem Post*. Retrieved from https://www.jpost.com/Arab-Israeli
-Conflict/Reporters-Notebook-By-the-Temple-Mount-we-sat-and-wept-as-we
-remembered-Zion-415605

Hertz, E.E. (2017, July 12). "The Geneva Convention as a Weapon against Israel." *Israeli Front-
line*. http://www.israelifrontline.com/2017/07/geneva-convention-weapon-israel.html

Herzog, M. (2017). "The Kerry Legacy: Inside the Black Box of Israeli-Palestinian Talks."
The American Interest, *12*(5). Retrieved from https://www.the-american-interest
.com/2017/02/27/inside-the-black-box-of-israeli-palestinian-talks/

Human Rights Voices. (2017, August 1). "Palestinian Child Terrorists: Children Who Kill
and Their Adult Enablers." Retrieved from http://www.humanrightsvoices.org/
assets/attachments/documents/Palestinian_child_terrorists_August_1_2017_final
.pdf

Inbari, M. (2007). "Religious Zionism and the Temple Mount Dilemma—Key Trends."
Israel Studies, 12(2), 29–47. https://doi.org/10.2979/isr.2007.12.2.29

Israel Ministry of Foreign Affairs. (2016, August 4). "Behind the Headlines: Hamas
Exploitation of *World Vision* in Gaza to Support Terrorism." Retrieved from http://
mfa.gov.il/MFA/ForeignPolicy/Issues/Pages/Behind-the-Headlines-Hamas
-exploitation-of-World-Vision-in-Gaza-to-support-terrorism-4-August-2016.aspx

Kittrie, O.F. (2016). *Lawfare: Law as a Weapon of War.* Oxford, UK: Oxford University Press.

Kramer, M. (2017, June 28). "The Balfour Declaration Was More Than the Promise of One Nation." *Mosaic.* Retrieved from https://mosaicmagazine.com/response/2017/06/the-balfour-declaration-was-more-than-the-promise-of-one-nation/

Makovsky, D. (2017, November 29). "70 Years after Partition, a Two-State Solution Is Still Possible." *Washington Post.* Retrieved from https://www.washingtonpost.com/news/global-opinions/wp/2017/11/29/70-years-after-partition-a-two-state-solution-is-still-possible/?utm_term=.bfabb70e0b19

Menenberg, A. (2014, June). "Terrorists and Kleptocrats: How Corruption Is Eating the Palestinians Alive." *The Tower,* no. 15. Retrieved from http://www.thetower.org/article/terrorists-kleptocrats-how-corruption-is-eating-the-palestinians-alive/

NGO Monitor. (2017, June). "Who Else Profits: The Scope of European and Multinational Business in the Occupied Territories." Retrieved from http://www.ngo-monitor.org/nm/wp-content/uploads/2017/06/WhoElseProfits_final.pdf

NGO Monitor. (2018, October 30). "Al-Haq." Retrieved from http://www.ngo-monitor.org/nm/wp-content/uploads/2017/06/WhoElseProfits_final.pdf,https://www.ngo-monitor.org/ngos/al_haq/

Philologos. (2006, January 27). "The Battle over 'Judea and Samaria.'" *Forward.* Retrieved from https://forward.com/culture/1568/the-battle-over-e2-80-98judea-and-samaria-e2-80-99/

Polisar, D. (2017, April 3). "Do Palestinians Want a Two-State Solution?" *Mosaic.* Retrieved from https://mosaicmagazine.com/essay/2017/04/do-palestinians-want-a-two-state-solution/

Pressman, J. (2017). "Throwing Stones in Social Science: Non-violence, Unarmed Violence, and the First Intifada." *Cooperation and Conflict, 52*(4), 519–36. https://doi.org/10.1177/0010836717701967

Reiter, Y. (2008). *Jerusalem and Its Role in Islamic Solidarity.* New York, NY: Palgrave Macmillan.

Reuters. (2014, July 14). "Watch: IDF Releases Video of Aborted Gaza Strikes to Prevent Civilian Casualties." *Jerusalem Post.* Retrieved from https://www.jpost.com/Operation-Protective-Edge/IDF-releases-video-of-aborted-strikes-in-Gaza-to-prevent-civilian-casualties-362733

Rostow, N. (2017, June 12). "How the Balfour Declaration Became Part of International Law." *Mosaic.* Retrieved from https://mosaicmagazine.com/response/2017/06/how-the-balfour-declaration-became-part-of-international-law/

Rubin, M. (2016, July 25). "The Truth about 'Settlement Growth.'" *Commentary.* Retrieved from https://www.commentarymagazine.com/foreign-policy/middle-east/how-much-are-settlements-growing/

Rumley, G. (2016, May 1). "Barack Obama's West Bank Strongman: Mahmoud Abbas." *Newsweek.* Retrieved from http://www.newsweek.com/obamas-west-bank-strongman-mahmoud-abbas-453311

Safian, A. (2011, September 22). "Palestinians Rejected Statehood Three Times, Claim Frustration—with Israel." *CAMERA.* Retrieved from http://www.camera.org/article/palestinians-rejected-statehood-three-times-claim-frustration-with-israel/

Savage, S. (2017, August 29). "Experts Say Upcoming UN 'Blacklist' of Companies Tied to Israel Invokes Antisemitism." *JNS.* Retrieved from https://www.jns.org/upcoming-un-blacklist-of-companies-tied-to-israel-invokes-anti-semitism-experts-say/

Sher, G., & Aviram, K. (2014, December 31). "A Veritable Battlefield: The Palestinians' Legal Warfare Strategy." *Institute for National Security Studies,* INSS Insight, no. 650.

Retrieved from http://www.inss.org.il/publication/a-veritable-battlefield-the -palestinians-legal-warfare-strategy/

Sher, G., & Ofek, L. (2013). "Dividing the Land, Not the People: Lessons from the Givat HaUlpana an Migron Evacuations." *Strategic Assessment*, 15(4), 37–51. https://www .gsher-law.com/webfiles/fck/file/Preventing%20internal%20conflict_Strategic %20Assessment%20INSS.pdf.

Sher, G., & Wolf, D. (2016, July 8). "Recognizing That Israel Is Not an Occupying Power in Gaza Is Good for Everyone." *War on the Rocks*. Retrieved from https://warontherocks .com/2016/07/recognizing-that-israel-is-not-an-occupying-power-in-gaza-is -good-for-everyone/

Shragai, N. (2016). *Protecting the Status of the Temple Mount in Jerusalem*. Jerusalem Center for Public Affairs. Retrieved from http://jcpa.org/status-quo-temple-mount/

Strawson, J. (2002). "Reflections on Edward Said and the Legal Narratives of Palestine: Israeli Settlements and Palestinian Self-determination." *Penn State International Law Review, 20*(2), 363–84.

UN Watch. (2015, June 12). *Key Preliminary Findings of the High Level International Military Group on the Gaza Conflict*. Retrieved from http://blog.unwatch.org/index .php/2015/06/12/key-findings-of-the-high-level-international-military-group -on-the-gaza-conflict/

Watson, G.R. (2000). *The Oslo Accords: International Law and the Israeli-Palestinian Peace Agreements*. Oxford, UK: Oxford University Press.

Wittes, B. (2015, December 15). "Israeli Targeting Procedures and the Concept of Proportionality." *Lawfare*. Retrieved from https://www.lawfareblog.com/israeli-targeting -procedures-and-concept-proportionality

PART II

Contemporary Debates

five
Refugees and Displacement

Displacement and dispossession have been two persistent and unjust features of the Israeli-Palestinian conflict. The most commonly discussed issue around displacement is that of those called refugees officially, defined by the Office of the United Nations High Commissioner for Refugees (UNHCR) as "someone who has left his or her country of origin and is unable or unwilling to return there because of a serious threat to his or her life or freedom" (Nicholson & Kumin, 2017; UNRWA, 2015). But internal displacement also remains a sticking point in efforts to seek social justice in Israel/Palestine.

As a result of the 1947–49 wars in Israel/Palestine, 800,000 Palestinian Arabs became refugees, dispossessed of their homes and land. Their forced removal at the hands of Jewish military forces, not only between 1947 and 1949 but also as a result of the 1967 war (when Israel conquered the West Bank and Gaza), defines their position within the dominant Palestinian narrative: their land was violently taken from them by another people. Even among those Palestinians who remained in what became Israel, some became internally displaced peoples (IDPs). Although not officially classified as refugees, IDPs retain an element of shared identity with those Palestinians who registered with the United Nations Relief and Works Agency for Palestine Refugees in the Near East (known as UNRWA) after its establishment in December 1949, and thus became refugees, despite the stigma attached to the refugee label within Arab communities generally and Palestinian communities specifically (Hahn Tapper, 2016 pp. 122–23, 196–97).

Jewish Israelis frequently point to the tens of thousands of European Jewish refugees who immigrated to Palestine in the 1930s and 1940s in connection with World War II. According to the Declaration of the Establishment of the State of Israel, Israel's founding in 1948 was a demonstration of "urgency" that helped solve the problem of "homelessness" for those Jews who became refugees as a result of the Holocaust. Many Jews look to this argument as the *de facto* justification for the Jewish state, a position, some say, buttressed by the approximately 800,000 Jews who immigrated to Israel from countries in the Middle East and North Africa (MENA) in the 1950s, many of whom identified as refugees despite not being officially classified as such. Some staunch advocates of Israel also argue that Arab-majority states should absorb the remaining Palestinian refugees just as Israel absorbed the Jews previously living in MENA countries. Put another way, for many, the question of who are the "true" refugees—and who must take responsibility for their displacement and dispossession—has come to define positions regarding the Israeli-Palestinian conflict.

This chapter touches on three aspects of the issue of displacement and dispossession in Israel/Palestine. Roula El-Rifai's essay, "Navigating the Palestinian Refugee Issue: An Insider's Guide," begins by laying out the nature of Palestinian refugee status, before examining the role the Canadian government has played in advancing diplomatic efforts to address the refugee issue, "a key component of any just and lasting resolution of the Palestinian-Israeli conflict." As a member of Canada's International Development Research Centre, El-Rifai offers personal observations about the "behind the scenes" parts of these Track II efforts, addressing some of the less discussed pieces of this puzzle, including identifying ten lessons learned from these experiences.

Shayna Zamkanei's piece, "Are Jews Displaced from Arab Countries 'Refugees'?," examines the claim that those Jews who immigrated to Israel in the 1950s from MENA countries identified as "refugees," including a discussion of the historical context of these Jews in 1950s and 1960s Israel. Thereafter, she identifies various reasons for the recent political trend in Jewish Israeli Zionist discourse to use the signifier "Jewish refugee," including ways this label interacts with the trope of the Palestinian refugee. She ends her essay by looking at the idea of refugees in the broader international context.

Finally, Safa Aburabia's "The Bedouin Struggle over Land in Palestine/Israel: Men of the *Nakba* Generation Narrate Their Attachment to Land" investigates a marginalized group within the Israel/Palestine paradigm, those Palestinian Bedouin who live in the Naqab (or Negev) region of southern Israel, many of whom identify as internally displaced peoples. Aburabia shows how members of these communities have resisted the theft of their land for more than seventy years, adding that the rituals used in this process also ensure that their progeny continue to have a relationship with the literal land that was taken from them.

References

Hahn Tapper, A.J. (2016). *Judaisms: A Twenty-First-Century Introduction to Jews and Jewish Identities.* Oakland, CA: University of California Press.

Nicholson, F., & Kumin, J. (2017). *A Guide to International Refugee Protection and Building State Asylum Systems* (Handbook for Parliamentarians, no. 27). Inter-Parliamentary Union/UNHCR. Retrieved June 18, 2018, from https://www.unhcr.org/3d4aba564.pdf

UNRWA (United Nations Relief and Works Agency). (2015). *The United Nations and Palestinian Refugees.* Retrieved June 25, 2018, from https://www.unrwa.org/userfiles/2010011791015.pdf

Navigating the Palestinian Refugee Issue: An Insider's Guide

ROULA EL-RIFAI

There are nearly 6 million Palestinian refugees worldwide (living mostly in Lebanon, Jordan, the West Bank, and Gaza), out of whom some 1.6 million live in refugee camps, mostly in Gaza and Lebanon. Resolving the Palestinian refugee issue remains a key component of any just and lasting resolution of the Palestinian-Israeli conflict. Both Palestinians and Israelis perceive the Palestinian refugee issue as existential. Unfortunately, little political progress has been made on such contentious issues as the right of return, resettlement, and compensation. Third parties can help this issue along. The refugee issue provides a case study in how a smaller state—in this case, Canada—has played a pivotal role.

For more than two decades the Canadian government has engaged with the Palestinian refugee issue as part of multilateral negotiations tracks within the Middle East peace process. As someone engaged in the search for solutions to the Palestinian refugee problem during this time, as part of Canada's International Development Research Centre (IDRC), I can offer some personal observations about the process.[1]

Canada has always aimed to ensure a resolution to the Palestinian refugee issue that does not leave people worse off and provides a sense of fairness and justice. The goal has been to increase knowledge and discussion around potential solutions by providing a cost-benefit stakeholder analysis, rather than a blueprint for a solution. More importantly, Canadians engaged in this process have striven to ensure that the voices of key stakeholders and parties were heard, especially the voices of those who do not formally sit at the negotiations table, such as the host countries where Palestinian refugees live as well as the Palestinians in these host countries.

Who Are Palestinian Refugees?

When Israel was established in 1948, some 800,000 Palestinians were expelled or fled their homes as a result of Israeli military action,[2] settling in the West Bank and Gaza, as well as in the neighboring countries of Jordan, Lebanon, and Syria. Some 300,000 were further displaced from the West Bank and Gaza during the 1967 war, and fled to Jordan, Syria, and Egypt. Today, there are nearly six million Palestinian refugees registered with the United Nations Relief and Works Agency for Palestine Refugees (UNRWA), which was established in 1949 to service registered refugees, many of whom live in 58 Palestinian camps in host countries. As the refugee issue continues to be unresolved, the Palestinian refugee population has grown.

According to UNRWA (2017), Palestinian refugees are defined as "persons whose normal place of residence was Palestine during the period 1 June 1946 to 15 May 1948, and who lost both home and means of livelihood as a result of the 1948 conflict." UNRWA provides services to all those who meet this definition and who are registered with the agency and need assistance. The descendants of original Palestine refugee males are also eligible for registration. This has generally been a contentious point for the Israeli government, which commonly argues that these descendants should not be allowed to retain their refugee status and that UNRWA is helping perpetuate the refugee problem. Given their special status with UNRWA, Palestinian refugees are excluded from the benefits of the 1951 Convention Relating to the Status of Refugees and the services of the Office of the United Nations High Commissioner for Refugees (UNHCR), which, unlike UNRWA, is mandated to pursue durable solutions and engages with the politics of refugee crises.

History of IDRC and Canadian Engagement with the Palestinian Refugee Issue

Following the launch of the Middle East peace process in Madrid in 1991, Canada was assigned the position of Gavel of the Refugee Working Group (RWG) in the peace process's multilateral negotiations.[3] Thus began more than two decades of Canadian diplomatic, developmental, and technical engagement with the Palestinian refugee issue.[4]

Between 2000 and 2007, Canada convened seven formal meetings of the RWG, in addition to convening the first in a series of meetings of the so-called No-Name Group, which provided a forum for international coordination in the absence of more formal channels. The No-Name Group members included key western donors and international agencies such as the World Bank. It aimed to coordinate approaches and public messaging, and to discuss issues that were considered too sensitive for the public domain.

In parallel, Canada moved to a lower-profile Track II process to encourage dialogue between various parties and stakeholders about sensitive issues in more flexible and informal settings, allowing participants to develop and test options. This type of process fit well with IDRC's mandate to generate knowledge and build capacity for policy research.[5] Along the way, IDRC published three volumes—in 2007, 2013, and 2014—on the issues of repatriation, development, compensation, and a synthesis of all policy issues (Brynen & El-Rifai, 2007, 2013, 2014). The aim was to ensure that the knowledge generated over this time was not lost and could be used as a resource when and if negotiations resumed.

Learning from the Process

The lessons I have learned from almost two decades of IDRC and Canadian engagement on the refugee issue are condensed below into ten key observations.

1. The Issues That Will Not Go Away

The refugee issue encompasses many vexing and complex problems that include the right of return and the future residency of Palestinians, refugee compensation and reparations, intangible needs and moral acknowledgement, and refugee expectations and Jewish claims. These and other issues will be discussed below. Many of the refugee issues are existential and part of the respective national identities of both Palestinians and Israelis. Until each and every one of these issues is addressed, the conflict will not be resolved.

2. Words Matter

Given the differing Palestinian and Israeli narratives and positions on the Palestinian refugee issue, agreement on basic terminology has often been intensely challenging. For example, the Israeli government commonly claims that any refugee who obtained citizenship from a host country or any other country should no longer be considered a refugee (as is the case with Convention refugees), while Palestinians use the term as a legal one, embedded in international law[6] and entitling Palestinians to rights, including the right of return. Further, when discussing Palestinian property losses, Palestinians consider the word "compensation" to be inadequate because it does not include an array of measures of redress, including the restitution of Palestinian property and compensation for nonmaterial losses such as psychological injuries; thus, for Palestinians the term "reparations" seems more apt. In contrast, Israelis prefer the term "compensation" because it does not carry the implication of past wrongdoing or moral responsibility. For example, when IDRC organized a conference in 1999 on the issue of compensation, the title had to be negotiated to say "Palestinian compensation as part of a solution to the Palestinian refugee problem" to allay any fears of an agenda-driven meeting.

Language and the meaning of words are important. When language for a preamble to a peace agreement was discussed, it was close to impossible to reconcile Palestinian and Israeli narratives and terminology. Palestinians demanded that Israel acknowledge "responsibility" for creating the Palestinian refugee problem, while Israelis wanted to only express "regret" for the suffering of Palestinian refugees. Canadians in the "Core Group" Track II meetings proposed language that referred to a "human tragedy" and "suffering"—which both parties had to acknowledge. to be able to move on—all while stating how central the involuntary exile experience has been to Palestinians.

A further complicating issue arose in 2007, when Israel introduced a new demand: that Palestinians had to acknowledge Israel as a "Jewish state." Palestinians have always argued that they made their greatest concession in 1993, when they officially recognized the State of Israel, and could not agree to this new demand. In 2001, during the Taba negotiations, compromise language was proposed, when Palestinians were asked to recognize Israel as the homeland for the Jewish people.[7] No significant progress has been made on this issue since then.

3. Technical Work Is Critical: The Devil Is in the Details

It is essential to work on technical issues during political processes in order to avoid raising false expectations that can threaten the success and sustainability of a solution. It also helps set into place practical and realistic implementation measures that demonstrate that a peace agreement is indeed possible. IDRC largely focused on supporting technical work on various aspects of the refugee issue. These efforts were not meant to undermine rights of Palestinians or Israelis, but rather present options for feasible solutions. The Palestinians meanwhile had created a Negotiations Support Unit, which provided negotiators with technical advice on such issues as refugees, borders, and Jerusalem.[8]

A case in point on the value of the technical work is the thinking around the implementation mechanism for any agreement, and its dedicated organizational and operational structure. The assumption is that a yet-to-be-defined mechanism would manage such processes as future residency options for Palestinians (Israel, Palestinian state, host countries, and third countries), and compensation and restitution claims for Palestinians and host countries.

IDRC worked closely with the International Organization for Migration (IOM) to help develop technical thinking around how to design a practical, realistic, and feasible implementation mechanism (Brynen & El-Rifai, 2014, pp. 15–53). Other technical issues included the issue of reparations and compensation with relevant technical work carried out regarding such sub-issues as types of losses (physical, mental, etc.), types of compensation (cash, etc.), determining inheritance rights, eligibility for compensation, determining a potential role for UNRWA to play in an agreement, and proposing options for addressing "intangible needs" in an agreement.

4. Intangibles Are as Critical as Tangibles

The Palestinian refugee issue is unlikely to be resolved only through practical measures such as compensation and future residential solutions. Both Palestinians and Israelis have "intangible needs" that must be addressed in any future agreement.

To begin, the clashing narratives held by many Palestinians and Israelis frame each party's understanding of historical events. For Palestinians, the national tragedy and trauma of *Al-Nakba* ("catastrophe" in Arabic) was a defining moment in the formation of Palestinian national identity in 1948, leading to the displacement of 800,000 Palestinians who became, along with their descendants, refugees. In this narrative, Israel must recognize its responsibility in creating the refugee problem and the suffering that has ensued ever since, and also acknowledge the right of return arising out of UN General Assembly Resolution 194 to correct this injustice. It is also important for Israel to acknowledge and compensate for both physical and material losses (land, property, and economic development) and immaterial, intangible losses (suffering, loss of dignity and legitimacy).

Meanwhile, from an Israeli perspective, Israel was not responsible for creating the Palestinian refugee problem. Rather, this was the result of a war thrust upon Israel and initiated by Arab countries when they rejected the UN partition plan. According to this narrative, their core needs in relation to the refugee issue are for Palestinians to recognize Israel as a Jewish state, to acknowledge that Israel is not solely responsible for the creation of the refugee problem, and to ensure any agreement brings an end to all claims.

Experts have proposed four options in dealing with these intangibles: avoiding them altogether in negotiations, attending to them after an agreement, addressing them in a diluted way, or tackling them head-on as a way to ensure success. There is also a danger that intangible issues could be used as a tactic to delay progress on other practical/material issues in the negotiations. So, while there is a strong connection between intangible needs and the attainment of practical solutions, experts have recommended that intangible issues be tackled separately and head-on as they address the critical perceptions, aspirations, grievances, and fears of both parties. It is also critical to avoid any equivalence between the two sides' perspectives, such as the equivalence of suffering endured by Palestinian refugees and by Jews who fled Arab countries.

5. Counterperceptions of a Zero-Sum Game

Often the perception of a zero-sum game prevents or is used as an excuse to prevent the two sides from coming to the table. For many Israelis, the recognition of the right of return is anathema and equivalent to delegitimizing the State of Israel. For Palestinians, their forced displacement in 1948 is a moral wrong and their right of return is enshrined in UN Resolution 194 and in international law.

Over the years, to deal with this major stumbling block, several ideas have emerged about how to bridge this gap, one of which is the concept of modalities of return. The 1999 unofficial Canadian Core Group paper suggests that "in recognition of the Palestinian demand to exercise the right of return to historic Palestine, both parties agree that: a) this shall primarily be achieved through the voluntary repatriation of Palestinians to the Palestinian state; b) Israel shall admit a number of Palestinians who will live peacefully with their neighbors, whether as citizens of Israel, dual citizens, or as Israeli permanent residents."

The 2000 "Clinton parameters," laid out under the administration of US president Bill Clinton, spelled out five future residential choices for Palestinians: the State of Israel, a Palestinian state, and integration in host countries, in third countries, or areas in Israel that would be transferred to a Palestinian state in a land swap. These parameters suggested that the parties recognize a right of return to "historic Palestine" or return to a "Palestinian homeland" and considered this outcome to represent an implementation of Resolution 194. Modalities under each of the residential options have also been discussed over the years, such as setting caps on numbers of returnees or setting the rules of return (i.e., based on age, a first-come, first-served basis, on area of residency, on need, on procedures determined by the implementation mechanism, or by using a lottery system).

6. All Refugee Issues Are Interconnected and the Refugee Issue Is Part of a Package Deal

When one is discussing specific aspects of the Palestinian refugee issue, such as the right of return, future residence, or compensation, it is critical to remember that all of these aspects are interconnected. Further, the refugee issue cannot be treated in isolation from other elements of the peace process. Movement on any one of these aspects or elements can provide an incentive to compromise on another.

It has become evident over time that Palestinian negotiators have never really expected that there will be a mass return to Israel following a deal.

Rather, they have signaled that securing Israeli recognition of the plight of Palestinians as refugees, acknowledgement of responsibility for creating the refugee problem, and a substantive compensation package could go a long way in achieving greater Palestinian willingness to compromise. This said, there has never been a clear agreement on how much return, even if limited, is enough for Palestinians. The willingness of Palestinians to compromise will also be greatly impacted if a peace deal grants them a sovereign state based on 1967 borders with East Jerusalem as its capital, and with full control of borders and immigration.

As for the issue of equivalence between Palestinian refugees and Jews who left or were expelled from Arab countries in 1948 and afterwards, which is discussed in Shayna Zamkanei's essay (this volume), it is widely accepted in Palestinian and Israeli negotiation circles that linking the two groups and their claims for property losses is not a subject for bilateral Palestinian-Israeli talks. Rather, Jewish claims should be pursued by Israel directly with relevant Arab governments.

Similarly, there is no overt connection between Bedouin land rights— discussed in Safa Aburabia's essay (this volume)—and Palestinian-Israeli negotiations. The Bedouin land rights issue, which bears some similarity to Palestinian refugee land rights in terms of narratives and need for redress, is considered by negotiators and analysts to be solely an Israeli domestic issue.

7. Engage with Palestinian Refugees and with the Israeli Public

Over the years, there has been a clear disconnect between Palestinian ne-gotiators and Palestinian refugees. It is critical that preceding and during a negotiation process, Palestinian negotiators engage with Palestinian refugees and inform them directly of their future options. The objectives are to seek their input and feedback (argued by Thea Renda Abu El-Haj, this volume); manage their expectations, since they may not be fully met; and maximize their choices within an agreement that will inevitably limit and constrain these choices. Palestinian refugees must believe that their negotiators are legitimate and credible and can properly represent them.

On the Israeli side, over time[9] there has been a hardening of public opinion on the refugee issue alongside a steadily increasing dehuman-ization of Palestinians and Palestinian refugees, making violence against Palestinians and abuse of their rights morally acceptable. In spite of this development, it is equally important, and perhaps more now than ever, to communicate with the Israeli public about possibilities for a compromise on the most sensitive issues, those that are existential for Palestinians and Israelis alike. It is vital for the peoples on both sides to feel that their values and needs have been recognized, and that an attempt has been made to address those values and needs fairly, in order for any negotiation to hold legitimacy with them.

8. Palestinian and Israeli Exceptionalism

Some analysts argue, somewhat problematically, that the Palestinian refugee problem is unique, and hence other refugee experiences have little to offer in terms of lessons learned. For example, on the Israeli side, there is a rejection of the application of international law as a framework to develop a solution to the Palestinian refugee problem. On the Palestinian side, there is reluctance to value comparative learning about refugee movements, especially of examples that show how few displaced peoples actually chose to return and live in their original homes in cases of protracted conflicts.

IDRC and Canada have focused on learning from comparative case studies to inform their work on providing policy options. While there are limits to comparative work, this approach has proved useful in highlighting the potential for similarities and differences with other protracted refugee experiences and how these are resolved in terms of structures, institutions, and processes, but also and more importantly in terms of human experiences, emotions, and the intangibles highlighted earlier. Examples of comparative work include IDRC support to the IOM in its research on implementation and compensation claims mechanisms, support to Exeter University in research on the repatriation and absorption of refugees, and support to the Forced Migration and Refugee Unit at Birzeit University.

9. Preserve the Knowledge in the Face of a Lack of Institutional Memory

Given the vagaries of the political peace process, and at times an absence of any process at all, much of the knowledge generated about options for solutions to the refugee problem has risked being lost. In order to preserve knowledge and extend its shelf life, and to ensure future negotiations do not start from scratch in the absence of institutional memory of stakeholders, IDRC has published the three aforementioned volumes covering all aspects of the refugee issue (Brynen & El-Rifai, 2007, 2013, 2014). The IOM has also published an IDRC-supported book on the experiences of claims programs in property restitution and compensation, while the Ramallah-based Palestinian Negotiations Support Unit has produced much knowledge and thinking about options and solutions.

10. Track II Works, Being Canada Works

The Middle East experience within Track II diplomacy has been rich and extensive over the last two decades, with Canada contributing to efforts to solve the Palestinian refugee issue. The use of discreet and informal Track II processes has proven to be an effective tool to develop technical knowledge and policy for solutions where traditional bilateral formal discussions could not deliver. These Track II processes have helped maintain a network of experts and policymakers engaged on the refugee issue and promoted thinking about solutions to key aspects of the refugee problem.

In such informal diplomacy, a sponsor needs to be perceived as neutral and without an agenda; it should promote an understanding of each side's perspectives and the possibility of reaching consensus. I believe Canada has provided such an approach and, as a soft power on the international stage, was a credible convener of Track II informal discussions. The Palestinian and Israeli stakeholders have not felt that Canada imposed an agenda on them, and they have valued that we were not a superpower while being close enough to the United States to be able to convey key messages from these Track II processes. The IDRC approach of providing knowledge to inform the negotiations process, by producing policy options rather than a blueprint, has also enhanced Canadian legitimacy among the stakeholders.

However, in hindsight, I believe that in our rich history of convening meetings on the refugee issue, we have missed out by not regularly including some of the hardliners on both sides in our meetings or in specific forums, including, for example, representatives from the Israeli settlers' movement. This would have ensured a dose of realism about what was realistic and what was not. Also, it is important to bear in mind that Track II discussions can never make up for lack of political will, which is an essential ingredient to achieve progress towards a solution. Such a political will has not yet materialized in a significant way.

Conclusion

Canada and IDRC have helped produce substantive knowledge about options for solutions to the refugee problem and have helped preserve that knowledge. We helped create a network of engaged Palestinians and Israelis, and brought refugees from host countries into a process in which those refugees were not otherwise formally represented. We also became a future resource, for when negotiations resume, to share our knowledge about what works, what does not work, and why.

Unfortunately, the combined effect of our technical work and Track II diplomacy has not yet translated into concrete political progress. Our efforts have been stymied by the larger failures of the peace process. We are nowhere near a solution to the Palestinian-Israeli conflict and the refugee question. Facts on the ground, mainly the illegal expansion of settlement activity in the West Bank and the illegal Israeli blockade of Gaza, cur-' rently make for an environment where there is little incentive for either party to compromise.

This lack of political progress does not detract from the value of the work carried out by Canada, IDRC, and others on the refugee issue over more than two decades. There will never be an end to the Palestinian-Israeli conflict if the Palestinian refugee issue is not addressed head-on. Regardless of the future framing of a deal—be it two states or one state or some other arrangement altogether—the issues that Canadian engagement has tackled will not disappear, and resolution of the refugee issue will be part and parcel of any future arrangement between Palestinians and Israelis. I believe that when the time comes, the decades-long efforts by Canada, IDRC, and many others will contribute to a resolution of the Palestinian refugee issue.

Roula El-Rifai is a senior program specialist with the Employment and Growth program at Canada's International Development Research Centre (IDRC). Her work supports civil society actors in the Arab world advocating for reform with a focus on youth, gender-based violence, and refugees and forced migration. She is an expert on the Palestinian refugee issue and the Middle East peace process and is co-editor of three volumes on the subject: *The Palestinian Refugee Problem: The Search for a Resolution* (Pluto Press, 2014); *Compensation to Palestinian Refugees and the Search for Palestinian-Israeli Peace* (Pluto Press, 2013); and *Palestinian Refugees: Challenges of Repatriation and Development* (I.B. Tauris, 2007). She has an MA in international relations from the University of Kent at Canterbury and an MSc in rural planning and development from the University of Guelph.

Notes

1 I speak in this essay in a personal capacity, and any opinions expressed are mine alone and are not intended to represent the views of the various institutions and individuals mentioned.
2 See Israel's New Historians: Flapan (1987), Morris (1988), Pappe (1988), and Shlaim (1988).
3 The multilateral track of the peace process was meant to complement bilateral negotiations and address issues that are regional and international

in nature. The other working groups are: water, environment, arms control and regional security, and regional economic development.

4 The Canadian effort, in what came to be known in scholarly literature as the "Ottawa process," involved Canada's foreign affairs department and development agency and a secretariat established at IDRC called the "Expert and Advisory Services Fund." Canada's participation was led by a series of veteran diplomats who served as Gavel from 1992 to 2009: Marc Perron, Andrew Robinson, Michael Molloy, Jill Sinclair, Peter McRae, and Douglas Fraser. Canada partnered with the United Kingdom's DFID, Chatham House, Norway's FAFO, the Swiss Development Agency, the World Bank, the European Union, Arab and western governments, and independent experts such as Rex Brynen and Nadim Shehadi.

5 IDRC supported a broad range of policy-relevant research and dialogue on almost all aspects of the refugee issue, and convened and financed the informal Track II discussions as well as three major stocktaking conferences on Palestinian refugee research. Canada's Core Group meetings produced elements later incorporated in formal negotiations documents at Camp David and Taba.

6 See the Geneva Conventions, the Universal Declaration of Human Rights, the International Covenant on Civil and Political Rights, and United Nations General Assembly Resolution 194.

7 See the Palestinian and Israeli non-papers as well as the Moratinos non-paper from the Taba talks.

8 The unit still operates today, albeit on a smaller scale and with fewer resources since 2011.

9 For example, on the issue of return of refugees to Israel, Israel has indicated in past negotiations (2001, 2007) that it may be willing to admit a token number of refugee returns (based on family reunification schemes, or for 1948 survivors, for example). These views do not represent the opinions of the majority of the Israeli Jewish population.

References

Brynen, R., & El-Rifai, R. (eds). (2007). *Palestinian Refugees: Challenges of Repatriation and Development*. London, UK: I.B. Tauris.

Brynen, R., & El-Rifai, R. (eds). (2013). *Compensation to Palestinian Refugees and the Search for Palestinian-Israeli Peace*. London, UK: Pluto Press.

Brynen, R., & El-Rifai, R. (eds). (2014). *The Palestinian Refugee Problem: The Search for a Resolution*. London, UK: Pluto Press.

Flapan, S. (1987). *The Birth of Israel: Myths and Realities*. New York, NY: Pantheon Books.

Morris, B. (1988). *The Birth of the Palestinian Refugee Problem, 1947–1949*. New York, NY: Cambridge University Press.

Pappe, I. (1988). *Britain and the Arab-Israeli Conflict, 1948–1951*. New York, NY: St Martin's Press.

Shlaim, A. (1988). *Collusion across the Jordan: King Abdullah, the Zionist Movement, and the Partition of Palestine*. New York, NY: Columbia University Press.

UNRWA (United Nations Relief and Works Agency). (2017). "Palestinian Refugees: In Figures." Retrieved from https://www.unrwa.org/sites/default/files/content/resources/unrwa_in_figures_2017_english.pdf

Are Jews Displaced from Arab Countries "Refugees"?

SHAYNA ZAMKANEI

In the past decade, there has been a resurgence of interest in the refugee question within the context of the Palestinian-Israeli conflict. For the Israeli government and organizations such as Justice for Jews from Arab Countries, however, the refugee issue is no longer limited to the status of Palestinian refugees, but has instead expanded in scope to include Jews who were displaced from "Arab" countries in the twentieth century.[1] In February 2010, the Israeli government adopted a law that instructs the government and prime minister to raise the issue of compensation for lost property and assets during peace negotiations. Indeed, some Israeli politicians and Jewish refugee activists have even argued that Jewish compensation and refugee claims should be deducted from those owed to Palestinians, since roughly the same number of Jews from Arab countries—850,000—were displaced.

Not surprisingly, Palestinian politicians (as well as a number of Jewish Israeli scholars and Jewish writers) have opposed Jewish refugee claims, arguing they are nothing more than a cynical ploy by the Israeli government. In spite of the troubling circumstances that prompted emigration—sometimes forced, sometimes coerced, and sometimes voluntary—Jews from Arab countries were not classified collectively as refugees by the State of Israel, or international organizations, at the time of their displacement.[2] Nevertheless, their efforts to achieve recognition as refugees, and compensation for stolen or appropriated property, can be traced back to the 1970s. Why, then, does it seem as if the refugee campaign was hatched more recently?

To determine whether Jews from Arab countries constitute a refugee group, one needs to examine the historical, political, and legal circumstances governing each wave of migration from each specific country—a task that should be at the center of the refugee debate, but is not. For this reason, I will first focus on the problem of terminology, and briefly touch on how Jewish refugees have been defined within the Zionist context over the decades. By examining the shifts in meaning of the term "refugee," we are better able to understand why it has become an increasingly accepted label over time. As I shall explain, when the "refugee" label as applied to Jews from Arab countries conflicted with Zionist interests, it was shunned or ignored by the mainstream Zionist establishment (i.e., the Israeli government and prominent mainstream Jewish organizations). Conversely, when the "refugee" label could serve Zionist interests, it was embraced. This equivocality becomes more apparent when we examine how the term "refugee" has been defined with respect to Jewish immigration to Israel (*aliyah*), the Holocaust, and the Palestinian-Israeli conflict. Once the shifts in meaning are understood within these particular contexts, it becomes clear why Justice for Jews from Arab Countries (JJAC), which spearheaded the most recent refugee recognition campaign, was able to garner significantly more traction than did its predecessor, the World Organization of Jews from Arab Countries (WOJAC).

The Refugee within the Context of *Aliyah*

Until the 2000s, the Zionist establishment—including the Israeli government, scholars, and policymakers—was extremely reluctant to define Jews from Arab countries as refugees. Much of this reluctance, I suggest, involved the perceived dichotomy between *olim* (immigrants) and refugees, and the difference between their active commitment to Zionism. Traditionally, *olim*, those who physically and metaphorically "ascended" to the land of Israel, were understood as ideologically committed to developing Palestine for Jews. Their children became "new Jews" or *sabras*, who were considered physically stronger and less superstitious than "old" or diasporic Jews. While the ideal of the *sabra* eroded in Israeli popular imagination in the 1960s and 1970s, *olim* were (and still are) expected to be ideologically committed to the Zionist project.

Not surprisingly, then, the categories of "*olim*" and "refugee" were often considered to be mutually exclusive, not only in the case of Holocaust survivors—as I address below—but also in the early organizational literature of Jews displaced from Arab countries. In the 1970s and 1980s, for instance, references to Jews from Arab countries who immigrated to Israel as "refugees" undermined the Zionist narrative that these individuals had yearned to make *aliyah*. For this reason, both government officials and Jews from Arab countries hesitated to use the term "refugee," even when they compared the status of Jews from Arab countries with that of Palestinians.

Mordechai Ben-Porat, the Baghdad-born former Zionist emissary to Iraq and founder of WOJAC, considered adopting the word "refugee" into the name of his organization, but ultimately decided against it. On the one hand, he sought to offer a corrective of the Zionist establishment's historical narrative concerning the departure and integration of Jews from Arab countries. In particular, he emphasized the reluctance of Jews from Arab countries to leave their homelands, the difficulties of absorption, and the squalor of "transit" camps—refugee camps in fact but not in name—in his correspondence with Israeli government officials. On the other hand, while he believed that Jewish refugee experiences might neutralize Palestinian claims, he worried that Jewish refugee claims would not serve Zionist interests at a time when the status of Palestinian refugees had gained momentum in the international arena.

Ben-Porat was not alone in struggling to negotiate the tensions of support-ing and criticizing the Zionist establishment. His colleague, Shlomo Hillel, a former Zionist activist in Iraq and eventual government minister, emphasized the voluntary nature of the migration, and saw *aliyah* as a term that included both the early pioneers and those who arrived as part of mass immigration. For Hillel, Jews from Arab states were both. Similarly, the report from WOJAC's Third International Conference described the reluctance of the Israeli govern-ment and Jews from Arab countries themselves to refer to the latter as refugees, instead opting for "immigrants motivated by Zionist ideals" (Dangoor, 1986, p. 6). Others, however, were more equivocal. Shimon Avizemer, a WOJAC member from Yemen, cited discrimination as a factor that prompted the mass migrations, and referred to the emigrants as "the Jews who left Arab countries as refugees and settled in Israel and other countries," or simply as "Jews origin-ating from Arab countries" (Avizemer, 1997, p. 21; Avizemer, 2001, p. 7).

Further complicating matters, the Zionist establishment tended to per-ceive refugees as passive, while *olim* were characterized as having agency. Consequently, Jews from Arab countries, including both proponents and critics of the refugee claims, have tried to steer clear of the negative connotation of being a "refugee." WOJAC members often emphasized the "voluntary" aspect of their departure. More recently, scholars like Yehouda Shenhav, author of *The Arab Jews*, have argued that the refugee label is "offensive" to Mizrahi (Middle Eastern) Jews worldwide because it characterizes them as "lacking motivation to move to Israel"; yet it is not evident why this should be consid-ered offensive, especially to non-Israeli readers (Shenhav, 2012).

Similarly, Rachel Shabi, the bestselling author of *We Look Like the Enemy: The Hidden Story of Israel's Jews from Arab Lands*, also claims that Middle Eastern Jews would be "angered" by being defined as "refugees" because they chose to leave. Taking this point further, she clarifies that Middle Eastern Jews cannot be both Zionists and refugees, since "the former label has agency and involves a desire to live in the Jewish state; the second suggests passivity and a lack of choice" (Shabi, 2008). Thus, the dichotomy between refugees and *olim* can be found not just in academic sources, but in popular works as well.

Influenced by the Zionist assumptions undergirding *olim*, Shenhav, Shabi, and other prominent scholars and writers exclude those who might have taken an active role in their departure—by seeking or accepting outside assistance—from the definition of "refugee." Yet this runs counter to other historical precedents. The flaw in this logic becomes clear when we consider specific instances where Palestinians fled in anticipation of war (i.e., 1947–49 and 1967), and were not necessarily forcibly removed from their homes. Neither scholars nor international organizations consider these Palestinians any less deserving of refugee rights than those who were expelled, raising the question of why, in the case of Jews from Arab countries, individuals who flee preemptively cannot be considered refugees.

To clarify, if refugees embody passivity, and passivity carries a negative connotation, then Jews from Arab countries should want to avoid that kind of negative identification, not seek it out as in the case of JJAC. To account for this apparent cognitive dissonance, critics accuse organizations and individuals who champion the Jewish refugee cause as being Zionist, and therefore insincere when it comes to refugee demands. From the critics' perspective, if refugee proponents are Zionist, then they cannot truly support the idea of refugee claims and the accompanying implications of passivity. Accusing the refugee proponents of being Zionist is a shorthand way of calling them disingenuous and insincere.

In short, both proponents and critics of the refugee question have adopted the Zionist understanding (and mutual exclusiveness) of *olim* and refugees. We see this in the case of WOJAC, whose members tried to negotiate the tension between being a refugee, with its connotation of passivity, and the idea of voluntary emigration. We also see this in the case of critics who frame the Middle Eastern Jewish refugee question in terms of agency, rather than the particular circumstances of displacement. In so doing, critics foreclose opportunities for public deliberation over the legitimacy of the claims being put forward by refugee organizations. Consequently, any potential consider-ations of international law are ignored, as is the question of whether the categories "Zionist" and "refugee" can be reconciled.[3]

The Refugee within the Context of the Holocaust

As in the case of *aliyah*, the idea of passivity figures prominently in Holocaust survivor discourse. The association of the refugee with Holocaust survivors provides yet another reason that Jews from Arab countries might have been reluctant to identify as refugees.

In the first few decades of Israel's statehood, "refugees" (or *plitim*) referred neither to Palestinians nor to Jews from Arab countries, but to Holocaust survivors. *Sabras* regarded them with contempt, accusing them of being led "like a lamb to the slaughter." The early Zionists thus disdained the passiv-ity of European Holocaust survivors who arrived thereafter, even though they constituted roughly one-third of the Jewish population on the eve of statehood. They had not arrived in the land of Israel as idealist *olim*, but as refugees, and were consequently vilified.

In the 1950s and 1960s, when the majority of Jews from Arab coun-tries immigrated to Israel, they encountered Holocaust survivors in transit camps, quickly becoming aware of their marginalization in society and, paradoxically, their political centrality in post-1948 Zionist discourse. If we consider this along with the fact that Jews from Arab countries did not situate the Holocaust within their own history at that time, it is no surprise that they shied away from the term "refugee."

In the 1980s and 1990s, however, the stigmatization of survivors began to wane, and the Holocaust became integral to the national ethos. In parallel, as Jews from Arab countries began to migrate from the socioeconomic periphery towards its center, they began to regard the Holocaust as a formative event in the overarching collective Jewish memory, and to embrace the hegemony of Holocaust memory within Israeli society.[4] Still, Jews from Arab countries largely continued to feel uneasy referring to themselves as refugees, or making political demands, in the presence of Holocaust survivors.

As the stigma of being a survivor declined, so too did the stigma of being a refugee. This allowed Jews from Arab countries to begin identifying as refugees, or at least as a population that had experienced widespread persecution, which also helped in positioning themselves within the larger Israeli national memory. Initially, WOJAC members might have struggled with the appropriateness of comparing the events of the Holocaust with events that had transpired in the Middle East. Over time, however, the 1941 attack on Baghdad's Jewish community—known as the *farhūd*—was frequently likened to the Holocaust.[5] Publications like *The Scribe* and *Yom leyom*, which were geared towards Jews from Arab countries, began to devote articles to Sephardic Jews who had perished during the Holocaust.

By 2012, JJAC likened the Holocaust to events in North Africa during World War II. The organization lamented the dwindling number of Middle Eastern Jewish survivors who had not offered their testimony, as well as the absence of a national memorial like Yad Vashem dedicated to their memory (see Kahalon, 2012). Around this time, as a result of legal and political pressure, the Israeli government notably chose to compensate Tunisian, Libyan, Moroccan, Algerian, and Iraqi Jews for "Holocaust-era persecution" (Aderet, 2015). The hardships that Jews from Arab countries had experienced had assumed a place within the public consciousness within and outside of Israel.

The Refugee within the Context of the Israeli-Palestinian Conflict

In recent years, critics and proponents of Jewish refugee claims alike have compared the status of Jews from Arab countries to the status of Palestinian refugees. Indeed, the Palestinian case is instructive for demonstrating how refugee claims can extend beyond the cessation or acquisition of citizenship to questions concerning future residency, compensation, reparations, and moral acknowledgement or culpability (see Roula El-Rifai, this volume).

For critics, however, Jewish refugee demands are simply a political tool intended to deny Palestinians justice.

Given that some Israeli government officials and Jewish refugee proponents have intended to use these claims to counter Palestinian demands,
these accusations are not unfounded; nonetheless, they can be reductionist.
At times, Jews from Arab countries have likened themselves to Palestinian
refugees in order to demonstrate their commitment to the Zionist project,
aiding the Israeli government in turn, thereby proving their worth as "good"
olim. For these reasons, critics are right to be suspicious. Nevertheless, critics
tend to assume that what benefits Israeli state interests cannot also benefit
Jews from Arab countries and vice versa, when in fact the interests of the two
can at times overlap.

For some critics, organizations like WOJAC or JJAC intend only to obvi-
ate Palestinian compensation demands or the right of return, never intending
to help Jews from Arab countries in this process. While these accusations
might be true of some individuals, they are not true of others. In WOJAC's
early years, some executive members argued that the State of Israel should
collect claims on behalf of Jews from Arab countries and use them in negotiations with Palestinians, but this stance was controversial within WOJAC,
and prominent members like Heskel Haddad, Raffaelo Fellah, and Naim
Dangoor strongly opposed Israel's intervention in this capacity, not just in
the 1970s but in subsequent decades (H. Haddad, personal communication,
October 2012). Dangoor even accused the Israeli government of exploiting
the property rights of Jews from Arab countries. Time and again, he emphasized that the rights of Jews from Arab countries were not intended to be
used in Palestinian negotiations (Dangoor, 1993).

At other times, however, Jews from Arab countries have tried to distance themselves from the Palestinian analogy entirely because of negative
stereotypes—specifically, how Palestinians are characterized as unproductive
or undesirable. For this reason, some proponents emphasize the contributions of Jews from Arab countries in Israel's success. Gina Waldman, the
founder of Jews Indigenous to the Middle East and North Africa, as well
as a member of JJAC, described Israel as "the largest and most successful
refugee camp in the Middle East." In a similar vein, the prime minister of
Israel, Benjamin Netanyahu, has argued that Arab states used Palestinians
as a "battering ram" and turned them into "pawns," whereas Israel turned
Jews from Arab countries into "productive citizens."[6] The rhetoric surrounding who constitutes a productive citizen helps explain why Jews from
Arab countries, who might emphasize their experiences of persecution
and forced displacement, are otherwise extremely reluctant to be called
"refugees."[7]

The Refugee within the International Context

As the cases above illustrate, the politics of whether Jews from Arab countries can be considered refugees, in whole or in part, have not focused on the history of their displacement, but rather on particular assumptions about what being a refugee entails within Zionist contexts. When we utilize a legal or human rights framework within the international context, however, the category of "refugee" loses these negative connotations. Accordingly, more audiences—Jewish, Israeli, and international—have been more receptive to Middle Eastern Jewish refugee claims when the focus remains on the nature of their departure, rather than whether their refugee status should have any bearing on Palestinian refugee status. This helps account for why JJAC has been more successful in campaigning for refugee recognition than WOJAC (US Congress, 2008).

Within international law, refugees and their rights are enshrined in the Convention relating to the Status of Refugees (UNHCR, 1951):[8] "A person who owing to a well-founded fear of being persecuted for reasons of race, religion, nationality, membership of a particular social group or political opinion, is outside the country of his nationality and is unable or, owing to such fear, is unwilling to avail himself of the protection of that country; or who, not having a nationality and being outside the country of his former habitual residence as a result of such events, is unable or, owing to such fear, is unwilling to return to it" (Article 1). Proponents of Middle Eastern Jewish refugee recognition base their claims on this definition, and on UN Security Council Resolution 242, which refers to a "just settlement of the refugee problem." According to former US secretary of state Cyrus Vance, the "refugee problem" outlined in UNSCR 242 referred to both "Arab" and "Jewish" populations alike (Working Paper, 1977). By referencing these international definitions, proponents are able to distance themselves from the value-laden understandings of the term "refugee" within Zionist contexts.

In contrast, critics—particularly those personally or professionally invested in Zionism or the Palestinian-Israeli conflict—overlook or dismiss the international definition in favor of their own Zionist assumptions. Thus, in "Exploiting Jews from Arab Countries," Lara Friedman (2012), the Washington lobbyist and director of policy and government relations at Americans for Peace Now,[9] acknowledges the international definition of the refugee but deems it insufficient in the case of Jews from Arab countries, since Jews have ostensibly always yearned to return to Israel.[10] Notwithstanding the relevance of this claim for individuals, the biblical notion of return should not eclipse the fact that many Middle Eastern Jews considered the communities in which they had lived—some of which dated back millennia—as their homelands.

Conclusion

In most cases, those who flee their homes because of persecution or fear of persecution on the basis of race, religion, or political beliefs are normatively considered to be refugees, regardless of whether they desire to return to their place of origin afterward. In the case of Jews from Arab countries who immigrated to Israel, however, Israel is treated as an exception by the international community, Israelis, and Palestinians alike—it is either the "homeland of the Jews" or "a generic country" that granted "permanent refuge to a group of foreigners (who happened to be Jewish) fleeing persecution" in the Arab world, but it cannot be both (Friedman, 2012).

This problematic dichotomy overlooks how Jews from Arab countries might use their memories and narratives to shape boundaries and overlapping notions of belonging (see Safa Aburabia, this volume and Aziza Khazzoom, this volume). Outside of a Zionist paradigm, it is not clear why "Zionist" and "refugee" are mutually exclusive categories. Within a Zionist paradigm, "refugee" is a category that, when applied to Jews from Arab countries, has both undermined and supported maximalist Zionist goals in different political contexts. At present, because proponents have appealed to the international legal definition, refugee claims have found greater resonance within the international community. So long as claims for justice are considered within the framework of a comprehensive regional peace agreement, and are not treated as a "zero-sum" outcome within the context of Palestinian-Israeli bilateral negotiations, acknowledging the claims of Jews from Arab countries may yet be productive for achieving a stable peace agreement.

Shayna Zamkanei is currently an Israel Institute Fellow at Princeton University. Prior to this, she earned a PhD in political science from the University of Chicago and was a Frankel Fellow at the Frankel Institute for Advanced Judaic Studies at the University of Michigan. Her research explores the impact of dislocation on Middle Eastern Jewish communities in the United States and Israel, and her findings have been published in the *International Journal of Middle East Studies*, *Israel Studies*, and *Jewish Culture and History*. She is currently working on a monograph exploring the politics of recognition of Jews from Arab countries.

Notes

1 In September 2012, Justice for Jews from Arab Countries, the World Jewish Congress, and the Israel Ministry of Foreign Affairs held a

conference in Jerusalem entitled "Justice for Jewish Refugees from Arab Countries and Iran."

2 During the Suez crisis and the 1967 war, the office of the United Nations High Commissioner for Refugees referred to Jews fleeing Egypt as "refugees."

3 This does not take into consideration the status of Zionists displaced from Palestine during World War I.

4 With the formation of the Israeli Black Panthers, the establishment prioritized the creation of a unified national identity, in the hope of reducing ethnic tension.

5 Archives of the *fārhūd* can be found at Yad Vashem, Israel's national Holocaust memorial.

6 Comments by Waldman and Netanyahu were made at the Justice for Jewish Refugees from Arab Countries and Iran conference, Jerusalem, 2012.

7 As expressed to me by Egyptian, Moroccan, and Iraqi Jews whom I interviewed in October and November 2012 in New York City.

8 The Convention also has its limitations. For instance, displaced persons must cross an international border to be considered "refugees."

9 Americans for Peace Now is the "sister movement" to Peace Now, Israel's preeminent peace movement and the most influential left-leaning Zionist organization in the United States.

10 "Strangers in a foreign land" is a biblical expression to describe the Jews in Egypt.

References

Aderet, O. (2015, December 4). "Israel to Compensate Iraqi, Moroccan, Algerian Jews for Holocaust-Era Persecution." *Ha'aretz*. Retrieved from http://www.haaretz.com/israel-news/.premium-1.690077

Avizemer, S. (1997, April). "WOJAC." *The Scribe: Journal of Babylon Jewry, 67*, p. 21. Retrieved from http://www.dangoor.com/TheScribe67.pdf

Avizemer, S. (2001, Autumn). "WOJAC." *The Scribe: Journal of Babylonian Jewry, 74*, p. 7. Retrieved from http://www.dangoor.com/TheScribe_74.pdf

Dangoor, N. (1986, October). "Third International Conference of WOJAC." *The Scribe: Journal of Babylonian Jewry, 20*, p. 6. Retrieved from http://www.dangoor.com/TheScribe20.pdf

Dangoor, N. (1993, December). "Middle East Peace—Refugees and Compensation." *The Scribe: Journal of Babylonian Jewry 60*, p. 4. Retrieved from http://www.dangoor.com/TheScribe60.pdf

Friedman, L. (2012, August 2). "Exploiting Jews from Arab Countries." *The Daily Beast*. Retrieved from http://www.thedailybeast.com/articles/2012/08/02/exploiting-jews-from-arab-countries.html

Kahalon, M. [Director general, Central Organization for Jews from Arab Countries and Iran]. (2012). *Opening Statement*. Justice for Jewish Refugees from Arab Countries and Iran Conference, Jerusalem, Israel.

Shabi, R. (2008, June 27). "Another Side to the Jewish Story." *The Guardian*. Retrieved from http://www.theguardian.com/commentisfree/2008/jun/27/religion.israelandthepalestinians

Shenhav, Y. (2012, September 25). "Spineless Bookkeeping: The Use of Mizrahi Jews as Pawns against Palestinian Refugees." *+972 Magazine*. Retrieved from http://972mag.com/spineless-bookkeeping-the-use-of-mizrahi-jews-as-pawns-against-palestinian-refugees/56472

UNHCR (United Nations High Commissioner for Refugees). (1951, July 28). *Convention Relating to the Status of Refugees*. Retrieved April 6, 2016, from http://www.ohchr.org/EN/ProfessionalInterest/Pages/StatusOfRefugees.aspx

US Congress. (2008, April 1). *House Resolution 185*. Retrieved July 3, 2014, from https://www.govtrack.us/congress/bills/110/hres185/text

Working Paper. (1977, October 5). Israel State Archives (ISA) 6862/6. http://www.archives.gov.il/wp-content/uploads/2017/04/No-More-War-President-Sadats-Visit-to-Jerusalem-1977-List-of-documents.docx.

The Bedouin Struggle over Land in Palestine/Israel: Men of the *Nakba* Generation Narrate Their Attachment to Land

SAFA ABURABIA

The Bedouin, a community of Palestinian citizens of Israel, are the original inhabitants of the Naqab region (*Naqab* is the Arabic version of the Hebrew word *Negev*). For countless generations, their livelihoods were based on intensive agriculture and pasturing. Along with the creation of the State of Israel in 1948 came the Palestinian catastrophe (*Nakba* in Arabic), which fundamentally reshaped the geographical and tribal reality among Bedouin in the Naqab. The *Nakba* is visible primarily in the decimation of the Bedouin population, from 100,000 inhabitants of specified tribal terrains in the Naqab region in 1948 to 10,000 in 1953, a drop of 90 per cent, which contributed to drastic changes in their social structure. This essay addresses how Bedouin in Israel have been dispossessed of land through a variety of institutionalized methods. Taken together, the aim of these methods has been to Judaize the Naqab, resulting in Bedouin being displaced from their historical territory and becoming subject to mobility restrictions.

For nearly 70 years, in the face of the violence and relentlessness of this systematic persecution, Bedouin have continued to resist. By visiting and marking their tribal territories, continuing to use the names of their villages (regardless of whether they still exist), and preserving documents attesting to their status as landowners, they have preserved their territorial identity and transmitted it to their children. These "return" practices and the historical narratives they are embedded in revolve around direct links to their historical land, raising a challenge to the image of Bedouin as a "nomadic," landless people, while presenting an alternative view of their lives and desires. As these voices of Bedouin resistance are generally missing from historical scholarship, this essay relies on oral histories, that is, on the "lived archives" of the 1948 generation and their descendants (the second generation of the *Nakba*), who continue to reside in the Naqab.

Contested Spaces[1]

The struggle for place in Israel is expressed along two main axes: on the one hand, the construction of a national Zionist hegemony from above, which removes and erases remnants of Palestinian history through formal and institutional discourse and practices that shape the space as if it were, and has always been, exclusively Jewish; and on the other, the continuous building of the Bedouins' connection to their historical uprooted lands through spatial practices from below, such as pilgrimage, locating remains, marking borders, and reviving the past as part of strengthening the link between memory, belonging, and space. This spatial struggle illustrates how memories and narratives define boundaries, presence, and belonging.

This essay describes the struggle for the place of the Bedouin in the Naqab largely from the perspective of the *Nakba* generation. These narratives are drawn from in-depth interviews with male owners of land from the 1948 generation who were resident on their lands before the *Nakba* and were uprooted from it. They also include their sons—the second generation of the *Nakba*—who were born after 1948 in Israel, most of whom currently live in the northwestern part of the Naqab. These interviews, which were conducted as part of my master's thesis (Aburabia, 2005), focus on the men's life stories (Shakedi, 2003; Tuval-Mashiach & Spektor-Marzel, 2010).

1948 and State Mechanisms of Exclusion of the Bedouin from Place

Bedouin in the Naqab have been excluded from their land for almost 70 years. The Palestinian *Nakba* that occurred at the same time as the creation of the State of Israel radically reshaped geographical and tribal realities in the Naqab, as 90 per cent of Bedouin were expelled from their historical lands, mainly relocated to Gaza, the West Bank, Jordan, and the Sinai. This left only 10,000 Bedouin who were permitted to stay and live in the new State of Israel. The newly formed Israeli military government carried out one of the first mechanisms of dispossession against the Bedouin with the enforced confinement of 10,000 Bedouin to the Siyag triangle, north and east of Beer Sheva (Amara, Abu-Saad, & Yiftachel, 2013).

During this period, Bedouin movements were restricted. They were also cut off from what remained of the Palestinian population and, above all else, were denied any possibility of returning to their land. The Bedouin connection to land was further attacked through the establishment of seven so-called permanent settlements, which were designed to concentrate them into the smallest possible space so as to make way for the construction of Jewish settlements in the newly established country. Only half of the Naqab Bedouin live in these settlements today; the remainder live in villages within Israel that are unrecognized by the government and lack basic economic and social infrastructure (e.g., water, electricity). These villagers live highly precarious lives, under constant pressure to move to permanent settlements. To make matters even more difficult, these residents' homes are regularly demolished by the Israeli government and their crops are habitually destroyed (Nasasra, 2011, 2015; Swirski & Hasson, 2006).

In addition to flexing its military muscle, the Israeli state has wielded a variety of legal means to dispossess the Bedouin of their land and transfer it to state ownership. Revisiting outdated regulations and laws, including the Ottoman Mawat Law (1858) and the Dead Land Ordinance (1921) of the British Mandate, the authorities classified all of the land of the Palestinian Bedouin in the Naqab as "uncultivated," thereby transferring it to state ownership (Meir, 2007). The Land Acquisition Law of 1953 further expropriated the lots of anyone not living on their land as of 1 April 1952. Since most Bedouin in the Naqab had been forcibly evicted from their land prior to that date, they had lost their rights to it, their ownership documents notwithstanding (Meir, 2007). Such displacement mechanisms amount to a systematic effort on the part of the Israeli authorities to sever the Bedouin from their land, simultaneously challenging their rightful claims of land ownership (Falah, 1989).

Another important tool for dispossessing the Bedouin has emerged out of city planning and the use of modernist discourse to shape space in the alleged service of the nation, resulting in the concentration of Bedouin in limited spaces around community centers (Fenster, 2007; Meir, 2003). From a legal point of view, the Israeli discourse constructs the Zionist project as a moral narrative aimed at redeeming land from the Bedouin, a population understood to be nomadic remnants who represent chaos and immorality (Kram, 2012; Shamir, 1996). Bedouin are portrayed as "others" who are invisible in the eyes of the law. In such a constructed reality, further constructed and enforced by legislation, Bedouin claims to their land—based on unwritten traditional laws—are rendered illegitimate (Kram, 2012; Shamir, 1996).

Popular Zionist scholarship is yet another mechanism for Judaizing the Naqab, in that it reinforces Bedouins' semiotic displacement by construing them as tribal nomads in an "empty" terrain (Ashkenazi, 1957; Ben-David, 1972). Discourse in dominant Zionist scholarship has consistently emphasized Bedouins' alleged connection to tribe over connection to land. It portrays Bedouin as constantly moving, lacking connection to land, ahistorical, homogenous, frozen in time, and detached from proximate cultures. The implication and sense of this flawed scholarship is that the forcible relocation of the Bedouin comes without social, economic, or political consequence. In reality, Bedouin attachment to their historical lands has continued over the past 70 years, despite their physical displacement, through spatial and oral practices of return to the land, which work simultaneously to strengthen their sense of belonging to it while alienating them from their contemporary living spaces.

Memory and Belonging: The Bedouin Sense of Place as Resistance to Exclusion

For first- and second-generation Bedouin in the Naqab, identity continues to be shaped by the events of the *Nakba*; they continue to perceive themselves as exiles and aspire to return to their land. This sense of self is embedded in their "sense of place" in regard to their historical villages, forming a connection between their identity and place. This dynamic stems from their need to belong to a particular place where they feel a sense of comfort, security, and refuge (Massey, 1995). The meaning of a space is expressed by walking through these lands, marking territory, acquiring knowledge about the place, remembering it, and gaining an intimate experience of it. This bond is supplemented by events from the past that connect childhood experiences to historical terrain (De Certeau, 1988; Fenster, 2004).

These Bedouin preserve their connection to their land through the return practices they have maintained for 70 years, now enacted alongside their children and grandchildren. Among the practices cultivated are visits to their former land with their families, with the trip symbolizing their lives before the *Nakba* and including stories being told of the past and the marking of tribal territories: "Our houses still exist, and our graves are there.... In order to get to know the area in which we lived, our parents show us how they lived.... We lived here, here was the well of water, here we would sit at night" (Abu-Shareb, second generation). N. Abu Shareb (first generation) describes the intensity of the literal sensation of the land: "They visit the soil, they feel the soil, kiss it.... They feel the land and [are] attached to it."

These visits, along with the sharing of narratives about a lost way of life, create an intimacy that links participants to the land while reconstructing the past (Halbwachs, 1992; Lowenthal, 1985). As Al-Azazma points out:

> Every year we go there to visit my grandfather's house and the old houses there. We take the children and tell them the memories and sit on our land. We explain to them: this is our land and our home; here we were born, and here we lived, on this land; here we planted lentils, and wheat here; and here we made a field with digging tools on the camel's back. I teach my children that this is the land of this tribe, and this is the land of that tribe, and we yearn for our lands so that they may know them.... This is our land.

The children of the *Nakba* generation are thus informed of what still belongs to them. In the words of N. Abu-Shareb: "When we go there, we bring her [the land] stones and bring her sand.... It is important to me that the youngest child knows.... We had land and when we take him to the land, his mother tells him, 'It was your land!'.... The place where we live now is not our land, this is our land, we are connected to this land."

Similarly, as Abu-Rqayeq explains:

> Thus they will have continuity to prove ownership of the land, no
> less and no more; I take them to show them where I was born,
> where I would drink water, where I lived; I pass on this information
> to them so that they will know that we do not accept our [fate], that
> we are still here and that we have no right to our land; I want them
> to know that we are deprived. They do not have to forget where
> they came from. They have to know that they were not born in Tel
> Al Sabea [the Bedouin village where they live today]; we are not
> from this land, our source and our property are elsewhere, and the
> government [keeps] them from us.

In visits to their former lands, Bedouin parents clarify to their children that the reality in which they are living today is not obligatory and that in the past they had land, which afforded them dignity and social status. As Abu-Siam tells of his father's repeated descriptions:

> This is not the first time he has told us the history; he has been
> telling us all along. Why do you think I know this by heart? Because
> he told us at every event to explain to us why we have a problem
> today, why we have no land, why we are today on the land of others.
> We cannot develop anymore, so it hurts.... Today we have a problem:
> the families around us have land, so why do we not have land? Why
> do we not have land?

These uprooted families also maintain evidence of their ownership of their lands, such as maps and aerial photographs from the time of the British Mandate, and documents from the 1930s and 1940s that prove their presence on their land. Abu-Sharab N. says:

> The[se] documents are sacred ... because this is our land that we
> sowed.... Our land today is empty, and we have proof that this is our
> land, we own it. I have photocopied the documents several times
> and arranged them ... in a folder. I put all my pages on the side....
> I register in my documents exactly what the borders are from the
> north to someone, and from the south to someone and so on....
> I have something orderly.

Turning the history of the *Nakba* generation into something that their children think about today is a way to keep the memory of their ownership of the land alive (Issa, 1997). The past thus becomes eternal, existing in the mind in the present (Warner, 2002) and guiding their future actions. At the same time, Bedouin opposition to the dispossession is reflected in their heightened sense of exile in and alienation from the places where they live today.

Bedouin exile manifests in two primary ways. The first is physical. The exiles are far from their land, which nevertheless remains the focus of their lives; they yearn to return to it. The second is a matter of consciousness, including the idea of not belonging and an incompleteness of self caused by the damage done to one's territorial identity. Life is experienced as temporary and unstable for inhabitants of unrecognized villages; concurrently, those in permanent settlements lead narrow and difficult lives. Therefore, these Bedouin continue to define themselves in terms of having been expelled, regardless of whether they live in recognized or unrecognized villages. For them, the loss is mental and physical, personal and collective. Since 1948, their world order has been radically changed. All at once they were turned from landowners to landless people: "We are considered expelled, without land.... We are foreigners in our homeland" (Al-Okbi).

Although many Bedouin live close to their original land, they feel exiled because of having lost it to another people. Their land symbolizes a utopian past and is connected to the future through hope for a more peaceful life after returning to their land and to "themselves." In this sense, the Bedouin in the Naqab feel that they are no less exiled than the Palestinians forced across the borders of the newly established State of Israel (i.e., into the West Bank, Gaza, and elsewhere) and barred from returning. Despite the physical presence of the Bedouin in their homeland, they are excluded. And, indeed, the new boundaries of Israeli space explicitly define them as foreigners *within* Israel itself.

Language is a major tool to express opposition, often used to illustrate a refusal to accept the hegemonic narrative (Wedeen, 1998) of Israel. In the words of one of the interviewees: "The state will ... take the most precious thing we have.... We are now a tribe against a state" (Abu Sharab). Language is also a means of expressing alternative explanations and a counternarrative to explain their situation: "Zionism ..., every *dunam* of land for the sake of new immigrants.... This is the height of racism. Our land is waiting for Jews for 100 to 150 years until they come. This is discrimination. They look at the Arab citizen with one eye and the Jewish citizen with another.... The Jew must protect the nation's land from the non-Jewish citizen" (Al-Okbi).

Alienation is also expressed in the concrete vision that is fostered of returning to their historical lands. For these Bedouin, their visions represent concrete, realistic plans for the future: "We have to return at any price, we must return to our homes.... If we gain our right while Israel continues, then that will be good. If not, we will get it later" (Al-Oqbi N.) Their plan to return to their historical land reflects their refusal to accept their current homes. It constitutes a tangible alternative reality for them, subject to fulfillment in the near or distant future.

Conclusion

"Identity of place" among the landowning Bedouin conveys their birth identity, defining who they are, not only in terms of where they came from but also their place in the world. This identity is derived from the material place (the tribal territory) that belongs to them and defines their cultural identity. Even 70 years after the dispossession of the *Nakba* of 1948, place continues to exist as an integral part of them. Preserving "identity of place" by means of oral practices and actual return to their lost land strengthens their affinity for it, reflected in the way they convey to their children the sense of land as something that both has been taken from them in the past and will return to them in the future. These practices of return likewise define their opposition to the lives they lead in the settlements in Israel where they reside today. They also find expression in the active agency they exercise in their intergenerational struggle against the removal from their land.

Readings of Bedouin silences and ignored histories of their territorial identity expose the mechanisms of ongoing dispossession, such as the biased Zionist representation of Bedouin as "nomads" who do not belong to any place. This rewriting of Bedouin history "from below," based on people's oral history testimonies, represents their indigenous identity and culture; it recognizes their historical presence in their own spaces. This is an alternative history that needs to be expressed and should be heard in more public and academic spaces.

As Roula El-Rifai (this volume) claims, the conceptual clash between the Israeli and Palestinian versions of events surrounding 1948, namely, the *Nakba* and the creation of the Palestinian refugee problem, gives shape to the narratives, the terminology, and the consciousness of both sides in different and contradictory ways. The same division provides the basis for conflicting aims in attempts to find an appropriate solution to the problem of refugees displaced from their villages and lands, whether as part of the diaspora or within the borders of the state that was established on their ruins.

Shayna Zamkanei's essay (this volume) on the definition of "refugees" in the internal Israeli context, specifically regarding the Jewish population from Muslim and Arab countries, raises a number of significant points regarding the location of these definitions and their consolidation in the dominant Israeli narrative. It should be noted that these internal Israeli discussions have a direct impact on Jewish-Arab relations and the problem of Palestinian refugees. I would suggest that the attempt to define Jews from Arab countries as refugees undermines the positive relations that existed between them and Arabs before 1948.

In addition, this process of redefining Jewish Israelis from Arab countries as refugees is an attempt to tell the story (again) of the Jews and their connection to place from the perspective of victims who had no alternative after having been brutally expelled from Muslim- and European-dominant countries. Thus, the arrival of Jews in Israel works to support the same unified Zionist narrative. Such narratives focus exclusively on Jewish refugees in order to "balance" their side against the Palestinian refugees, and to claim that all Jews were expelled from their countries on the journey to a homeland that would redeem them from their suffering.

In this way, the Zionist narrative becomes an exchange of populations: while the Arabs have 22 states, the Jews have only one. Ignored in this narrative is the historical, cultural, and social uniqueness of Palestinians, in favor of clearly prioritizing the Zionist story and the Jewish connection to place over that of others. It is another Israeli attempt to introduce "balance" into the Israeli-Palestinian conflict, which only further widens the gap between the two sides. My research suggests that broadening the definition of "refugees" to include Bedouin citizens of Israel is antithetical to Israel's harsh policy towards them. Conversely, excluding Bedouin citizens of Israel in discussion around "refugees" reinforces the lack of need to deal with them justly. The Israeli perception of Bedouin as nomads with no connection to place underlies policies that have forced, and continue to force, them off their land.

Yet the Bedouin who were uprooted from their lands in the Negev define themselves as internally displaced and dispossessed. Their profound connection to place shapes their identity and their place in the world, a consideration that is absent from the way the issue is framed in Israeli policy. Moreover, for the Negev Bedouin, the *Nakba* is not something that ended in 1948, since their dispossession continues through physical displacement today, 70 years later (e.g., the settlements of Al-Arakib have been destroyed more than 100 times by now; the population has repeatedly been expelled so the state can plant a forest. Umm al-Hiran is another village where the population is being expelled to build a Jewish village on the ruins). This dispossession and expulsion continues through the symbolic expropriation that defines Bedouin as nomads, belonging everywhere and yet nowhere.

The Bedouin perceive their return to their former territories as a realistic vision that must be implemented. In the years since the *Nakba*, the 1948 generation, along with their children and grandchildren, have visited their lands, marked their boundaries, and narrated their past lives to succeeding generations, thus maintaining the connection to land as theirs. The reclamation of place by these return practices shapes the identity of the Bedouin as owners of the land at the same time that the identity of the place is reshaped as Bedouin. As this identity is passed from generation to generation, it strengthens their resistance to their dispossession and displacement.

Safa Aburabia has been a postdoctoral fellow in the anthropology department at Harvard University, and a Fulbright Fellow (2016–17) and Israel Institute Fellow (2016–18). Her current work applies a gender perspective to Bedouin collective memory and representations of 1948 and the subsequent struggle over land through the lens of internal social structure, gender, and class tension. She is also working on a research project entitled "Between Israeli Institutions and Bedouin Tribalism: The Struggle for Land among the Third Generation of the *Nakba* in the South of Palestine/ Israel." It focuses on the Bedouins' struggle with the state over land rights; the participation of young Bedouin men and women in the struggle; and their experience reconstructing their social, intergenerational, and gender identities in contexts of displacement and internal migration. The project is a collaboration with Professor Avinoam Meir, and is funded by the Israeli Science Foundation (ISF).

Note

1 The spatial struggle in Israel must be understood as occurring between competing spaces (Kuper, 2003), in the sense of a social and political conflict centered on sites representing collective myths. The core contention in such a struggle is about having the right to control resources and to determine the future of sites based on their past, and to have control over how they are represented and understood culturally. Typically, this conflict finds expression in two ways. First is the construction of the way sites are remembered through the exercise of a state monopoly over public spaces, enabling states to impose official and popular memories while simultaneously weakening contradictory histories. Second is the institutionalization and marketing of tourist sites, which are crucial to maintaining ideological hegemony in support of strengthening national identity.

References

Aburabia, S. (2005). *Exiled in Our Homeland: The Diasporic Identity of the Negev Bedouin* (Master's thesis). Beer Sheva, Israel: Ben-Gurion University of the Negev, Israel. [In Hebrew]

Amara, A., Abu-Saad, I., & Yiftachel, O. (2013). *Indigenous (In)Justice: Human Rights Law and Bedouin Arabs in the Naqab/Negev.* Cambridge, MA: Human Rights Program at Harvard Law School.

Ashkenazi, T. (1957). *The Bedouin: Their Origins, Life, and Customs.* Jerusalem, Israel: Reuven Mas. [In Hebrew]

Ben-David, Y. (1972). *Bedouin Tribes in Southern Sinai* (Master's thesis). Hebrew University in Jerusalem, Jerusalem, Israel. [In Hebrew]

De Certeau, M. (1988). *The Practice of Everyday Life.* Berkeley, CA: University of California Press.

Falah, G. (1989). "The Spatial Pattern of Bedouin Sedentarization in Israel." *Geojournal, 11*(4), 361–68. https://doi.org/10.1007/bf00150770

Fenster, T. (2004). "On Belonging and Spatial Planning in Israel." In H. Yacobi (ed.), *Constructing Sense of Place: Architecture and the Zionist Discourse* (pp. 285–302). Aldershot, UK: Ashgate.

Fenster, T. (2007). "Memory, Relevance, and Spatial Planning in Israel." *Theory and Criticism, 30,* 189–212.

Halbwachs, M. (1992). *On Collective Memory.* Chicago, IL: Chicago University Press.

Issa, M. (1997, December). "Decoding the Silencing Process in Modern Palestinian Historiography." Paper presented at Worlds and Visions: Perspectives on the Middle East Today, Local and National Histories Conference, Aarhus, Denmark.

Kram, N. (2012). "The Naqab Bedouins: Legal Struggles for Land Ownership Rights in Israel." In A. Amara, I. Abu-Saad, & O. Yiftachel (eds), *Indigenous (In)Justice: Human Rights Law and Bedouin Arabs in the Naqab/Negev* (pp. 126–56). Cambridge, MA: Human Rights Program at Harvard Law School.

Kuper, H. (2003). "The Language of Sites in the Politics of Space." In S.M. Low & D. Lawrence-Zuniga (eds), *The Anthropology of Space and Place: Locating Culture* (pp. 247–63). Malden, MA: Blackwell.

Lowenthal, D. (1985). *The Past is a Foreign Country.* Cambridge, UK: Cambridge University Press.

Massey, D. (1995). "The Conceptualization of Place." In D. Massey & P. Jess (eds), *A Place in the World? Places, Cultures, and Globalization* (pp. 45–86). Milton Keynes, UK: Open University Press.

Meir, A. (2003). *From Planning Advocacy to Independent Planning: The Negev Bedouin on the Path to Democratization in Planning.* Beer Sheva, Israel: Negev Center for Regional Development, Ben Gurion University of the Negev (Hebrew).

Meir, A. (2007). "An Alternative Examination of the Ground Conflict in the Negev between the Government and the Bedouin." *Land, 63,* 14–51.

Nasasra, M. (2011). "The Southern Palestine Bedouin and British Mandate Relations, 1917–1948: Resistance to Colonialism." *Arab World Geographer Journal, 4*(14), 305–35.

Nasasra, M. (2015). "Ruling the Desert: Ottoman and British Policies towards the Bedouin of the Naqab and Transjordan Region, 1900–1948." *British Journal of Middle Eastern Studies, 42*(3), 261–83. https://doi.org/10.1080/13530194.2015.1011452

Nora, P. (1993). "Between Memory and History: On the Problem of the Place." *Zmanim, 45,* 4–19.

Shakedi, A. (2003). *Words Trying to Touch.* Tel Aviv, Israel: Ramot. [In Hebrew]

Shamir, R. (1996). "Suspended in Space: Bedouins under the Law of Israel." *Law and Society Review*, *30*(2), 231–56. https://doi.org/10.2307/3053959

Swirski, S., & Hasson, Y. (2006). "Invisible Citizens: Government Policy towards Bedouins in the Negev." ADVA Center. Retrieved January 7, 2019, from https://adva.org/wp -content/uploads/2014/09/NegevEnglishSummary.pdf

Tuval-Mashiach, R., & Spektor-Marzel, G. (2010). *Narrative Research: Theory, Creation, and Interpretation*. Jerusalem, Israel: Magnes Press. [In Hebrew]

Warner, B. (2002). "Beyond the Boundaries." In N. Abdo (ed.), *Women and the Politics of Military Confrontation* (pp. 111–18). New York, NY: Berghahn Books.

Wedeen, L. (1998). "Acting 'As If': Symbolic Politics and Social Control in Syria." *Comparative Studies in Society and History*, *40*(3), 503–23. https://doi.org/10.1017/ S0010417598001388

six

Apartheid

In recent years, debate over the conflict in Israel/Palestine has taken on an added dimension with the injection of the word "apartheid" by some of Israel's critics to describe Israel's rule over the Palestinians. Originating in the context of South Africa, it's admittedly a controversial and loaded term, with "Israeli Apartheid Week" on various university and college campuses worldwide being one example of how it has been used to galvanize activists while placing many advocates of Israel on the defensive. This chapter seeks to assess the comparison of Israel/Palestine to apartheid in a scholarly way, showing where the designation may or may not hold.

Some proponents of the apartheid label use the term to describe the experience of Palestinian citizens of Israel; some use it to describe Palestinians living under Israeli occupation in East Jerusalem, the West Bank, and Gaza; and some proponents of the label argue that Israel's ongoing occupation is enough to classify the whole country as an apartheid state no matter how many rights Palestinian citizens of Israel enjoy relative to their East Jerusalem, West Bank, and Gazan counterparts.

The two essays in this chapter primarily restrict their analysis to Israel's rule in the West Bank. Oren Kroll-Zeldin argues that the situation there—namely, the near-permanent status of occupation supported by institutionalized and systemic oppression—merits the apartheid label. He contends that the widely accepted definition of apartheid, embodied in various international conventions, is an apt descriptor of the situation in the West Bank, as the occupation relies on two separate legal systems, one privileging Jewish citizens and the other oppressing Palestinian residents. Kroll-Zeldin acknowledges that while "some claim that this is simply a semantic debate, describing Israel's rule over the Occupied Palestinian Territories as apartheid is fundamental to questioning the morality of Israel's occupation and applying a rights-based discourse to the Palestinian-Israeli conflict."

By contrast, in their essay, Zeina M. Barakat and Mohammed S. Dajani Daoudi argue that the apartheid label does not fit. They prefer the term "occupation"—full stop. They say that "Israel is not oppressing the Palestinians in the West Bank and East Jerusalem as minority citizens of the state, but as an occupying force of territories acknowledged by the United Nations and international law as occupied." They interpret the settlement policies, for example, as motivated by "political cleansing, not ethnic cleansing." They further suggest that it "is the norm and custom of an occupation-state that an occupier does not invest heavily in the territories it occupies because the occupying force perceives their presence to be provisional."

While Kroll-Zeldin sees the apartheid label as important to bringing about human rights in Israel/Palestine, Barakat and Dajani Daoudi contend that the apartheid label is not only misleading, but could divert energy from ending the occupation. In their own words: "The fact that the occupation is immoral, that it elicits violent resistance, and that it breeds home-grown terrorists, is overshadowed and marginalized by adopting the apartheid analogy."

For our purposes, we are interested in the following question: what's at stake in this debate? From a scholarly perspective, debating the apartheid label can point to areas of comparative analysis and help trace processes of internal and external political change. From a social justice perspective, some activists argue that applying the label could serve to accelerate and intensify an international response to Israel's unequal treatment of Palestinians. Using the label also lends credence to the tactics of the BDS (Boycott, Divestment, Sanctions) movement (chapter 8), which gets much of its energy from the legacy of using international pressure to help bring about an end to South African apartheid. On the other hand, some opponents of the label—whatever their social justice leanings—simply feel that the term "apartheid" is misplaced in this case. And still others, especially those within staunch Israel advocacy circles, decry what they see as a rhetorical move meant to unfairly malign Israel; they view those who use the apartheid label as participating in a pernicious attempt to "delegitimize" the world's only Jewish state.

As in the case of the settler-colonialism discussion (chapter 3), the apartheid debate in the context of Israel/Palestine provides a prime opportunity to consider the question of what the relationship might be, or should be, between academic assessments and political sensibilities.

Does Israel Function as an Apartheid State? Critically Engaging the Complexities of the Apartheid Debate in Palestine/Israel

OREN KROLL–ZELDIN

Since its inaugural event at the University of Toronto in 2005, Israeli Apartheid Week has fomented widespread protest and consternation among students and faculty on university campuses across the world, which have become embroiled in a battle of campus politics over the term "apartheid" and its applicability (or not) to the situation in Palestine/Israel. Israeli Apartheid Week, which now takes place in over 200 cities worldwide, is comprised of a series of events that seek to raise awareness of what its organizers commonly refer to as "Israel's apartheid system over the Palestinian people" and to build support for the global Boycott, Divestment, and Sanctions (BDS) movement (Israeli Apartheid Week, 2017). Lauded by some for its human rights advocacy and counterhegemonic narrative (Ziadah & Hanieh, 2010) and derided by others as anti-Semitic in its attempt to delegitimize Israel (Weinryb, 2008), Israeli Apartheid Week often acts as a campus proxy for the conflict in Palestine/Israel. It has become such a contentious issue that many people on campuses have started using the phrase "the A word" in order to avoid the controversy altogether over the term "apartheid."

This organized week of lectures and direct actions did not arise out of the founders' anti-Semitism, as some of its detractors contest, but rather from a serious concern for the human rights of Palestinians who are subject to those Israeli policies that systematically and institutionally discriminate against them while privileging Jews. It also stems from the long-standing connection between the State of Israel and the apartheid government in South Africa, the latter of which lasted from 1948 to 1994.[1] These official ties between the State of Israel and apartheid South Africa illuminated for many the similarities in the institutionalized separation defining the two societies. This subsequently gave rise to the extension of the apartheid label to the State of Israel alongside its widely accepted use to describe a particular era in South Africa (Polakow-Suransky, 2010). The alliance between these two regimes, which dates back to the 1970s, has enabled scholars, activists, and politicians to make a clear link between the policies of separation of whites and blacks in South Africa and Israel's discriminatory policies towards Palestinians (Badran, 2010; Bishara, 2001; Pappe, 2015; Soske & Jacobs, 2015).

Furthermore, the term "apartheid" is not only used by critics of Israeli policies, but has also been commonly repeated by Israeli and United States politicians alike. Former Israeli prime ministers Ehud Olmert (McCarthy, 2007) and Ehud Barak (McCarthy, 2010) each warned that Israel, vis-à-vis its occupation of the Palestinian Territories, was on the path to becoming an apartheid state, as did former foreign minister Tzipi Livni (Derfner, 2013). Even US Secretary of State John Kerry used "the A word" in 2014 during his unsuccessful attempt to broker peace between Israel and Palestine (Rogin, 2014).

Perhaps the biggest firestorm in this regard came after President Jimmy Carter published a book called *Palestine: Peace Not Apartheid* and went on a speaking tour on college campuses across the United States to discuss the dire human rights situation in Palestine/Israel. His tentative yet provocative use of the word—in the title of his book, no less—described what he witnessed in the Occupied Palestinian Territories; he argued that one of the options Israel faces is "a system of apartheid, with two peoples occupying the same land but completely separate from each other, with Israelis totally dominant and suppressing violence by depriving Palestinians of their basic human rights" (Carter, 2006, p. 215). The unfettered use of "apartheid" to refer to the policies of the State of Israel by such prominent politicians, including Israeli prime ministers, points to the legitimacy of using the term, rather than its use having stemming from vitriol towards Israel or from anti-Semitism.

Though the concern over a hostile campus climate evident during Israeli Apartheid Week must be taken seriously, calls to abolish Israeli Apartheid Week or charges of anti-Semitism against its organizers ignore the fact that there is significant evidence demonstrating the numerous ways in which Israel actually functions as an apartheid state. In order for students to fully understand and engage with the events on campuses and in the larger world, it is essential to critically engage with the term "apartheid" and to have a rigorous conversation about the ways in which it applies to the State of Israel. Though some claim that this is simply a semantic debate, describing Israel's rule over the Occupied Palestinian Territories as apartheid is fundamental to questioning the morality of Israel's occupation and applying a rights-based discourse to the Palestinian-Israeli conflict.

Defining Apartheid and Its Application to the State of Israel

"Apartheid," which literally means "apartness," is the Afrikaans word used most often to describe the institutionalized system of racial segregation and discrimination in South Africa between 1948 and 1994. In November 1973, the United Nations General Assembly passed the International Convention on the Suppression and Punishment of the Crime of Apartheid, thereby codifying the term "apartheid" within international legal systems as a crime against humanity. The Apartheid Convention, which became law on 18 July 1976, defines apartheid as "inhuman acts committed for the purpose of establishing and maintaining domination by one racial group of persons over any other racial group of persons and systematically oppressing them" (United Nations, 1973). According to this convention, apartheid practices are not limited to South Africa alone; rather, they are understood as "similar policies and practices of racial segregation and discrimination as practiced in southern Africa." In the 2002 Rome Statute, another important international legal document, the "crime of apartheid" is included as one of the recognized crimes against humanity. The Rome Statute defines apartheid as "inhuman acts ... committed in the context of an institutionalized regime of systematic oppression and domination by one racial group over any other racial group or groups and committed with the intention of maintaining that regime" (United Nations, 2002).[2]

There are three important elements to the legal definition of apartheid that help us determine its applicability to the case of Israel. First, it is essential to understand that, as stated above, the Apartheid Convention clearly stipulates that the crime of apartheid is not exclusive to South Africa but also pertains to policies and practices that are "similar" to those used in apartheid South Africa. The term "apartheid," which was clearly created in the South African context and is most often associated with South Africa, is not monolithic nor is it limited by time and space. In fact, "the prevailing scholarly view is that, while the Apartheid Convention was drafted with southern Africa in mind, it was meant to be universal in character and not confined to the practice of apartheid as seen in southern Africa" (Tilley, 2012, p. 124).

Second, for a set of policies to be considered apartheid, they must be systematic and institutionalized. In a comprehensive article that examines the applicability of apartheid in international law to the Occupied Palestinian Territories, John Dugard and John Reynolds (2013), both from South Africa, contend that "the essence of the definition of apartheid is thus the systematic, institutionalized, and oppressive character of the discrimination involved, and the purpose of domination that is entailed. It is this institutionalized element, involving a state-sanctioned regime of law, policy, and institutions, that distinguishes the practice of apartheid from other forms of prohibited discrimination" (p. 881). After even a cursory examination of everyday life in the Occupied Palestinian Territories, as will be done below, it would be problematic to deny that Israel does not have clear-cut policies that systematically oppress Palestinians with the intention of maintaining its regime of power over them while simultaneously preserving a Jewish demographic majority.

Lastly, though not overtly obvious, the international legal definitions of apartheid broaden the term "racial group" in a way that makes the term applicable to the State of Israel. One key argument *against* the application of the Apartheid Convention to Israel is that apartheid applies only to "racial groups," and neither Jews nor Palestinians are considered today to be a racial group. In other words, Israel cannot maintain its regime based on "racial discrimination." However, the International Convention on the Elimination of All Forms of Racial Discrimination, which is invoked in the Preamble of the International Convention on the Suppression and Punishment of the Crime of Apartheid, defines "racial discrimination" as any distinction, exclusion, restriction, or preference based on race, color, descent, or national or ethnic origin that has the purpose or effect of nullifying or impairing the recognition, enjoyment, or exercise, on an equal footing, of human rights and fundamental freedoms in the political, economic, social, cultural, or any other field of public life (United Nations, 1965).

If racial discrimination includes groups of national or ethnic origin, then it is most certainly applicable to Israel, whose policies systematically oppress noncitizen Palestinians, an ethnic and national group (Tilley, 2012).

A Note on the Politics of Comparison

Scholars and activists often use the comparative method to develop scholarly and political arguments that illuminate certain similarities and differences between distinct cases. Though I believe that the method of comparison is appropriate in the context of Israeli apartheid, it is not always an appropriate tool of analysis. According to Julie Peteet (2016), "comparisons must be situated in a context of commensurability, or a purposeful field of analysis, rather than strewn haphazardly across time and space" (pp. 254–55). She argues that since both Israel and South Africa are settler colonial societies (Veracini, 2010), the comparisons are both appropriate and legitimate. In this context, the value of comparison lies in its ability to "make things seem familiar by highlighting the broad resemblances or approximations between them" (Peteet, 2016, p. 255). Furthermore, a comparative approach serves to de-exceptionalize both Israeli and South African forms of apartheid while highlighting possibilities for change and conflict transformation (Bakan & Abu-Laban, 2010).

Polemical use of the term "apartheid," as it is often employed in activist communities, does not help elucidate the legitimate legal applications of the term to the Palestine context. The phrase must be used judiciously, based in a careful examination of its legal definitions and the ways in which Israel's policies vis-à-vis Palestinians constitute apartheid. For example, we must remember that apartheid in Israel is different from the way it existed in South Africa. Yet this does not mean that it is inappropriate to use the term in the Israeli case, especially since the legal definition allows for the term to be applied outside of South Africa. Since the particular form of apartheid in Israel is different from that in South Africa, perhaps it may be useful to say "Israeli apartheid," always using the signifier "Israeli" to point to the specificities and particularities of Israel's apartheid system. Though many differences between the two systems of apartheid exist, they all stem from the particularities of the social, historical, and political context. The most obvious and prominent example is in the privilege given to one group over another based on racial and ethnic identity. While in South Africa the racial and ethnic differentiations were based in a white/non-white binary, in Israel the main marker of difference is Jewish/non-Jewish.

Lastly, a word of caution—it is essential to avoid engaging in a conversation over which form of apartheid, Israeli or South African, was better or worse. Though the comparison is apt, it must be done in a context that refuses to compare levels of suffering, oppression, and victimhood. Suffering is suffering and oppression is oppression. As Audre Lorde reminds us, there is no hierarchy of oppression (Lorde, 1983, p. 9). A critical engagement with the complexities of the apartheid debate in Palestine/Israel must therefore remain focused, specific, and nonpolemical. Using the comparative method, below I make the case that Israel functions as an apartheid state not with the intention to argue that Palestinians have it better or worse than blacks did in South Africa, but rather as a critical intervention into the very specific forms of occupation and colonization in Palestine that can be legitimately described as apartheid.

Israeli Apartheid

Before we can examine some of the ways Israel functions as an apartheid state, it is important to clarify the boundaries of this country. Even among those who agree that it is legitimate to apply the term "apartheid" to Israel there is disagreement over whether or not it functions as an apartheid state only within the territories that it illegally occupies (Gaza, West Bank, East Jerusalem) or if Israeli apartheid extends also to the pre-1967 borders of the state and the Palestinian citizens of Israel. While legitimate arguments can be made for both claims, I will focus solely on the Israeli apartheid system in the Occupied Palestinian Territories. This is not to obfuscate Israeli responsibility for the institutionalized discrimination against Palestinian citizens of Israel, but rather to focus on more clearly agreed upon international borders and legal issues.

The 1949 Armistice Lines that formally ended the Arab-Israeli War, also referred to as the Green Line, define the internationally recognized borders of the State of Israel. After the 1967 Arab-Israeli War, Israel extended its rule beyond the Green Line, occupying the Gaza Strip, West Bank, and East Jerusalem (as well as other territories not directly relevant to the conversation at hand). In the half century since, Israel has steadily and systematically extended its rule over "Greater Israel," with different rights given to the people living there based on their citizenship. In the geographical area between the Jordan River and the Mediterranean Sea, Israel rules over 8.7 million citizens with full civil and political rights, 75 per cent of whom are Jewish and 20 per cent of whom are Palestinian (Israeli Central Bureau of Statistics, 2017), and 4.8 million stateless Palestinian subjects (3 million in the West Bank and 1.8 million in Gaza) who have neither citizenship nor full civil and political rights (OCHA OPT, 2017). The institutionalized and systematic denial of equal rights to these 4.8 million Palestinians and the privileging of Jews over Palestinians in the Occupied Palestinian Territories forms the core of the argument that an Israeli apartheid exists.

On the broadest level, Israel imposes a separate and unequal regime in the occupied territories that institutionally and systematically oppresses Palestinians while privileging Jews. The state does so to maintain its dominance over Palestinians because in order to preserve its identity as a Jewish state, it must have a Jewish demographic majority. Domination over Palestinians has been an essential element of the Zionist vision even prior to the establishment of the State of Israel. As a result, it is thought to be essential for the state's identity to pursue policies that maintain this domination, making it function as an apartheid state. Put another way, "an apartheid regime is not created out of 'misunderstanding,' but to serve a group's survival agenda by physically excluding other groups—a policy that has little to do with the nature of others except that they are, by definition, others" (Tilley, 2012, p. xiv).

One specific way that Israel functions as an apartheid state is through its separate legal systems for Jewish Israelis and Palestinians in the West Bank, which give different rights and privileges to each group (Association for Civil Rights in Israel, 2014).[3] Jews are subjected to civil law while Palestinians live under military law in the same territory. At the most fundamental level, Israeli Jews who live in the West Bank, who number some 382,000, are citizens of the State of Israel and, as such, have the right to vote in Israeli elections.[4] They have the privilege of participating in the democratic processes that impact their everyday lives. Palestinians in the West Bank do not have citizenship and are therefore barred from voting rights, making it all but impossible for them to influence Israeli policies and practices that directly impact their lives on a daily basis.

Furthermore, if a Jewish Israeli citizen and a Palestinian noncitizen were both accused of committing the same crime in the West Bank, they would be sentenced under different guidelines and sent to different prisons. An Israeli Jew would be subject to civil law and sent to a prison in Israel, while a Palestinian would go to a military court and prison in the West Bank. Additionally, a Jew in the West Bank has the right to engage in political protest, while Palestinians do not. Lastly, if a Jew in the West Bank marries an Israeli citizen, they are allowed to reside anywhere in Israel to live with their spouse. If, on the other hand, a Palestinian in the West Bank marries an Israeli citizen, they would not be allowed to move to Israel (i.e., within the Green Line) to live with their spouse. These examples evidence the ways that the same laws apply differently based on one's national or ethnic origin.

Another key element of Israel's apartheid rule is the slow but steady attempts to "Judaize Jerusalem" (Yiftachel, 1999) in order to preserve a Jewish demographic majority in the city. Judaizing Jerusalem refers to the practice of making the city distinctly more Jewish Israeli in its culture, politics, language, and geography. One of the key methods Israel uses to maintain the city's character is the systematic revocation of the permanent residency rights of Palestinians (Kroll-Zeldin, 2018). Palestinians in East Jerusalem are permanent residents of Jerusalem, which is a form of "quasi-citizenship" (Jefferis, 2012) that is distinctly different from the legal classification of Palestinian citizens of Israel or stateless Palestinians in Gaza and the West Bank. East Jerusalem is also different from the other Occupied Palestinian Territories since Israel annexed East Jerusalem in 1967, thereby extending Israeli law over the eastern section of the city. Though Palestinian permanent residents in Jerusalem are afforded some rights, such as access to Israeli national health care and freedom of movement, among others, their permanent residency status makes them vulnerable to processes of exclusion and discrimination that separate them from Jewish Israeli citizens in Jerusalem, who have full citizenship rights.

The potential revocation of one's permanent residency status forces Palestinian Jerusalemites to abide by the "center of life policy," which states that Palestinians must maintain Jerusalem as the center of their life in order to retain their residency rights. What exactly "center of life" means remains ambiguous and has never been codified into law (Jefferis, 2012). However, at its most fundamental level, the center of life policy means that if a Palestinian East Jerusalemite does not live their everyday life in Jerusalem, their residency may be revoked. Essential to the apartheid debate is that this policy systematically and intentionally targets Palestinians while privileging Jews by preventing the former from living according to the same laws. While Palestinians are systematically excluded from the city, Israel's law of return of 1950 allows any Jew in the world to obtain Israeli citizenship, including its benefits and privileges, such as the right to live in Jerusalem and to access the resources available to citizens. Israel explicitly engages in an unequal application of rights for the purpose of establishing and maintaining its domination and demographic majority over Palestinians, which is precisely the definition of apartheid.

These are just a few examples of the ways in which Israel functions as an apartheid state; a more comprehensive look would examine other instances of acts committed with the intention of establishing and maintaining Israel's domination over Palestinians, such as the permit regime and the Separation Wall. In her recent book examining Israel's permit regime in the occupied West Bank, Yael Berda (2017) notes that there are 101 different permits that govern the lives and restrict the freedom of movement of Palestinians in Gaza, the West Bank, and East Jerusalem, while there are none for Jewish Israelis (pp. 82–83). Unlike Palestinians, Jews can freely move throughout Israel and almost every part of the West Bank, nor are they subject to the same searches and stops at military checkpoints.

The Separation Wall, which many Palestinians and activists refer to as the Apartheid Wall, is perhaps the most visual mechanism of apartheid rule in the Occupied Palestinian Territories. Though the justification for the wall is Israeli security, it separates Palestinians from each other and from their land as much as it separates Palestinians from Israel and Israeli settlements in the West Bank. The length of the wall is approximately 700 km, which is more than twice the length of the Green Line, a "border" existing on maps only. Due to the wall's meandering route, 85 per cent of it is in Palestinian territory (rather than following the Green Line), which *de facto* annexes that land to Israel (Matar, 2012).

Though the examples listed here are many, they do not mention some of Israel's other apartheid policies in the West Bank, such as separate road systems for Israelis and Palestinians, unequal access to land, water, and other resources, and the Israeli settlements that have rendered the viability of an independent Palestinian state far more uncertain (Farsakh, 2005), the result of which is catastrophic for Palestinians and Jewish Israelis alike, particularly as there is no end in sight to the existence of these policies.

The Failure of the Occupation-Not-Apartheid Argument

The claim made by Zeina M. Barakat and Mohammed S. Dajani Daoudi (this volume)—that the situation in Palestine is occupation, not apartheid—is legitimate, but also fails to acknowledge the institutionalized and legal mechanisms of separation and discrimination that target Palestinians and privilege

Jews. Though the two authors do not necessarily do so in their essay, this argument is often used to minimize the severity of the dire circumstances facing Palestinians in their everyday lives, and too often seems to absolve the occupying regime of responsibility. Though it is correct to say that the situation in the Palestinian Territories is a military occupation, which is legally and politically different from apartheid, Israel actually functions as an apartheid state due to the ways in which the military occupation imposes mechanisms of separation and discrimination.

This argument is furthered by UN Special Rapporteur John Dugard (2007) in his "Report of the Special Rapporteur on the situation of human rights in the Palestinian territories occupied since 1967," where he claims that Israel's occupation of the Palestinian territories contains elements of "colonialism, apartheid, and foreign occupation" (p. 22). In other words, it is not sufficient merely to claim that Israel's policies towards Palestinians are only a form of military or foreign occupation, since they also contain elements of colonialism (see Ghanem and Khateeb, this volume) and apartheid. Referring to the situation as merely occupation ignores the legal definitions of apartheid, the similarities to (and differences from) apartheid in South Africa, and the institutionalized separation and discrimination integral to Israel's continued domination over Palestinians.

Furthermore, the argument is based on the assumption that this military occupation is temporary. After more than half a century and no negotiated settlement on the horizon, there is no evidence to support such an assumption. Israel is not merely a settler-colonial society that has engaged in a military occupation since 1967; it also functions as an apartheid state in continuing its institutionalized regime of systematic oppression and domination that maintains its regime.

Conclusion

In 2012–13 I lived in Jerusalem conducting doctoral research on the impacts of the systematic exclusion of Palestinians from the city. At the end of nearly two years in the contested city, crossing the Green Line every day, I traveled to South Africa for two weeks, in part because I wanted to explore the history of apartheid more deeply. I was also motivated by the desire to make sense of the analogy between apartheid South Africa and the State of Israel, to see for myself if indeed the comparisons were fitting. The Apartheid Museum in Johannesburg, the preeminent museum dedicated to the history of apartheid in South Africa, was the first place I visited. As I went through the exhibitions, deliberately stopping to read every single description of photos and artifacts, I was struck by the incredible similarities between the experiences of blacks in apartheid South Africa and Palestinians in Jerusalem and the West Bank, the latter of which I had witnessed during the preceding years. I found the similarities between so many different elements of each regime incredible, from the "pass" system used in South Africa and the permit regime used in the West Bank to the dual road systems, separate legal procedures, and unequal access to water and other natural resources that differentiated blacks from whites in South Africa and Palestinians from Jews in the West Bank.

As I went through the museum, I could not avoid recalling a statement that Archbishop Desmond Tutu had made while speaking in a New York synagogue in 1989: "If you changed the names, the description of what is happening in the Gaza Strip and the West Bank would be a description of what is happening in South Africa" (quoted in Murray, 2008, p. 137). Though I was trying to learn about apartheid, I inevitably thought of my Palestinian friends who experience similar forms of institutionalized and systemic discrimination as encountered by blacks in apartheid South Africa. Like Tutu, I felt that if I just changed the names, faces, location, and time, what I saw in that museum could easily have been documenting the experiences of Palestinians today.

I say this not to argue that what happened in apartheid South Africa is exactly what is happening in Palestine/Israel today, but rather to demonstrate the ways in which the analogy is valid. It is clear to me that Israel functions as an apartheid state, albeit in ways far different from the apartheid system in South Africa. My experience at the Apartheid Museum, and later in Soweto, Robben Island, and other locations throughout South Africa, showed me that the claim levied against Israel as an apartheid state must be taken seriously. Such an argument stems from a legitimate connection between the ways in which apartheid South Africa and Israel discriminate against "the other" in their societies. These experiences further taught me that in order for students to fully understand the social and political complexities surrounding the events on campus during Israeli Apartheid Week and in the larger world, it is essential to critically engage with the term "apartheid." Once we are ready for such a conversation, perhaps it may be possible to formulate a counterhegemonic narrative about Israel's occupation of Palestine and understand Israeli Apartheid Week as a strategic political intervention committed to justice, equality, and human rights.

Oren Kroll-Zeldin is the assistant director of the Swig Program in Jewish Studies and Social Justice at the University of San Francisco, where he is also an assistant professor in the Department of Theology and Religious Studies.

Notes

1 There is a debate whether the apartheid laws ended in 1991, when the process of dismantling apartheid laws began; 1993, when the negotiations basically ended; or 1994, when the post-apartheid regime began (Dubow, 2014).

2 Israel is not a party to the Rome Statute, meaning that it never ratified the treaty. The Rome Statute is therefore not binding on Israel.

3 Though Israel also occupies East Jerusalem and the Gaza Strip, it applies its laws differently in those territories than it does in the West Bank. In the West Bank Palestinians are subject to Israeli military law, while in East Jerusalem, which Israel officially annexed in 1967, Palestinians are subject to Israeli civil law. Israel does not exert any legal jurisdiction over Palestinians in Gaza, though it remains an occupied territory due to Israel's military blockade of the entire area.

4 This figure only applies to the Jewish Israeli citizens living in the West Bank and does not include the Jewish Israelis living in East Jerusalem, of which there are currently 205,000. Jewish Israelis living in the Occupied Palestinian Territories, including East Jerusalem, are called settlers, meaning that they have settled in the disputed territories beyond the Green Line.

References

ACRI. (2014). *One Rule, Two Legal Systems: Israel's Regime of Laws in the West Bank.* Retrieved from https://www.acri.org.il/en/wp-content/uploads/2015/02/Two-Systems-of-Law-English-FINAL.pdf

Badran, A.D. (2010). *Zionist Israel and Apartheid South Africa: Civil Society and Peace Building in Ethnic-National States.* London, UK: Routledge.

Bakan, A.B., & Abu-Laban, Y. (2010). "Israel/Palestine, South Africa, and the 'One-state Solution': The Case for an Apartheid Analysis." *Politikon, 37*(2–3), 331–51. https://doi.org/10.1080/02589346.2010.522342

Berda, Y. (2017). *Living Emergency: Israel's Permit Regime in the Occupied West Bank.* Stanford, CA: Stanford University Press.

Bishara, M. (2001). *Palestine/Israel: Peace or Apartheid, Prospects for Resolving the Conflict.* London, UK: Zed Books.

Carter, J. (2006). *Palestine: Peace Not Apartheid.* New York, NY: Simon and Schuster.

Derfner, L. (2013, July 2). "Tzipi Livni Joins the 'Israel Apartheid' Club." *+972 Magazine.* Retrieved from https://972mag.com/tzipi-livni-joins-israel-apartheid-club/74951/

Dubow, S. (2014). *Apartheid: 1948–1994.* Oxford, UK: Oxford University Press.

Dugard, J. (2007). *Report of the Special Rapporteur on the Situation of Human Rights in the Palestinian Territories Occupied Since 1967.* Retrieved from https://digitallibrary.un.org/record/583071/files/A_HRC_2_5-EN.pdf

Dugard, J., & Reynolds, J. (2013). "Apartheid, International Law, and the Occupied Palestinian Territory." *European Journal of International Law, 24*(3), 867–913. https://doi.org/10.1093/ejil/cht045

Farsakh, L. (2005). "Independence, Cantons, or Bantustans: Whither the Palestinian State?" *Middle East Journal, 59*(2), 230–45. https://doi.org/10.3751/59.2.13

ICBS (2017). *Population of Israel on the Eve of 2018—8.8 Million.* Retrieved from www .cbs.gov.il/www/hodaot2017n/11_17_387e.docx

Israeli Apartheid Week (2017). "About." Retrieved October 5, 2017, from http:// apartheidweek.org/

Jefferis, D.C. (2012). "Institutionalizing Statelessness: The Revocation of Residency Rights of Palestinians in East Jerusalem." *International Journal of Refugee Law, 24*(2), 202–30. https://doi.org/10.1093/ijrl/ees026

Kroll-Zeldin, O. (2018). "Separate, Excluded, Unequal: Struggle and Resistance for Palestinian Permanent Residents in East Jerusalem." In C.M. Lyon & A.F. Goebel, (eds), *Citizenship and Place: Case Studies on the Borders of Citizenship* (pp. 143–68). London, UK: Rowman & Littlefield.

Lorde, A. (1983). "There Is No Hierarchy of Oppressions." *Bulletin: Homophobia and Education, 14*(3-4), 9.

Lorenzo, V. (2010). *Settler Colonialism: A Theoretical Overview.* New York, NY: Palgrave Macmillan.

Matar, H. (2012, April 9). "The Wall, 10 Years on: The Great Israeli Project." *+972 Magazine.* Retrieved from https://972mag.com/the-wall-10-years-on-the-great -israeli-project/40683/

McCarthy, R. (2007, November 30). "Israel Risks Apartheid-like Struggle If Two-State Solution Fails, Says Olmert." *The Guardian.* Retrieved from https://www.theguardian .com/world/2007/nov/30/israel

McCarthy, R. (2010, February 10). "Barak: Make Peace with Palestinians or Face Apartheid." *The Guardian.* Retrieved from https://www.theguardian.com/world/2010/feb/03/ barak-apartheid-palestine-peace

Murray, N. (2008). "Dynamics of Resistance: The Apartheid Analogy." *MIT Electronic Journal of Middle East Studies, 8,* 132–48. https://dome.mit.edu/bitstream/handle/ 1721.3/177980/MITEJMES_Vol_8_Spring2008.pdf?sequence=1

OCHA OPT (United Nations Office for the Coordination of Humanitarian Affairs in the Occupied Palestinian Territories). (2017). *Occupied Palestinian Territory: Humanitarian Facts and Figures.* Retrieved from https://www.ochaopt.org/sites/default/ files/factsheet_booklet_final_21_12_2017.pdf

Pappe, I. (ed.). (2015). *Israel and South Africa: The Many Faces of Apartheid.* London, UK: Zed Books.

Peteet, J. (2016). "The Work of Comparison: Israel/Palestine and Apartheid." *Anthropological Quarterly, 89*(1), 247–82. https://doi.org/10.1353/anq.2016.0015

Polakow-Suransky, S. (2010. *The Unspoken Alliance: Israel's Secret Relationship with Apartheid South Africa.* New York: Pantheon Books.

Rogin, J. (2014, April 27). "Exclusive: Kerry Warns Israel Could Become 'an Apartheid State.'" *The Daily Beast.* Retrieved from https://www.thedailybeast.com/exclusive -kerry-warns-israel-could-become-an-apartheid-state

Soske, J., & Jacobs, S. (eds). (2015). *Apartheid Israel: The Politics of an Analogy.* Chicago, IL: Haymarket Books.

Tilley, V. (ed.). (2012). *Beyond Occupation: Apartheid, Colonialism, and International Law in the Occupied Palestinian Territories.* London, UK: Pluto Press.

United Nations. (1965). *International Convention on the Elimination of All Forms of Racial Discrimination.* Retrieved from http://www.ohchr.org/EN/ProfessionalInterest/ Pages/CERD.aspx

United Nations. (1973). *International Convention on the Suppression and Punishment of the Crime of Apartheid.* Retrieved from https://treaties.un.org/doc/publication/unts/volume%201015/volume-1015-i-14861-english.pdf

United Nations. (2002). *Rome Statute of the International Criminal Court.* Retrieved from https://www.icc-cpi.int/nr/rdonlyres/ea9aeff7-5752-4f84-be94-0a655eb30e16/0/rome_statute_english.pdf

Weinryb, A. (2008). "At Issue: The University of Toronto—The Institution Where Israel Apartheid Week Was Born." *Jewish Political Studies Review, 20*(3-4), 107–17. https://www.jstor.org/stable/25834802

Yiftachel, O. (1999). "'Ethnocracy': The Politics of Judaizing Israel/Palestine." *Constellations, 6*(3), 364–90. https://doi.org/10.1111/1467-8675.00151

Ziadah, R., & Hanieh, A. (2010). "Collective Approaches to Activist Knowledge: Experiences of the New Anti-apartheid Movement in Toronto." In D. Kapoor & A. Choudry (eds), *Learning from the Ground up: Global Perspectives on Social Movements and Knowledge Production* (pp. 85–100). New York, NY: Palgrave Macmillan.

Israel and Palestine: Occupation Not Apartheid

ZEINA M. BARAKAT AND MOHAMMED S. DAJANI DAOUDI

This essay sheds light on the sensitive political issue of comparing Israel to apartheid South Africa due to its impact on reconciliation, conflict resolution, and peace. In dealing with this topic, we will address the following questions: What constitutes an apartheid state? Is Israel an apartheid state in its policy and its legal and structural relationship between its Jewish citizens and Palestinian residents of the West Bank and East Jerusalem? Is Israel the heir of South Africa, as claimed by those calling for its boycott through the Boycott, Divestment, and Sanctions (BDS) movement?[1] What are the implications of this label for the Palestinian struggle to end Israeli occupation of Palestinian territories and reach a peaceful, just settlement? What lessons ought Palestinians to learn from the South African experience, taking into consideration that the Palestine/Israel and South African contexts are different? What would apply within the Israel/Palestine context?

We evaluate the claim, made by some of Israel's critics and by Oren Kroll-Zeldin (this volume) that Israel is an apartheid state. Here, like Kroll-Zeldin, we wish to make clear that we are not focusing on all of Israel (including the policy and legal and structural relationships between Jewish and non-Jewish citizens in Israel proper), but only on the West Bank and East Jerusalem. We argue that neither in the West Bank nor in East Jerusalem does the apartheid label fit. While there are problematic policies and institutional discrimination in Israeli occupation policies, the situation does not warrant application of the apartheid label. In the West Bank and East Jerusalem as well as in the Gaza Strip before unilateral Israeli withdrawal in 2005, the more fitting term is "occupation."

"Occupation" here refers to one state seizing through military acquisition and holding territories not internationally recognized as belonging to it. As a result of Israel's military conquest of the Gaza Strip, the West Bank, and East Jerusalem in the June 1967 war, Israel has illegally occupied these Palestinian territories for more than 50 years. Israel's blockades of Gaza, ongoing since 2005, and its continued military presence in the West Bank are illegal acts by international law and UN Security Council Resolution 242 (passed after the 1967 war), requiring Israel to withdraw from territories it occupied during that war. In other words, Israel is required to vacate these Palestinian territories because they are militarily occupied—illegally—not because they are instances of apartheid.

Defining "Apartheid"

In 2006, former United States president Jimmy Carter used the term "apartheid" in the subtitle of his book *Palestine: Peace Not Apartheid* to describe the Israeli occupation of Palestinian territories, generating a great deal of controversy and criticism of its author for the use of that term. In a CNN interview, Carter defended his word choice by saying that "forced segregation in the West Bank and terrible oppression of the Palestinians create a situation accurately described by the word. I made it plain in the text that this abuse is not based on racism, but on the desire of a minority of Israelis to confiscate and colonize Palestinian land" (CNN, 2007).

Ten years later, in March 2017, a United Nations report titled "Israeli Practices towards the Palestinian People and the Question of Apartheid" labeled Israel an "apartheid state" because of its treatment of Palestinians. The report, which covered both Israel proper and the Occupied Palestinian Territories, stated it had concluded, on the "basis of scholarly inquiry and overwhelming evidence, that Israel is guilty of the crime of apartheid." Rather than addressing specific components of the report, Israel condemned the report altogether, with Israeli UN ambassador Danny Danon commenting, "The attempt to smear and falsely label the only true democracy in the Middle East by creating a false analogy is despicable and constitutes a blatant lie" (*Times of Israel*, 2017).

The authors of the 2017 report, Richard Falk and Virginia Tilley, base their definition of apartheid primarily on Article 2 of the 1973 International Convention on the Suppression and Punishment of the Crime of Apartheid, which states:

> The term "the crime of apartheid," which shall include similar policies and practices of racial segregation and discrimination as practiced in southern Africa, shall apply to the following inhumane acts committed for the purpose of establishing and maintaining domination by one racial group of persons over any other racial group of persons and systematically oppressing them.

Significantly, Falk and Tilley in their report underscore that the "crime of apartheid" consists of discrete inhuman acts that acquire the status of crimes against humanity only if they intentionally serve the core purpose of racial domination. Yet both examples cited in the report—the Israeli law that allows "spouses of Israeli citizens to relocate to Israel but [prohibit] this option in the case of Palestinians from the occupied territory or beyond," and the Israeli policy of rejecting "the return of any Palestinian refugees and exiles to territory under Israeli control"—are motivated by Israeli security concerns and reflect occupation control politics rather than apartheid policies. While they may seem in effect like apartheid policies, their purpose is to foster colonialization, expansion, and illegal settlement on territories of another people in the West Bank and East Jerusalem.

A more thorough critique of this report or other arguments that the term "apartheid" applies to the situation in Israel/Palestine necessitates an analysis of the meaning of the concept itself. Generally speaking, "apartheid" means a system of institutionalized, legalized racial segregation and ethnic discrimination. It refers to a unified political system in which one group uses the judicial system to segregate another people of different ethnic origin or race by law, tradition, and custom. In South Africa, it involved the segregation of public facilities and social events, as well as housing, schools, sports, and employment opportunities by race. South African apartheid was constructed along a white/nonwhite binary, instigated by feelings of racial superiority. Under that system, 53 million nonwhite South Africans, who comprised more than 80 per cent of the total population, were unable to own land, move freely, and vote in public affairs.

In her book *Zionist Israel and Apartheid South Africa*, Amneh Badran (2010) compares the two ethnic-national "apartheid" states in South Africa and Israel, highlighting the economic relationship between the dominant and dominated side, as well as the legitimacy of the ideology in power (i.e., apartheid in South Africa and Zionism in Israel). She points out that while the South African peace agenda in the post-apartheid era adopted a vision of a united nonracial democratic South Africa, the Israeli-Palestinian peace agenda supports an exclusively Jewish state with a neighboring Palestinian state, a so-called two-state solution. In theory, if this separation occurred Israel could not be labelled an apartheid state as regards the West Bank.

The comparison with South Africa is helpful in thinking about whether the term "apartheid" can be applied to the situation in Israel/Palestine. For instance, when addressing the human rights of Palestinians living under Israeli occupation who are subject to Israeli policies that systematically discriminate against them while privileging Jews, we need to clearly distinguish between two types of Palestinians subject to Israeli policies.

The first category encompasses those Palestinians subject to Israeli rule since 1948, when the *Nakba* of Palestine[2] took place and the State of Israel was established, who became minority citizens of the State of Israel; this category also includes their descendants. These Palestinian citizens of Israel can own land and vote in Israeli elections. There aren't any specific laws in the State of Israel that prohibit Palestinians from purchasing land. However, in some Jewish neighborhoods in Israel proper, Israelis do practice housing discrimination, preventing Palestinian Arabs from living in Jewish communities, renting, or buying homes.

The second category is those Palestinians subjected to Israeli rule since 1967, when the Israeli army occupied the West Bank, the Gaza Strip, and East Jerusalem, most of whom have retained their Palestinian identity and never held Israeli citizenship.

It is this second category of Palestinians that we consider in this essay. We will consider whether Israeli laws discriminate against Palestinians as an ethnic minority group of the State of Israel, or as an occupied people to promote Israeli control over certain territories and to gain further territory. We argue that the term "occupation" is more fitting in this context, as Israel is not oppressing the Palestinians in the West Bank and East Jerusalem as minority citizens of the state, but as an occupying force of territories acknowledged by the United Nations and international law as occupied.

The 2002 Rome Statute of the International Criminal Court specifies in its definition of "apartheid" the presence of an "institutionalized regime" serving the "intention" of racial domination. Thus, for the description to fit, the following elements need to apply:

1. Discrimination is institutionalized.
2. The reason for discrimination is racial.
3. There is segregation of public facilities and social events.
4. Separation is enforced by the legal system.
5. Any violation of the status quo is punished by law.

Based on this definition, if discrimination by the state against an ethnic or religious group within society is not institutionalized, is not racial, and is not enforced by legal measures prohibiting the use of public facilities and participating in social events, then such a system is not labeled as apartheid.

The Apartheid Analogy

In the Palestinian-Israeli context, the conflict is between two different ethnic and religious groups over land and is characterized as a national liberation struggle for an independent nation-state outside the borders of Israel proper, recognized as a member of the United Nations. Those accusing Israel of running an apartheid regime in the Palestinian territories of the West Bank confuse occupation policies with apartheid. For instance, the Israeli military dismantled a Dutch-funded agricultural project on the West Bank, including tools and sheds. This project, in which the Netherlands invested ten million Euros, involved teaching Palestinians how to use the land to grow their crops. This action was motivated by occupation-based repressive policies and not "apartheid." A second example is the cement wall Israel built to separate Israelis from Palestinians. The BDS movement describes it as an "apartheid wall," though a more fitting description is a "separation wall," since it was constructed in 2002 in the wake of suicide-bombing attacks targeting the Israeli civilian population; the wall was intended to separate Palestinians from Israelis for political and security reasons. It is more of a "border barrier" than an "apartheid wall" built to enforce ethnic and racial segregation. Palestinians condemned the wall because it cuts deep into Palestinian territory, has resulted in the confiscation of large areas of fertile Palestinian land, and has cut off thousands of Palestinians from their families, social services, schools, and farmland, not because it was an apartheid wall.

In March 2017, the Israeli Knesset passed a law barring the entry of any person who calls for a boycott of Israel or is actively engaged in the BDS movement. (This act became the model of several anti-boycott laws passed in some US states and European countries.) More specifically, the Israeli law bars entry into Israel of foreign nationals who have both knowingly and publicly called for a boycott of Israel or who represent an organization that calls for such a boycott. Though this law violates the fundamental human rights of freedom of speech and freedom of expression and undermines the Israeli democratic system, it can hardly be viewed as part of apartheid policy.

The 1993 Oslo Accords

The 1993 Oslo Accords transferred portions of Gaza and the West Bank to Palestinian control. These accords divided the West Bank into three main administrative areas: Area A, exclusively administered by the Palestinian Authority (but not with full sovereignty, since the Israeli military can enter at will); Area B, administered by both the Palestinian Authority and Israel; and Area C, administered by Israel and containing the Israeli settlements. Any Palestinians in Area C are living under full Israeli military and civil control. The Israeli settlers enjoy full protection from the Israeli military, giving them a free hand in developing and expanding their settlements—most of which are built on publicly and privately owned Palestinian land. In contrast, the Palestinian residents in Area C do not enjoy similar privileges and rights (Berger, 2017). The motivation behind this policy is political cleansing, not ethnic cleansing, though the line separating the two is quite thin. It is the norm and custom of an occupation-state that an occupier does not invest heavily in the territories it occupies because the occupying force perceives their presence to be provisional. Israeli policies towards the Palestinians in the West Bank are not oppressive and discriminatory due to their ethnic background or the color of their skin, but rather because these policies aim to ensure Israeli security and the legalization of occupied annexed territories.

In Area C, Israel retains near exclusive control, including over law enforcement, planning, and construction, allowing for illegal settlements to grow and spread. In Area A, Israeli laws do not apply to Palestinians in the West Bank occupied territories where Palestinian laws are enforced and where Palestinian citizens resort to Palestinian courts and laws to uphold and protect their legal rights. As for East Jerusalemite Palestinians, they must resort to Israeli courts and laws to protect their lawful rights. For example, the Dajani family was able to regain its property rights over the tomb of its ancestor, Sheikh Ahmed Dajani (1459–561), located in Mamilla Cemetery in Jerusalem, through the Israeli judicial system. A court order forced the Israeli occupiers to evict the premises of the tomb, and the Israeli police restored the property to its rightful owners.

Though this may seem like an isolated incident, it could imply the absence of apartheid laws. In September 2009, a Palestinian Arab family from Jaffa (Israel proper), the Siksiks, reopened a Jaffa mosque that the family had built in 1838. The mosque had been taken over by Israeli authorities in 1948, the same year the State of Israel was founded. Jaffa residents decided to open this mosque, and the Siksik family agreed to take care of the renovations. In a separate case, in February 2017, the Israeli Supreme Court rejected an appeal presented by Regavim, a pro-settler nongovernmental organization, that demanded a mosque in southern Hebron be demolished after claiming it was illegally built. In 2000, the Supreme Court of Israel ruled that the town of Katzir could not deny the right of the Arab Ka'adan family to live in the town simply on the basis that they were not Jewish. This was the first time that Palestinian citizens of Israel successfully challenged the legality of "Jewish-only" communities in the state, generating cautious optimism that it could set an important precedent for Palestinian rights in land and housing. However, in September 2014, these hopes were dashed when the Supreme Court permitted Jewish committees to refuse residency based on any "undesired" identity, including being Palestinian, Sephardic, African, gay, religious, or secular, among others (Iraqi, 2014). The incentive behind such laws was to subdue the perceived threat Palestinian citizens posed to the Jewish character of the state. Such antisocial behavior is not necessarily reflective of widespread prejudice found among all Jewish Israelis, but *de facto* points to inequity, arising from behavior rooted in conflict. Similar prohibitions are practiced by Palestinians living in the West Bank and East Jerusalem, who consider permitting Jewish Israelis to buy Palestinian homes or land to be akin to high treason, a crime punishable by random killing.

The Apartheid Label Is Not Helpful

Some argue that calling Israel an apartheid state increases the urgency of outside actions, possibly pushing Israel to end the occupation, as was the case in South Africa. In the case of Palestine, however, intensified external pressure would damage the cooperative relationship with those Israelis seeking peace with the Palestinians and an end of the occupation. Accusing Israel of being an apartheid state does not serve the more substantial Palestinian cause since it diverts attention from Israel's occupation, whose time, at more than a half-century, must come to an end. Palestinians need to be granted their right to self-determination. The occupation feeds the fear of mortal danger and the siege mentality that keeps the Israeli right-wing minority parties in power.

The principal method by which Israel imposes an occupation regime and not an apartheid regime is the strategic fragmentation of the Palestinian people. Those who claim that Israel is an apartheid system in its West Bank policies are committing an act of profound ignorance of the nature of the beast. The Israeli–Palestinian conflict is not about racial segregation, but military occupation. Israel's Jewish national-identity-based activism reflects Zionist aspirations to create a homeland for the Jews on Palestinian territories, and not apartheid inclinations of racial superiority over another group. On the other side of the coin, the ongoing Palestinian struggle is for freedom, self-determination, dignity, identity, and justice, and not an end to ethnic and racial discrimination and desegregation against them. Palestinians living in East Jerusalem, the West Bank, and Gaza Strip demand not the cessation of racial separation, but an end to the military occupation of their territories, with recognition of their human rights to freedom, independence, and statehood. Israeli sovereignty and security can coexist permanently and peacefully with Palestinian identity, statehood, and nationhood.

The Oslo Accords assert that Palestinian identity can be reconciled with the existence of a Jewish national sovereign independent state. The fact that Jews believe in a Jewish homeland in Palestine should not be viewed as being apartheid unless Israel seeks to become so and Jews declare it to be so, as was the case in South Africa. At their core, both Zionism and Palestinian nationalism are liberation movements that need not be incompatible with one another. The false claim that these movements cannot coexist is part of a traditional pan-Arab paradigm that views Israel as an imperialist dagger in the heart of the Arab nation. This old traditional perception must be replaced with a recognition of the State of Israel as part of the Middle East. To play up the apartheid analogy to downplay the occupation's harsh reality, and thus ignore the plight of Palestinians as victims of a repressive occupation, is misleading. The fact that the occupation is immoral, that it elicits violent resistance, and that it breeds home-grown terrorists, is overshadowed and marginalized by adopting the apartheid analogy.

The Nation-State Law

As the right-wing Israeli government continues to make laws that are construed to be racist and discriminatory, the descriptor "apartheid state" will become more applicable to Israel proper. In labeling Israel an "apartheid state," its critics confuse the State of Israel and the State of Palestine, dealing with both entities as if they represent one unified body, as was the case in South Africa. The distinction became more evident with the adoption of the nation-state law on 19 July 2018, which officially declared the State of Israel the national home of the Jewish people. The law restricts the right to self-determination in the State of Israel to the Jewish people, although "every resident of Israel, without distinction of religion or national origin, is entitled to work to preserve his culture, heritage, language and identity" and "the state may allow a community, including members of the same religion or national origin, to have separate communal settlements." The law also downgraded Arabic from an official language to one having "special status" only.

The Expanding Borders of Israel

While "apartheid" is not an accurate description of the situation of Palestinians living in the West Bank, a major problem with many Israeli laws is that they are written without specifying the borders of Israel (and there is no Israeli constitution specifying those borders). Consequently, Israeli laws are viewed as including all lands of Mandatory Palestine—from the Jordan River to the Mediterranean Sea. However, Israel did in fact acknowledge in its UN commitments, the 1993 Oslo Accords, and peace treaties with Egypt and Jordan (not to mention international law) that part of this land belongs to the Palestinians and is agreed to house the State of Palestine. The Palestinians view the West Bank and East Jerusalem, areas captured by Israel in 1967, as parts of their future independent state. In December 2016, the UN Security Council passed a resolution that declared all settlements in both areas to be illegal. Furthermore, as a political entity, the State of Palestine already exists in the West Bank and the Gaza Strip *de facto* though not *de jure*, even though more than 100 UN member nations acknowledge it. Israeli laws do not acknowledge Palestinian rights to self-determination and statehood in the West Bank, Gaza, and East Jerusalem.

De Facto Discrimination

The Israeli government often treats Palestinians who do not hold Israeli citizenship differently from Israeli citizens. For lack of education of what apartheid means, such practices are perceived as symptoms of an apartheid system. As a result of the occupation, Palestinians from Gaza and the West Bank who are not Israeli citizens are tried in military courts for political and criminal offenses while Israeli citizens are tried in civilian courts. Sentences for similar offenses are harsher for Palestinians than for Jewish Israelis, even though Palestinian lives, liberties, and personal security are *de jure* protected, allegedly equally with that of Jewish Israelis. Palestinian political prisoners face torture and degrading treatment, whereas Jewish Israeli prisoners are handled better. Palestinians suffer from arbitrary administrative arrest and incarceration without trial while Jewish Israelis do not. Additionally, Palestinians do not exercise the human right to freedom of movement in and out of Palestine, whereas Jewish Israeli settlers are permitted this freedom and are provided with army protection to build and expand illegal settlements in the West Bank and East Jerusalem, on illegally confiscated Palestinian land, no less. While Jews worldwide enjoy the privilege of the law of return, Palestinians living in the diaspora cannot exercise the same right even to the Palestinian territories or the state of Palestine.

The Israeli military at times enforces a "shoot to kill" policy when targeting Palestinian demonstrators or terrorist suspects; no similar policy is applied to Jewish Israelis. When the Israeli military confiscates Palestinian land, Palestinians are allowed to file lawsuits against the state to regain their lands or compensation, but such suits are often dismissed on the grounds of security, often without any compensation.

While Jewish Israelis enjoy freedom of expression on social networks, Palestinians are held criminally accountable when they attack or criticize Israel or when their posts are deemed to support violence, incite terrorism, call for a boycott of Israel, or deny the existence of Israel. Offenders from East Jerusalem are jailed, even though Jewish Israelis are not held accountable for similar offenses.

While rarely would a Jewish Israeli resident of Jerusalem have his or her residency status annulled, revocation of East Jerusalem residency status is a persistent nightmare for Palestinians. As of 1998, Israel bars family unification, prohibiting West Bank and Gaza Palestinian spouses of Israeli citizens from acquiring citizenship. The Israeli police and military forces violently disperse peaceful Palestinian protests in East Jerusalem while peaceful Jewish Israeli protestors are permitted, though at times they do clash with the Israeli police.

While deeply problematic, these Israeli practices against Palestinian citizens of the West Bank and East Jerusalem are not motivated by a superiority ethos but rather by mistrust, fear of the other, and feelings of insecurity. These examples may justifiably lead Palestinians to believe that what the Jewish state has in mind for Palestinians living in the West Bank and East Jerusalem is ethnic cleansing by continuing to deny their existence and their national identity. These perceptions fuel advocates of the apartheid model, as well as the antinormalization movement, making the challenge for peacemakers more formidable. However, should the occupation be terminated, most probably such practices would lose their rationale. This should strengthen the resolve to continue on the path of moderation and reconciliation in the midst of conflict to pave the path for conflict resolution, peace, democracy, security, and prosperity.

Lessons from the South African Experience

When looking at the South African experience, Palestinians and Israelis need to focus on the bright post-apartheid period rather than the dark apartheid regime era. After his release from prison, Nelson Mandela (1918–2013) called upon his people to throw away their weapons and abandon their strategy of violence. The approach not only won him the presidency, but also earned him deep respect at home and worldwide. As the first president of a democratic South Africa, he convincingly argued that violence breeds violence, that bloodshed should cease and reconciliation pave the way to coexistence and peace. Mandela advised that none of the parties should be regarded as right or wrong. This is the lesson Palestinians and Israelis should learn from the South African experience, if the conflict is to end and healing to take place. The voices of moderation among Palestinians need to become more and more vocal.

Acting with collective moral responsibility is crucial. What is at stake is the existential identity of nations threatened by the rising tide of extremism and terrorism. Nelson Mandela's visionary leadership is desperately needed in these times, and his inspirational words always invite reflection. The South African leader set a high standard; he served his nation for the greater good. He created a strong sense of national identity that united South Africa across racial and ethnic lines. National unity and reconciliation were at the heart of his rainbow vision for a new South Africa, and began in his own heart: he appointed former enemies as his aides and even his bodyguards.

Think of the peaceful transformation in South Africa, of the great march for peace in Cape Town in 1989, and of the fall of the Berlin Wall in November 1989, when people suppressed under the communist dictatorship walked out, assembled in churches, and marched with candles in their hands and not weapons, bringing the Berlin Wall down. It was the wax of the candles that dripped on the ground, not blood.

Imagine if the Palestinian people were to take constructive moves towards a better future, to learn from such examples the right way to go about nation-building. Moderation does not mean surrender; instead, it reflects a strong belief in the cause. This is the lesson to be learned from South Africa, to motivate Palestinian youth to carve a path towards a better future.

Conclusion

The thrust of this essay is that the elephant in the room is not apartheid but the occupation of Palestinian Territories of the West Bank and East Jerusalem, as well as the ongoing blockade of the Gaza Strip. To every Palestinian, Israeli occupation policies are the crux of the present conflict. There are two lessons to learn from the South African experience. The first is that it is wrong-headed to compare today's Israel to the apartheid regime in South Africa (though we do not exclude the possibility of Israel becoming an apartheid state, given the ongoing policies of its right-wing government, which run counter to the values Israel embraced at its founding). The second lesson lies in adopting the inspiring vision of Nelson Mandela, with his focus on reconciliation and coexistence.

Palestinian citizens are denied the full human and legal rights enjoyed by citizens of Israel not because of apartheid, as was the case in South Africa, but as a result of the occupation. The suffering, dispossession, and dispersion of the Palestinian people from their homeland should arouse genuine concern for peace with justice for both conflicting parties. No doubt, dialogue, diplomacy, and peace negotiations are the only legitimate channels that can produce an agreement based on justice and security for all parties, one that would accommodate the national aspirations of both peoples, thereby embodying the historical, religious, and psychological connections of both Israelis and Palestinians to this ancient Holy Land.

Zeina M. Barakat is a Jerusalem-born Palestinian who holds a doctorate in reconciliation studies from Friedrich-Schiller University in Jena, Germany, where she is currently a postdoctoral fellow and where, since 2013, she has been project coordinator of "From Heart of Stone to Heart of Flesh." She studied at al-Quds University in Jerusalem and has taught at Friedrich Schiller University in Jena and Europa-Universität Flensburg. She is the author of many books and articles, including *Sexual Harassment* (Al Quds University Press, 2012), one of the few books in Arabic dealing with this taboo topic in Arab society. Her latest book is *From Heart of Stone to Heart of Flesh: Evolutionary Journey from Extremism to Moderation* (Uty Verlag, 2017).

Her research interests include gender, narratives, reconciliation, empathy, and collective memory.

Mohammed S. Dajani Daoudi is a Palestinian scholar born in Jerusalem, where he currently lives. He was the founding director of the American Studies Graduate Program, and general director of libraries at al-Quds University in Jerusalem. In 2007, he established the Wasatia moderate Islamic movement, which aims at promoting moderation, coexistence, and interfaith dialogue as a pathway to reconciliation. He has gained international recognition for his work to spread moderation culture and to raise awareness concerning the Holocaust. In March 2014, he found himself at the center of a heated controversy when he took 27 Palestinian students to the Nazi concentration camp in Auschwitz. A Palestinian public outcry led to his resignation from his posts at the university. He is currently the founding director of the Wasatia Academic Institute, which aims at establishing an interdisciplinary doctoral program for Palestinian students on the topics of reconciliation, moderation, empathy, and ethics.

Notes

1 BDS was created as an organization in 2005 by a coalition of Palestinian civil society organizations to force Israel to recognize Palestinian rights and end its occupation of Palestinian territories.
2 *Nakba* is an Arabic term that Palestinians use to refer to their 1948 loss of land and property and forced expulsion from what used to be Palestine.

References

Badran, A.D. (2010). *Zionist Israel and Apartheid South Africa: Civil Society and Peace Building in Ethnic-National States.* Abingdon, UK: Routledge.
Berger, Y. (2017, August 23). "Revealed: Nearly 3,500 Settlement Homes Built on Private Palestinian Land." *Haaretz.* Retrieved from https://www.haaretz.com/israel-news/premium-revealed-3-500-settlement-homes-built-on-private-palestinian-land-1.5445036
Carter, J. (2006). *Palestine: Peace Not Apartheid.* New York, NY: Simon & Schuster.
CNN. (2007, January 21). [Interviews with Jimmy Carter and Walter Mondale]. *CNN Late Edition with Wolf Blitzer.*
Iraqi, A. (2014, September 18). "Contradicting Its Own Ruling, Israel's Supreme Court Legalizes Segregated Communities." *+972 Magazine.* Retrieved from https://972mag.com/contradicting-itsown-ruling-israels-supreme-court-legalizes-segregated-communities/96817/
Soske, J., & Jacobs, S. (2015). *Apartheid Israel: The Politics of an Analogy.* Chicago, IL: Haymarket Books.

Tilley,V. (ed.). (2012). *Beyond Occupation:Apartheid, Colonialism, and International Law in the Occupied Palestinian Territories*. London, UK: Pluto Press.

United Nations, ESCWA (Economic and Social Commission for Western Asia). (2017). "Israeli Practices towards the Palestinian People and the Question of Apartheid." *Palestine and the Israeli Occupation*, no. 1.

Times of Israel. (2017, March 15). "Israel Fumes as UN Board Slams Its 'Apartheid, Racial Domination' over Palestinians." *Times of Israel*. Retrieved from https://www.timesofisrael.com/israel-fumes-as-un-board-censures-apartheid-and-racial-domination/

seven

Intersectional Alliances

Similar to other international conflicts, there are multiple parties involved in the Israeli-Palestinian conflict. It has connections—positive and negative, in the form of enemies and allies—with local and global players around the world. Solidarity manifests between groups within Israel/Palestine, while simultaneously the conflict has been exported to and relived in different countries worldwide, such as the United States (Hahn Tapper, 2011). There are a range of systems, on both macro and micro levels, that help explain this interconnectedness.

Globalization aside, which surely plays a central role in this phenomenon, one of these structures is firmly ideological, rooted in the idea of intersectionality. As we know, intersecting things cross or pass through one another. Intersectionality, which builds upon this idea, is "the interconnected nature of social categorizations such as race, class, and gender as they apply to a given individual or group, regarded as creating overlapping and interdependent systems of discrimination or disadvantage" ("Intersectionality," n.d.).[1]

There are numerous communities involved in the Israeli-Palestinian conflict, some dominant, others subordinated, and many who have identified as being marginalized. The search for social justice in Israel/Palestine points to a need to look at the relationships between some of these groups. Indeed, since well before the State of Israel was established and the *Nakba* occurred, many of these groups—regardless of their power—developed relationships with one another, some positive and others not. This chapter includes three essays, each focusing on a different example of how intersectional solidarity manifests in the Israeli-Palestinian conflict.

The first two essays look at the intersectional alliances of groups connected to Israel/Palestine who consider themselves to be on the margins; in one case the relationship is transnational, and in the other it is local. Joey Ayoub's "Black-Palestinian Solidarity: Towards an Intersectionality of Struggles" examines relatively new alliances being made between Palestinians and African American activists in an arrangement that he refers to as an "intersectionality of struggles." Using a "transnational solidarity framework," Ayoub uncovers some of the conditions that have allowed such solidarity to take place by tracing "the historical context of both struggles" and exposing their shared components. He ends his piece by hypothesizing that a "black-Palestinian bond may prove to open up spaces for joint struggles against oppression in both the United States and Israel/Palestine while allowing Ashkenazi Jews (Jews who trace their lineage back to Europe and Russia) and Mizrahi Jews (Jews of pre-1948 Middle Eastern descent) in the United States and Israel-Palestine, respectively, to build new links independently from the policies of the State of Israel (or as an explicit rejection of them)."

The second essay, Aziza Khazzoom's "Cultural Commonalities, Colonial Divisions: On Sources of Solidarity between Palestinians and Jews from the Middle East," explores the local relationship between Palestinians and Mizrahim. Whereas Ayoub underscores a current emerging transnational alliance that is perhaps less surprising, Khazzoom addresses a potential partnership that is arguably more radical. She suggests that Mizrahi Jewish Israelis could align with Palestinians in a common cause that challenges Ashkenazi Jewish Israeli dominance. Because roughly half of Israel's Jewish population identifies as being of Middle Eastern and North African descent, such a possibility, she argues, could be a powerful force for change. Drawing from her own Iraqi Jewish ancestry, Khazzoom looks at the complicated relationship Mizrahi Jews have had with Arabs generally and Palestinian Arabs specifically, as well as how both groups—relative to Ashkenazi Jewish Israelis—share a commonality of exclusion. She ends her essay by suggesting ways such commonalities can play a positive role in bringing greater justice to Israel/Palestine.

The third and final essay places these discussions in an interstate context by examining the United States–Israel bilateral relationship. Yousef Munayyer's "Alternate Bipolarity: How Israel Found Itself on the Wrong Side of the Global Divide," traces the "processes that contributed to how Israel, once considered part of the liberal democratic global order, found itself increasingly associated with authoritarianism and ethnocracy." More specifically, Munayyer explains the waxing and waning of Israel's relationship with the United States by presenting it through four historical periods, moving from tensions (pre-1967 period) to strong allyship (post-1967 period) to weak allyship (post–Cold War "clash of civilizations" period) to a seemingly strong but actually vulnerable relationship in which Israel's "privileging [of] its Jewishness over democratic principles" may lead social justice–minded Americans to eventually turn away from Israel.

In an effort to uncover some of the central strands of intersectional alliances at play in the Israeli-Palestinian conflict, this chapter highlights a small selection of associations and coalitions—real and theoretical, past and present—playing important roles in this Middle Eastern struggle.

Note

1 There are intense scholarly debates regarding the best definition of the term "intersectionality." For more on this critical term see, for example, Collins (1990), Crenshaw (1989a, 1989b), and Hancock (2016).

References

Collins, P.H. (1990). *Black Feminist Thought: Knowledge, Consciousness, and the Politics of Empowerment*. New York, NY: Routledge.

Crenshaw, K.W. (1989a). "Demarginalizing the Intersection of Race and Sex: A Black Feminist Critique of Antidiscrimination Doctrine, Feminist Theory, and Antiracist Politics." *University of Chicago Legal Forum, 140,* 139–67. http://chicagounbound.uchicago.edu/uclf/vol1989/iss1/8

Crenshaw, K.W. (1989b). "Mapping the Margins: Intersectionality, Identity Politics, and Violence against Women of Color." *Stanford Law Review, 43*(6), 1241–99. http://www.jstor.org/stable/1229039

Hahn Tapper, A.J. (2011). "The War of Words: Jews, Muslims, and the Israeli–Palestinian Conflict on American University Campuses." In R. Aslan & A.J. Hahn Tapper (eds), *Muslims and Jews in America: Commonalities, Contentions, and Complexities* (pp. 71–92). New York, NY: Palgrave Macmillan.

Hancock, A.-M. (2016). *Intersectionality: An Intellectual History*. New York, NY: Oxford University Press.

"Intersectionality." (n.d.). In *Oxford Living Dictionaries*. Retrieved January 3, 2019, from https://en.oxforddictionaries.com/definition/intersectionality

Black-Palestinian Solidarity: Towards an Intersectionality of Struggles

JOEY AYOUB

In October 2015, more than 60 African American and Palestinian intellectuals and activists launched a statement of "black–Palestinian solidarity," declaring in a video that "when I see them, I see us" (Black-Palestinian Solidarity, 2015). This new solidarity movement between blacks in the United States and Palestinians in Israel/Palestine was born in the context of the July–August 2014 Israeli military assault on Gaza and the murders of Eric Garner in New York City on 17 July 2014 and Michael Brown in Ferguson, Missouri, on 9 August 2014, two of the killings largely credited for launching the Black Lives Matter movement.[1]

The simultaneity of these events sparked a number of public statements of solidarity from both Palestinians and African Americans towards each another. For example, on 14 August 2014 Palestinians from the West Bank tweeted advice about dealing with tear gas to protesters in Ferguson under the hashtag #Palestine2Ferguson (Molloy, 2014); over 1,100 black activists, artists, scholars, students, and organizations signed the "2015 Black Solidarity Statement with Palestine" declaring their "reaffirmed solidarity with the Palestinian struggle and commitment to the liberation of Palestine's land and people," published in October 2015 (Black-Palestinian Solidarity, 2015). Though they were different ethnic-national groups in distinct countries fighting for freedom and justice against separate powers, both collectives deeply identified with one another based on resistance to a politics of oppression.

In order to understand the politics and potential of black-Palestinian solidarity and explore the potential of an "intersectionality of struggles," it is important to uncover the conditions that have allowed such solidarity to take place. The aim of this essay, therefore, is twofold: to trace the historical context of both struggles and to expose the shared components of these respective struggles. This would then allow us to uncover their relationship within a politics of a transnational solidarity framework.

Tracing Geographies of Liberation in a Historical Context

Paul Gilroy once suggested that a component of African American identity is rooted in what he called the "Black Atlantic," which he defined, in Philip Kaisary's words, as a "specifically modern cultural-political formation that was induced by the experience and inheritance of the African slave trade and the plantation system in the Americas, and which transcends both the nation-state and ethnicity." He viewed it as "a distinctively modern, cultural-political space that is not specifically African, American, Caribbean, or British, but is, rather, a hybrid of all of these at once" (Kaisary, 2014). The Black Atlantic consciousness, he argues, could "produce an explicitly transnational and intercultural perspective" (Gilroy, 1993, p. 15). Gilroy's thesis has had its critics, but one aspect that is particularly relevant to considering African American and Palestinian solidarity is the idea of transnationalism.

This transnationalism is present in both oppressive and, consequently, resistant forms. The politics of oppression take a transnational form through the framework, and under the logic, of international neoliberal capitalism as corporations and governments work hand in hand to subdue racialized populations. As #Blacks4Palestine member Kristian Davis Bailey wrote shortly after visiting the West Bank, referring to the post-9/11 law enforcement exchanges between the Israeli and US governments, "our governments literally share resources and tactics with each other that directly harm our respective communities" (quoted in Ball, 2014). Indeed, as one journalist described it: "Thousands of American law enforcement officers frequently travel for training to one of the few countries where policing and militarism are even more deeply intertwined than they are here: Israel" (Speri, 2017).

Consequently, the internationalization of methods of oppression has given birth to the internationalization of methods of resistance. Complementing this transnationalism is the globalization of the Palestinian struggle, particularly in the West, as a struggle against the forces of (specifically) Western settler colonialism. As Israeli historian Ilan Pappe argues, the fact that Zionism could be academically and intellectually assigned the label of settler colonialism has "enabled activists to better see the resemblance between the case of Israel and Palestine with that of [apartheid] South Africa, and to equate the fate of the Palestinians with that of the Native Americans" (Pappe & Chomsky, 2015, p. 33). Indeed, upon visiting the West Bank, Black Lives Matter co-founder Patrisse Cullors said, "This is an apartheid state. We can't deny that and if we do deny it we are a part of the Zionist violence" (quoted in Bailey, 2015).

This phenomenon was described by American scholar, activist, and former Black Panthers leader Angela Davis, who claimed "a political kinship" between African Americans and Palestinians as practicing an "intersectionality of struggles" (quoted in Johnson & Lubin, 2017). Such a view was relatively common among African American intellectuals as early as the 1970s.

In 1972, for example, James Baldwin wrote, "and if I had fled, to Israel, a state created for the purpose of protecting Western interests, I would have been in a yet tighter bind: on which side of Jerusalem would I have decided to live?" (quoted in Farber & Lang, 2016). Six years prior, in 1966, Baldwin penned an essay describing his hometown of Harlem as "occupied territory," declaring, "Occupied territory is occupied territory, even though it be found in that New World which the Europeans conquered, and it is axiomatic, in occupied territory, that any act of resistance, even though it be executed by a child, be answered at once, and with the full weight of the occupying forces." That Baldwin penned this a year before Israel began its actual occupation of East Jerusalem, the West Bank, and Gaza (as well as the Sinai and Golan Heights), an outcome of the 1967 war, is especially poignant. What would Baldwin think of the relationship between Ferguson and Palestine today?

The processes of institutionalized racism against and dehumanization of African Americans in the United States and Palestinians in Israel/Palestine have been extensively documented, thereby facilitating a belief in a common struggle against oppression. To give a common example for both, one can point to the mass incarceration of black men in the United States and of Palestinians in Israel/Palestine. The former was explored by Michelle Alexander in her 2010 book *The New Jim Crow: Mass Incarceration in the Age of Colorblindness*, in which she detailed how millions of African Americans get trapped by a criminal justice system rigged against them. Indeed, in April 2016, one of former US president Richard Nixon's top advisors, John Ehrlichman, revealed that the administration "knew we couldn't make it illegal to be either against the war or black, but by getting the public to associate the hippies with marijuana and blacks with heroin, and then criminalizing both heavily, we could disrupt those communities" (Baum, 2016).

As for the institutionalized discrimination against Palestinians in Israel/Palestine, the evidence is quite clear. Statistics provided by the Jerusalem-based NGO Addameer (2017) speak for themselves: "Since the beginning of the Israeli occupation in 1967, Israeli forces have arrested more than 800,000 Palestinians, constituting almost 20% of the total Palestinian population in the occupied Palestinian territories. With the majority of these detainees being men, about 40% of male Palestinians in the occupied territories have been arrested." This excludes the years between 1967 and the foundation of the State of Israel in 1948, known to Palestinians as the *Nakba* (catastrophe), during which time over 700,000 Palestinians—80 per cent of the population of the land that became Israel—were forced out of their homes (Sadi & Abu-Lughod, 2007, p. 3).

In *Apartheid Israel: The Politics of an Analogy* (Soske & Jacobs, 2015), twenty African studies scholars reflected on whether the apartheid South Africa/Israel analogy held water. Sean Jacobs, one of the book's editors, elsewhere wrote the following: "Both apartheid South Africa and the Israeli state originated through a process of conquest and settlement largely justified on the grounds of religion and ethnic nationalism. Both pursued a legalized, large-scale program of displacing the earlier inhabitants from their land. Both instituted a variety of discriminatory laws based on racial or ethnic grounds" (2014). (The question of apartheid is debated elsewhere in this volume by Oren Kroll-Zeldin, who takes one view, and Zeina M. Barakat and Mohammed S. Dajani Daoudi, who take another.)

That being said, tracing back to a single common political link between African Americans and Palestinians is an impossible task. The attitudes of African American intellectuals towards Israel/Palestine have themselves changed over time. African American intellectuals, including many who placed themselves on the political far left, seem to have been sympathetic towards Zionism until at least the 1960s. This, Alex Lubin (2014) explains, is largely due to the "strong bond within the U.S. civil rights movements uniting African Americans and Jews," which came at a time where "African-Americans increasingly turned their political activities away from the pan-Africanist projects of Black internationalism to nation-bound movements for civil rights within the framework of the liberal state" (pp. 12–13). Essentially, at the risk of over-simplifying, we can discern at least two tendencies among black intellectuals here. The first, a nation-oriented one, tended to sympathize with Zionism as a form of national liberation. The second, an internationalist or transnationalist one, empathized with, and sometimes actively supported, the Palestinian struggle.

Evidence of the latter strain emerged in the 1960s in the era of radical antiwar movements in the United States. In the 1967 war, as African countries continued the process of decolonization begun in the 1950s, Israel captured the Egyptian Sinai (returned in 1982), the Syrian Golan Heights, and, notably for our purposes, the West Bank and Gaza. After 1967, once it became clear that the State of Israel planned on maintaining control over these lands, Israel's emergence as a colonial state and an occupying power contrasted sharply with the prevailing anticolonial sentiment of the era. This reinforced the idea among many African Americans that Israel was, to quote Baldwin again, there for the purpose of "protecting Western interests." Foreseeing this, the Israeli scholar Yeshayahu Leibowitz, critical of his state's trajectory, said in 1968 that Zionism would reproduce "the corruption characteristic of every colonial regime" (quoted in Cohen, 2016).

The aftermath of the 1967 war helped forge a link between the two best-known liberation movements to come from the African American and Palestinian struggles, respectively: the Black Panthers Party (BPP), founded in 1966, and the Palestine Liberation Organization (PLO), founded in 1964.

Shortly after the war, the BPP established links with the PLO, putting into practice what BPP co-founder Huey P. Newton called intercommunalism, which was "the Panthers' understanding of how local communities were sutured together by global processes of imperialism and racial capitalism" (Lubin, 2014, p. 112).

The key takeaway here is the link between the local and the global, for it represents a shift from looking at communities as belonging to a single nation within borders, to attempting to deconstruct the oppressive forces that have created capitalist nation-states and, in the process, oppressed racialized bodies. In *Shadow Over Palestine: The Imperial Life of Race in America*, Keith P. Feldman (2017) writes, "Black Power's Palestine ... engaged the Palestine problem to reveal racial and colonial violence's spatial dispensation." This is why Palestinian American scholar Noura Erakat argues that each group faced "completely different historical trajectories, but both ... resulted in a process of dehumanization that criminalized them and that subject their bodies as expendable" (quoted in Tharoor, 2015).

Mapping Black-Palestinian Solidarity Today: "When I See Them, I See Us"

Much more could be written about the sociopolitical contexts that have given birth to this transnational solidarity between African Americans and Palestinians. Moving forward to the present, we are left wondering whether black–Palestinian solidarity can develop beyond the (albeit important) symbolic rhetoric and move into the realm of concrete struggle within the framework of resistance to the politics of oppression. While it remains too soon to assess that, and one may disagree over *how* such a question is assessed, it is certainly true that black–Palestinian initiatives have grown more vocal over the past few years.

On 23 September 2012, the "Freedom Bus" collective issued a press release from the Palestinian town of Jenin in the West Bank, launching a "ground-breaking West Bank ride" inspired by the Freedom Rides of the American civil rights era (Freedom Bus Palestine, 2012). Like the historical American versions launched to oppose racial segregation, the West Bank Freedom Bus rides were planned to call attention to segregated roads in the occupied West Bank—as of 2012, 79 kilometers of West Bank roads were accessible only to Israeli citizens in addition to 155 kilometers that had restricted access for Palestinians (Visualizing Palestine, 2012).

This was a distinct action, irrespective of an increasing number of tours organized by African Americans in the occupied West Bank, which often end in condemnations of Israeli practices (Sheppard, 2014). These tours consolidate the narrative of "when I see them, I see us" as declared by the Black-Palestinian Solidarity group, promoting comparisons between, say, life in Ferguson and life in a West Bank city like Hebron.

Furthermore, pro-Palestine protests in the United States accelerated during and following the 2014 Israeli war on Gaza, which was perceived by many as having been particularly brutal, even compared to previous wars. In reaction to happenings observed in Indiana, Bill Mullen wrote, "In response to the Israeli massacre in Gaza in summer 2014, we had hundreds of people out in the streets protesting. Since then, we have three brand new Students for Justice in Palestine chapters in Indiana, and a Jewish Voice for Peace chapter" (Mullen, 2015). The rate of new pro-Palestine groups, notably Jewish-identified ones, formed after the 2014 war has been quite impressive. Indeed, at the time of writing, there are over 60 chapters of the anti-occupation and intersectional Jewish Voice for Peace in the United States alone (Jewish Voice for Peace, 2017).

Given the importance of the African American-Jewish American bonds formed during the civil rights era, the rise of anti-Zionist, post-Zionist, and non-Zionist Jewish American groups has helped create a greater emphasis on the Palestinians' oppressed status while challenging the Israeli state's claim of representing all Jews. If we also add the 1,100 black activists, artists, scholars, students, and organizations who signed the "2015 Black Solidarity Statement with Palestine" under the hashtag #Palestine2Ferguson to everything mentioned to far, we start to form a concrete picture of not only a black-Palestinian Solidarity movement being built, but a Jewish-allied one as well.

One could choose to frame the movement as "Jewish-allied black-Palestinian solidarity" as a deliberate attempt to open up the conversation on the increasing number of Jewish voices consciously using their Jewishness as a source of inspiration for their antiracist, anticolonial, and anti-Zionist activities, groups such as Jewish Voice for Peace. In addition to the reasons mentioned above, highlighting such voices is also an attempt to provide an alternative to the increasingly vocal alt-right, which, fueled by the presidency of Donald Trump, has created an uneasy alliance between white nationalists and pro-Israel advocates in the United States. As Naomi Dann (2017), reflecting on white nationalist Richard Spencer's self-identification as a "white Zionist," declared: "What's so chilling about Spencer's comparison of white supremacy to Israel" is not only its anti-Semitism "but the kernel of truth at its core." She argues that "Richard Spencer, whose racist views are rightfully abhorred by the majority of the Jewish community, is holding a mirror up to Zionism and the reflection isn't pretty."

This has become all the more obvious given the Israeli government's reluctance to condemn white nationalists who claim to support Israel. The Israeli government's "tepid reaction" (Shalev, 2017) to the neo-Nazi show of force in Charlottesville, Virginia, in August 2017 has been interpreted as a wake-up call by many Jewish activists. Ben Lorber, campus coordinator for Jewish Voice for Peace, writes that "we are in transition towards a future where our communal identity will not be defined by support for Israel, nor will it rest primarily upon markers of blood" (Lorber, 2017).

Furthermore, labeling this emerging phenomenon "Jewish-allied black-Palestinian solidarity" allows us to open up the discussion further to add to the already-explored links between Mizrahi (Middle Eastern) Jews and Palestinians, a dimension of explicit solidarity, even if discussed as potential rather than actual. In her essay, Aziza Khazzoom (this volume) acknowledges that the "more positive stances" Mizrahi Jews hold "towards putatively 'eastern' Arab culture can offer new ways of including Palestinians irrespective of Israel's status as Jewish." As we saw with black-Palestinian ties, shining a light on these very mechanisms could help us identify the links between Mizrahi Jews and Palestinians, and in the process decolonize Jewishness as understood to be dominated by Ashkenazim. This would be a Jewishness that is, in this context, no longer defined by the "de-Arabization" priorities of Zionism or by the other historical and actual pressures listed by Khazzoom, but is instead built on a shared common culture between Mizrahi Jews and Palestinians.

And one can even take it further. Khazzoom touches upon the increasing identification among Ethiopian Israelis with the "Black Atlantic" consciousness. In making this point, Khazzoom quotes Steven Kaplan, who writes that "young Ethiopians are able to tap into a resource with far greater prestige than the Ethiopian heritage of their parents ... by claiming as their own a powerful, globalized, sophisticated, militant transnational Black identity" (Kaplan, 2002). Given the current dominance of African American life in the Black Atlantic, and taking into account the narrative of "when I see them, I see us" vis-à-vis African Americans and Palestinians, is it not within the realm of possibility to see a movement that links all three? And if the material basis undermining Mizrahi-Palestinian ties is identified and challenged, could this not open up discussions of an even broader, inclusive movement?

Conclusion

This essay argues that a more expansive black-Palestinian solidarity framework is likely to emerge, given the rich historical and contemporary context that has produced an undeniable pattern of transnational political philosophy among African American and Palestinian intellectuals and activists based on a shared resistance to the politics of oppression. A black–Palestinian bond may prove to open up spaces for joint struggles against oppression in both the United States and Israel/Palestine while allowing Ashkenazi Jews and Mizrahi Jews in the United States and Israel-Palestine, respectively, to build new links independently from the policies of the State of Israel (or as an explicit rejection of them).

Whether this will have an impact on state policy is yet to be seen. But given the increased participation of both African Americans and Jewish Americans in supporting Palestinian rights, we may be witnessing a shift from the dominance of pro-Israel politics in mainstream American discourse into a new territory where such notions are openly challenged and rejected. One factor that may be inadvertently accelerating this process, as argued by Yousef Munayyer (this volume), is the recent change in American governmental leadership. "Today, Israel fits neatly alongside Trump's ethno-nationalist politics, even though the 'Trump phenomenon' will likely be both reactionary and ephemeral in the United States because the key constituencies supporting and benefiting from ethno-nationalist politics are becoming a minority." As this ethno-nationalism is by definition whiteness, it could accelerate the building of these very links.

Joey Ayoub is a doctoral student at the University of Edinburgh researching cinema in postwar Lebanese society. He is the regional editor for the MENA region at Global Voices and IFEX and is a freelance writer focusing on Lebanon, Syria, and Israel/Palestine.

Notes

1 The author notes that the identities "African American" and "Jewish," which are used throughout this essay, are not mutually exclusive. Similarly, neither are the categories of "Arab" and "Jewish" or "Palestinian" and "Jewish." For the purpose of this piece, the overlap of such identities (e.g., African American Jew) is not explored. Nonetheless, the author believes that including such analyses in future work would enrich the conversation on intersectionality.

References

Addameer. (2017). "On Administrative Detentions." Retrieved January 10, 2019, from http://www.addameer.org/israeli_military_judicial_system/administrative_detention

Bailey, K.D. (2015, January 15). "Dream Defenders, Black Lives Matter, and Ferguson Reps Take Historic Trip to Palestine." *San Francisco Bay View*. Retrieved December 21, 2017, from http://sfbayview.com/2015/01/dream-defenders-black-lives-matter-and -ferguson-reps-take-historic-trip-to-palestine/

Baldwin, J. (1966, July 11). "A Report from Occupied Territory." *The Nation*. Retrieved December 21, 2017, from https://www.thenation.com/article/report-occupied -territory/

Ball, C. (2014, July 31). "Israel or Palestine? Do Black People Have a Stake in the Conflict?" *Madame Noire*. Retrieved December 21, 2017, from http://madamenoire .com/452865/israel-palestine-black-people-stake-conflict/

Baum, D. (2016, April). "Legalize It All." *Harper's Magazine*. Retrieved December 21, 2017, from https://harpers.org/archive/2016/04/legalize-it-all/

Black-Palestinian Solidarity. (2015, October 14). [Press release]. Retrieved December 21, 2017, from http://www.blackpalestiniansolidarity.com/release.html

Cohen, R. (2016). *The Girl from Human Street: Ghosts of Memory in a Jewish Family*. London, UK: Bloomsbury.

Dann, N. (2017, August 17). "Richard Spencer Might Be the Worst Person in America. But He Might Also Be Right about Israel." *The Forward*. Retrieved December 21, 2017, from https://forward.com/opinion/380384/richard-spencer-israel/

Farber, J.B., & Lang, J. (2016). *James Baldwin: Exile in Provence*. Gretna, LA: Pelican.

Feldman, K.P. (2017). *Shadow over Palestine: The Imperial Life of Race in America*. Minneapolis, MN: University of Minneapolis Press.

Freedom Bus Palestine. (2012, September 22). [Press release]. Retrieved December 21, 2017, from https://freedombuspalestine.wordpress.com/2012/09/19/34/

Gilroy, P. (1993). *The Black Atlantic: Modernity and Double Consciousness*. London: Verso.

Jacobs, S. (2014, November). "Apartheid Israel: The politics of an analogy." Retrieved January 13, 2019 from https://africasacountry.com/2014/11/the-apartheid-analogy/

Jewish Voice for Peace. (2017). "Interested in Joining or Starting a JVP Chapter?" Retrieved December 21, 2017, from https://jewishvoiceforpeace.org/chapters/#section -Chapters

Johnson, G.T., & Lubin, A. (2017, September 1). "Angela Davis on Black Lives Matter, Palestine, and the Future of Radicalism." *Literary Hub*. Retrieved December 21, 2017, from http://lithub.com/angela-davis-on-black-lives-matter-palestine-and-the-future -of-radicalism/

Kaisary, P. (2014, September 18). "The Black Atlantic: Notes on the Thought of Paul Gilroy." *Critical Legal Thinking*. Retrieved December 21, 2017, from http://criticallegalthinking .com/2014/09/15/black-atlantic-notes-thought-paul-gilroy/

Kaplan, S. (2002). "Black and White, Blue and White and Beyond the Pale: Ethiopian Jews and the Discourse of Colour in Israel." *Jewish Culture and History*, 5(1), 51–68. https://doi.org/10.1080/1462169x.2002.10511962

Lorber, B. (2017, October 20). "A Spot at the Kotel Won't Save Us: A Crisis in American Judaism." *Doikayt*. Retrieved December 16, 2017, from https://doikayt .com/2017/10/20/a-spot-at-the-kotel-wont-save-us-a-crisis-in-american-judaism/

Lubin, A. (2014). *Geographies of Liberation: The Making of an Afro-Arab Political Imaginary*. Chapel Hill, NC: University of North Carolina Press.

Molloy, M. (2014, August 15). "Palestinians Tweet Tear Gas Advice to. Protesters in Ferguson." *The Telegraph*. Retrieved December 21, 2017, from http://www.telegraph

.co.uk/news/worldnews/northamerica/usa/11036190/Palestinians-tweet-tear
-gas-advice-to-protesters-in-Ferguson.html

Mullen, B.V. (2015, December 14). "Black Lives Matter and BDS." *Socialist Worker.*
Retrieved December 21, 2017, from http://socialistworker.org/2015/12/14/black
-lives-matter-and-bds

Pappe, I., & Chomsky, N. (2015). *On Palestine.* London, UK: Penguin Books.

Sadi, A.H., & Abu-Lughod, L. (2007). *Nakba Palestine, 1948, and the Claims of Memory.*
New York, NY: Columbia University Press.

Shalev, C. (2017, August 21). "Israel's Rash Embrace of Trump Accelerates the Jewish
Schism." *Haaretz.* Retrieved December 16, 2017, from https://www.haaretz.com/
us-news/1.807936

Sheppard, F. (2014, February 10). "I Traveled to Palestine-Israel and Discovered There Is
No 'Palestinian-Israeli Conflict.'" *Huffington Post.* Retrieved December 21, 2017,
from https://www.huffingtonpost.com/ferrari-sheppard/i-traveled-to-palestine
_b_4761896.html.

Soske, J., & Jacobs, S., eds (2015). *Apartheid Israel: The Politics of an Analogy.* Chicago, IL:
Haymarket Books.

Speri, A. (2017, September 15). "Israel Security Forces are Training American Cops Despite
History of Rights Abuses." *The Intercept.* Retrieved December 21, 2017, from https://
theintercept.com/2017/09/15/police-israel-cops-training-adl-human-rights-abuses
-dc-washington/

Tharoor, E. (2015, October 14). "Lauryn Hill Joins Black, Palestinian Activists in Solidarity Video." *Al Jazeera America.* Retrieved December 21, 2017, from http://america
.aljazeera.com/articles/2015/10/14/lauryn-hill-joins-black-palestinian-activists-in
-solidarity-video.html

Visualizing Palestine. (2012, May). "Israel's System of Segregated Roads in the Occupied Palestinian Territories." Retrieved December 21, 2017, from https://visualizingpalestine
.org/visuals/segregated-roads-west-bank

Cultural Commonalities, Colonial Divisions: On Sources of Solidarity between Palestinians and Jews from the Middle East

AZIZA KHAZZOOM

Just before my son was born, my father visited me in Israel. We went to the market in Jerusalem's Old City to buy a trunk made of inlay from Syria to store my son's birth records. Watching my father was fascinating. As a child growing up in San Francisco with him and my white Anglo-Saxon Protestant mother, I sometimes saw my father, a Jewish immigrant from Iraq, as awkward. Like many immigrants, he used odd words, wrong phrases, his timing was often off. But in the market, speaking Arabic with shopkeepers, my father looked comfortable, the looks, jokes, laughter all in sync. In one shop, my father asked a Palestinian shopkeeper for an "Iraqi price." The shopkeeper, responding to an earlier part of the conversation, asked that my father express pride in his Iraqi heritage first. My father took the man's hand, looked at him, and said, "They did not treat us well in Iraq." The shopkeeper nodded, and the conversation moved on. We finally found the trunk at a store on the Via Dolorosa. That shopkeeper was Armenian. My father said that he had an Armenian dentist in Iraq. I cringed—"Dad, not all Armenians know each other!," I thought—but they got right down to reviewing family trees, found the link between vendor and dentist, and sat back, satisfied.

This paper traces dynamics that build and undermine a sense of solidarity that Jews of Middle/Near Eastern origin[1] (Mizrahim) might feel with Palestinians. Though we often think of Israel as a creation of European Zionism populated by Jews from Europe (Ashkenazim), for much of the State of Israel's history, close to half its Jewish population has been of Middle Eastern origin. The Jews who arrived from the Middle East were *of* the region. They came from long-standing communities that often predated Islam, they spoke local languages, and their cultures developed over centuries in interaction with other local Muslim and Christian cultures. When Europe began colonizing the Muslim Middle East in the eighteenth century, ethno-religious minorities like Jews and Armenians underwent occupation along with Muslims, though the consequences differed for them. At least a few (some say many) Middle Eastern Jews identified *as* Arabs, Turks, Persians, or Iranians.

In Israel, Mizrahim often argued that because of their rootedness in the Middle Eastern context, they should have had a greater role in negotiating with local populations and societies in the region. The exchange about the

Iraqi price—in which common culture facilitated personal connection and honest exchange—shows what they meant. Experiences in Iraq do not always apply to Israel/Palestine, but the interaction with the Armenian shopkeeper shows how relevant they can be. My father's game of "Middle Eastern geography" plugged into a multicultural Middle Eastern social fabric that extends to Israel but is rarely accessible to Israeli Jews. Moreover, a second bond with Palestinians—common experiences of discrimination—is fully rooted in Israel/Palestine. It is by now widely agreed that in the 1950s European Jewish state-builders discriminated against Mizrahi immigrants because they seemed too "Arab." My father's anger at this discrimination led him to reimmigrate to the United States, and his perception of Ashkenazi state-builders—as culturally intolerant bullies who hoarded resources—tempered his right-leaning politics on Israel. Fifty years later, I have very different experiences of Israel. I move in an academic world that is respectful of non-Ashkenazi experiences, I value Israel's pro-family ethos, collective orientation, and political engagement, and when I needed support I experienced the deeply humane side of the Jewish society. But still, my father's memories predispose me to take seriously Palestinian complaints about labor market discrimination, degradation at checkpoints, broken contracts, and invasive behavior.

But my father's interactions in the Old City also reveal chasms, similarly rooted in Jewish experiences in Muslim societies. My father's memory of Iraq is dominated by stories of oppression he experienced as a Jew. In the interaction with the Palestinian shopkeeper he seeks acknowledgement of his minority status in Iraq. There is intense debate about how marginalized Jews were in Middle Eastern societies, with some pointing to limitations on Jewish building, praying, dress, and government service, and others pointing to the high levels of Jewish autonomy and Jewish/Muslim cooperation. Still, some sense of marginalization is present in most Mizrahi reconstructions of life in the Middle East. For many, that memory limits identification as Arab and informs support for an exclusively Jewish state.

There are additional chasms my father does not mention, but which I study. Europe began colonizing the Muslim Middle East in the late eighteenth century, starting with Egypt. When Europeans occupied a Muslim society they often treated local minorities—Jews, Armenians, and others—as allies, rewarding them for cooperating with Europeans. This divide-and-conquer strategy increased Jewish marginalization from the Middle Eastern societies in which they lived. When these Jews immigrated to Israel several generations later, economic and military divisions between Jews and Palestinians further limited potential identification. Finally, Jewish privilege—that multifaceted system that advantages Jews over non-Jews[2]—creates additional political and emotional distance.

In short, the origin of Mizrahim in Middle Eastern societies has important yet multidirectional implications for the likelihood of identification or solidarity with Palestinians in Israel. In this essay, I review those connections. I use the terms "identification" and "solidarity" loosely, to mark anything from recognition and empathy when Palestinians describe oppression in Israel (identification) to outright joining of Palestinian causes evidenced in political behavior (solidarity). Although this paper is about Mizrahi identification with Palestinians, my own work suggests that Ashkenazi and Mizrahi identification are both tied to the Jewish encounter with European colonialism—and the very strong overlap between Orientalism and anti-Semitism in European Christian thinking—and that therefore Mizrahi and Ashkenazi lines of identification are more related than they originally seem. An analysis that puts Mizrahim at the center, therefore, gives us more insight into how *all* Jews relate to Palestinians and to the Middle Eastern context.

The Current Status?

It is difficult to assess current levels of Mizrahi solidarity with Palestinians. Quantitative work has studied its opposite, antipathy, and found that ethnicity makes little difference. Levels of antipathy are high for all groups of Jews, suggesting little potential for solidarity. "Antipathy" in this literature is variably measured as unwillingness to cede territory for peace; grant political rights or extend the social net to Palestinians; cooperate with neighboring Palestinians on communal projects; or engage in social integration by living in the same neighborhood as Palestinians, being friends with Arabs, inviting them into one's home, or allowing one's child to become romantically involved with one.[3] This literature is useful, but given the intensity of the push and pull factors I outlined above, summary measures can hide important dynamics. For this reason, the "state of the art" discussion of Mizrahi solidarity is not in the numbers, but in explication of the push and pull factors.

Colonialism, the East/West Line, and Jewish Identification

These push-and-pull factors are embedded in Jews' relationship to European colonialism and putative Western culture. There are many ways to think about Israel using a colonial frame. Some scholars, including many Israeli Jewish ones, read the Jewish settlement of Israel as another chapter in the large, multicentury European project of exploring, settling, conquering, or economically exploiting large swaths of the globe (which also includes the interwar British occupation of Palestine). In that reading, Jews displaced natives, developed a separate economy for themselves, and set up military governments to rule natives while they themselves enjoyed democratic rights, and this is parallel to the behavior of other European colonial groups.

However, attending to ethnicity among Jews complicates the picture. In her seminal article "Zionism from the Point of View of Its Jewish Victims," Ella Shohat (1988) kept the colonial frame but split Jewish groups, arguing that the colonizers were Ashkenazi state-builders. Though Shohat perceived Palestinians as more severely victimized than Mizrahim, she argued that Ashkenazi state-builders sought to make both groups cheap labor for a privileged Ashkenazi society. There is a great deal of archival evidence of this intent. For example, Ben-Gurion proclaimed that "we need people who are born workers.... The Oriental Jews['] ... standard of living and their needs are lower than the European workers" (quoted in Khazzoom, 2008, p. 52). Moreover, in both cases Ashkenazi state-builders referenced the Orientalist discourse, which constructs Middle Eastern societies as inferior to those of Europe, to shape and justify their monopolization of land, education, political power, residence in urban centers, and high-status occupations.

Shohat's answer to the solidarity question is therefore clear: Mizrahi and Palestinian interests are intrinsically aligned because both are oppressed by Ashkenazi Zionists. As to why Mizrahim have not, generally, engaged in collective action with Palestinians, Shohat argued, first, that they *had* expressed solidarity, and second that Ashkenazi state-builders used divide-and-conquer strategies, particularly in the first decades of statehood, to minimize that solidarity. One such strategy was to place Mizrahim on the literal border of the state, where they were likely to be direct targets during border skirmishes with Palestinians and other Arabs. Another was to foster a common Jewish culture through intensive Hebrew training, schools, and the army, which would make Mizrahim disidentify with Arabs and identify with Ashkenazim.

Chetrit (2009) and Roby (2015) study Mizrahi protest in Israel, and support Shohat's contention that at least some Mizrahim identified their struggle with that of Palestinians. Roby's evidence is compelling because he uses police files, which were intended to document all protest systematically, and often recorded what the protestors wrote on signs. It is on the basis of this evidence that Roby argues for identification. Manifestos and movement publications also confirm that movement leaders—of the protest movements of the 1950s, the Israeli Black Panthers of the 1970s, and the academic group Keshet from the 1990s—used sophisticated postcolonial theory to articulate these connections. Finally, the evidence Hazkani (2010) adduces is compelling. He analyzed a complete set of letters sent from Israel to Morocco by Israeli soldiers during the 1950s and showed that during some time periods some urged their family members to stay in Morocco with their "brothers" who accept them, rather than come to Israel and be excluded by Europeans who condescend to Middle Eastern culture. This is strong evidence that despite pressures to the contrary, common discrimination has also elicited Mizrahi identification with Palestinians.

My research suggests a different relationship between European colonialism, Mizrahim, and Ashkenazim (Khazzoom, 2008). I note that it is possible for Israeli exclusion of Palestinians to be colonial—in the sense that it relies on relegation to secondary labor markets, high levels of segregation, and a sense of permanence—without it being *European* colonial. This distinction does not always matter, but it is crucial for analyzing lines of potential solidarity. In essence, I argue that Mizrahim and Ashkenazim belong in the same category as each other vis-à-vis European colonialism and are neither European colonizers nor its primary victims. This conceptualization makes more room for Jews' status as minorities, both in the Middle East and in Europe, than other conceptualizations do.

The key here is the experience of a protégé. This is a formal or informal status that European colonizers gave to some groups in the societies they occupied, usually groups that had been marginalized prior to European invasion. In the Middle East, Jews were such a group. Protégés were given economic benefits in return for supporting European rule, and they often became Europhilic, seeing Middle Eastern lifestyles as backward, seeking to emulate their benefactors' putatively Western culture, and engaging in exclusion of those who appeared more "native" than themselves. Middle Eastern Jews developed this desire to become Western prior to the move to Israel. To highlight their increasing westernization, many stressed their differences from Muslim Arabs. This means that they began to disidentify with Arabs prior to the move to Israel. Therefore, disidentification emerged from an interaction between European colonialism and their status as ethno-national minorities in Muslim societies, as much as from their experience in Israel.

Although European Jews were not colonized militarily, European Christian intellectuals initiated a similar identity dynamic with the "Jewish question" when they cast Jews as Oriental, sometimes in cahoots with the Muslim enemy, and demanded that Jews prove their fitness for equal rights by becoming culturally similar to bourgeois western European Christians. Like Jews in the Middle East, Jews in Europe accepted the characterization and became intent on rooting out the "Oriental" from Jewish life. Zionism absorbed this "westernization project." The state-builders then arrived in Israel determined to marginalize people and things they read as eastern, including Mizrahim, who were dark, spoke with Arabic accents, and otherwise appeared to reflect the eastern state European Jews believed they had only recently left behind. In my empirical work I show that Mizrahim who had attended colonial schools, and therefore could self-present as westernized, did not experience labor market discrimination. This suggests that when

Mizrahim did experience labor market discrimination it was because they appeared too "eastern" and suggests that exclusion in Israel was about making the country western.

Ultimately, I follow Shohat in treating Ashkenazi state-builders as the excluders and Mizrahim and Palestinians as the targets of exclusion. However, both Mizrahim and Ashkenazim desire to make Israel western, with consequences for the exclusion of Palestinians. Studies of the Jewish Enlightenment often point to the internalized anti-Semitism involved in the project of Jewish cultural change, and this suggests that it is in the interest of all Israeli Jews to rethink the project. From this perspective, Yousef Munayyer's essay (this volume) can be seen as an explication of how Israel's alliance with the West—and attachment to Orientalism as a frame for understanding the world—has hurt Israel as much as it has helped it.

Yehouda Shenhav's (2006) concepts of "entry tickets" and "de-Arabization" also address the consequences of westernization projects for alliances between Mizrahim and Palestinians or the larger Middle East region. By "de-Arabization," Shenhav means Ashkenazi Zionists' push to make Mizrahim more recognizably Jewish by becoming less recognizably Arab. To de-Arabize, and obtain their entry ticket to Israeli society, Mizrahi immigrants were expected to change putatively eastern names, behaviors, accents, mentalities, traditions, musical tastes, family formations, and the like. Some entered intelligence occupations and went undercover in Arab countries, or monitored news broadcasts from Arab countries, looking for areas of weakness. In this sense they build on cultural commonality with Arabs to become *not* Arab, and therefore full members of the Jewish society.[4]

As with Shohat's divide-and-conquer dynamics, there is evidence that de-Arabization was not fully successful, at least for the immigrant generation. Recent work has argued that Mizrahi immigrants in Israel continued to use Arabic in daily life, to produce literature in it, and to remain attached to the music, food, and other cultural products they knew from their pre-immigration life (Bashkin, 2017; Meir-Glitzenstein, 2015; Snir, 2006). Often, participation in Arab culture was surreptitious, and relegated to the privacy of the home. Some work, such as Levy's (1997) research on Moroccan Jews who travel back to Morocco after years in Israel, reference ambivalence towards the culture they encounter there, including both identification and a sense of distance. Regarding the Israeli-born, multiple directions have been observed. On the one hand, evidence of a post-ethnic identification on the part of the Mizrahi middle class would suggest that younger generations have lost the cultural basis for identification and solidarity with Palestinians and the Middle Eastern region. On the other hand, the phenomena of Mediterranean music and *ars poetica* are often read as an attempt to retain or re-create those cultural connections. Similarly, the academic group Keshet is made up largely of second-generation Mizrahi immigrants, many of whom experience more solidarity towards Palestinians than their parents' generation. Thus again, the pressures towards identification and disidentification remain strong, and belie any simple summary measures.

Ethiopians

Ethiopian Jewish Israelis provide an interesting counterpart to this discussion of Mizrahim. While Mizrahim can identify with Palestinians through pan-Arab connections, Ethiopian Jewish Israelis appear to be developing a sense of belonging to the Black Atlantic. This identification is understood to be a reaction to both discrimination and the cachet of Western culture (Kaplan, 2002). As Kaplan writes, "young Ethiopians are able to tap into a resource with far greater prestige than the Ethiopian heritage of their parents ... by claiming as their own a powerful, globalized, sophisticated, militant transnational Black identity" (p. 56).

Joey Ayoub's essay (this volume) looks towards the "Black Atlantic" for support for Palestinian causes. This suggests more of an alliance with Ethiopians through the Black Atlantic than with Mizrahim through common culture. It also raises questions about which "outside" identities are useful, for whom, and in what ways. I would suggest that for all groups concerned, the Black Atlantic is useful for highlighting "resource injustice," or that global tendency to give brown people *less*—less political power, money, housing, education—as well as to subject them to higher rates of imprisonment and state violence. While it suggests a kind of ganging up on Israel, the idea that all brown people are excluded in similar ways worldwide also underscores that exclusionary practices in Israel are not unique or unusual for modern industrialized societies. If the Black Atlantic underscores economic issues, attention to Orientalism underscores issues of cultural valuation. I suspect that when it comes to the value Palestinians are accorded in Israeli society, a Mizrahi-Palestinian alliance is more powerful. In fact, given the effect Oriental stigmas had on Ashkenazi identities, all Israelis have interests in shaking off this common yoke of oppression.

Conclusion

On the day my father and I were in Jerusalem, we had lunch near an Ashkenazi ultra-Orthodox *yeshiva* that had just moved into the Muslim quarter. As the *yeshiva* residents walked around, my father reflected on how their domineering body language rekindled the anger from his first years in Israel. He spoke of a sense of cultural loss, as an Israeli site that reminded him of home in its rhythm and sound gave way to rhythms and sounds that he found foreign and invasive. His comments fit well with post-Zionist and Palestinian perspectives, which emphasize invasion and erasure of Middle Eastern cultures in Israel/Palestine. When I pointed this out, my father did not object, but rather began speaking about oppression of Jews in Iraq. He argued that while Jews may have been well treated in most of the Middle East, they were never equal. In line with Zionist ideology, he thinks that for Jews to be equal they must have a Jewish state. This conversation showcases not just the strength of push and pull factors for my father, but the inability of either Zionism or postcolonialism to fully encapsulate his thinking. He moves back and forth between frames, never fully attaching to either.

From Shohat in 1988 to Roby in 2015, the focus of post-Zionist research on the Mizrahi experience has been to disentangle Mizrahi subjectivity from the Zionist narrative by showing the ambivalence, alternative identities, and outright resistance to Zionism that had been erased by those in power. This is appropriate. However, the use of Palestinian and Middle Eastern anticolonial struggles to frame alternative Mizrahi subjectivities can also generate its own form of invisibility and erasure, because these discourses do not always incorporate the experiences of those Jews as minorities in the Middle Eastern societies from which they immigrated. To fully understand the potential for Mizrahi solidarity with Palestinians, we need to examine Mizrahi talk for the ways that it is out of step with both discourses. This analysis must be conducted on different communities separately because stances vary by generation, country of origin, and class.

In my own research, comparing life stories of bourgeois-origin Polish and Iraqi Jewish women who immigrated to Israel as young adults in the 1950s, I have made a few observations. First, there are two projects embedded in Zionism: the production of a Jewish state and the production of a Western society. Zionism blends Judaization and westernization but my Iraqi respondents do not, and they are more attached to the Jewish than the Western component. Second, what my respondents mean by "Jewish" may differ. I am examining the hypothesis that my Polish and Iraqi respondents mean different things when they talk about a Jewish state. Iraqis appear to have expected a larger version of the autonomous Jewish community they knew in Baghdad, while Poles use Zionist ideas of cultural pride. Palestinians prefer that Israel not be a Jewish state. However, Mizrahim may be sources of new, indigenous conceptions of what a Jewish society means, which changes the conversation. Moreover, their more positive stances towards putatively "eastern" Arab culture can offer new ways of including Palestinians irrespective of Israel's status as Jewish.

Finally, I began this essay with an argument that it is useful for Israeli Jews to rethink their alliance with the West, and that I see this is as a source of potential solidarity between Jews—by which I mean all Jews—and Palestinians. In fact, the protégé dynamic—in which subgroups that were offered special privileges by European colonialism responded by becoming Europhilic—is not limited to Jews. Watenpaugh (2014) posits that it is a consequential but understudied dynamic in the Middle East generally. If Israel's protégé dynamic is *Middle Eastern*, the result of a shared experience of European colonialism and Orientalism, then there is significant common ground for all Israeli Jews and non-Jews to address a common problem, which we can call the shadow of the West. In this sense, the question around which this essay is organized is an incorrect one. It is misleading to ask about potential solidarities between Mizrahim and Palestinians because that implies that Mizrahi and Ashkenazi relationships to Palestinians are shaped by different dynamics. In fact, however, they are shaped by very similar dynamics.

Aziza Khazzoom obtained her BA from Wellesley College and her PhD from UC Berkeley. She is currently an associate professor of Near Eastern Languages and Cultures at Indiana University, Bloomington, and was previously a senior lecturer of Sociology at Hebrew University of Jerusalem, and an assistant professor of sociology at University of California, Los Angeles. She is the author of *Shifting Ethnic Boundaries and Inequality in Israel; Or, How the Polish Peddler Became a German Intellectual* (Stanford University Press, 2008), and is currently analyzing life stories of Polish and Iraqi Jews who immigrated to Israel in the 1950s. She has held a National Science Foundation doctoral dissertation grant, an Israel Science Foundation research grant, and various other grants and postdoctoral fellowships.

Notes

1 "Near East" includes the Middle East, North Africa, Turkey, and Iran. It is the correct term for the origin of Mizrahim. However, following colloquial usage, I will refer to the Middle East rather than Near East.
2 Meaning Jewish privilege relative to Palestinian citizens of Israel as well as those in the territories. Jewish advantage accrues on multiple sites, from the distribution of resources for education or other services, to the ease of getting past security barriers, to the psychological effect of belonging to the Jewish nation. Among Israeli citizens, unequal distribution of resources is often indirect. In the territories, exclusion is more

direct. That is, whether out of necessity or not, Israel often actively limits access to labor markets, schools, water, electricity, and the like.

3 Early studies found that Mizrahim expressed slightly higher rates of antipathy than Ashkenazim. That finding became a truism in the larger Israeli worldview, but in fact the effects were weak and later work concluded that they were neutralized by nonethnic, class-related factors. Mizrahim tend to be religious and live in the periphery, which are themselves associated with antipathy.

4 Ashkenazi immigrants were also expected to jettison diaspora cultures to create a unified Jewish Israeli culture. However, there was more concern about Mizrahim, because their putatively Arab characteristics undermined the Westernness of the Jewish society. Moreover, de-Arabization has a political impact that assimilation of Ashkenazim does not have, in that potential cultural connections with Palestinians were reduced.

References

Bashkin, O. (2017). *Impossible Exodus: Iraqi Jews in Israel*. Stanford, CA: Stanford University Press.

Chetrit, S.S. (2009). *Intra-Jewish Conflict in Israel: White Jews, Black Jews*. New York, NY: Routledge.

Hazkani, S. (2010). "*Arab Mothers Also Cry*": *Conformity and Dissent in Israeli Soldiers' Letters from the Suez Crisis, 1953–1957* (Master's thesis). Georgetown University, Washington, DC.

Kaplan, S. (2002). "Black and White, Blue and White and Beyond the Pale: Ethiopian Jews and the Discourse of Colour in Israel." *Jewish Culture and History, 5*(1), 51–68.

Khazzoom, A. (2008). *Shifting Ethnic Boundaries and Inequality in Israel: Or, How the Polish Peddler Became a German Intellectual*. Stanford, CA: Stanford University Press.

Levy, A. (1997). "To Morocco and Back." In E. Ben-Ari & Y. Bilu (eds), *Grasping Land: Space and Place in Contemporary Israeli Discourse and Experience* (pp. 25–46). Albany, NY: State University of New York Press.

Meir-Glitzenstein, E. (2015). "Longing for the Aromas of Baghdad: Food, Emigration, and Transformation in the Lives of Iraqi Jews in Israel in the 1950s." In A. Helman (ed.), *Jews and Their Foodways* (pp. 89–109). New York, NY: Oxford University Press.

Roby, B. (2015). *The Mizrahi Era of Rebellion: Israel's Forgotten Civil Rights Struggle, 1948–1966*. Syracuse, NY: Syracuse University Press.

Shenhav, Y. (2006). *The Arab Jews: A Postcolonial Reading of Nationalism, Religion, and Ethnicity*." Stanford, CA: Stanford University Press.

Shohat, E. (1988). "Sephardim in Israel: Zionism from the Standpoint of Its Jewish Victims. *Social Text, 19/20*, 1–35. https://doi.org/10.2307/466176

Snir, R. (2006). "'Till Spring Comes': Arabic and Hebrew Literary Debates among Iraqi-Jews in Israel (1950–2000)." *Shofar, 24*(2), 92–123.

Watenpaugh, K.D. (2014). *Being Modern in the Middle East: Revolution, Nationalism, Colonialism, and the Arab Middle Class*. Princeton, NJ: Princeton University Press.

Alternate Bipolarity: How Israel Found Itself on the Wrong Side of the Global Divide

YOUSEF MUNAYYER ·

In this essay I trace the processes that contributed to how Israel, once considered part of the liberal democratic global order, found itself increasingly associated with authoritarianism and ethnocracy. I will argue that historically Israel fit relatively neatly into the Western side within the global bipolarity. But this bipolarity ran into great tension with the ascendant politics of multiculturalism in the West, concurrent with disastrous Western foreign interventions in Muslim countries, forcing an abrupt reevaluation of the dichotomous framing that produced a new bipolarity of universalism and particularism where ideology, not geography, served as the most active delineating variable.

Historically, Israel's relations with the world and, most importantly, with the United States and the former Soviet Union can be divided into four periods; the pre-1967 era, the post-1967 era, the "clash of civilizations era," and the multicultural era. I trace events in each period that characterize Israel's global positioning. In the first period, Israel's relationship with the outside world did not place it neatly on either side of the global divide. While the global divide itself adjusted over the following two periods, Israel eventually found itself on the same side as the United States. In the most recent period this is less clear. I argue that, over time, Israel will continue to find itself further alienated from the side of the global divide that it had long fit into alongside the United States. Ultimately, as Israel continues its abusive policies towards Palestinians, Americans valuing freedom, justice, and equality will turn away from Israel, leading to an erosion in political support for the United States-Israel alliance.

The Pre-1967 Era

From Israel's 1948 founding through the 1967 war, several key events shaped its relationship with both superpowers. The first was recognition it received from the United States and the Soviet Union. While the Truman Doctrine, launching the Cold War, was announced in early 1947, it was in its initial stages at this time, while international debate around the creation of a Jewish state had preceded the Truman Doctrine, dating back to the Balfour Declaration (1917) and the King-Crane Commission (1919). After Israel was recognized by the Soviet Union and the United States in 1948, it had an opportunity to develop relationships with both superpowers. For many reasons, including an established and growing Jewish American community that helped push Truman towards recognition (Judis, 2014), the State of Israel was able to build unique ties with the United States during this period without becoming a client state, something that would develop as the Cold War proceeded (Ganin, 2005). During this time several issues generated tension between Israel and the United States. This included a key event following its establishment, which was Israel's response to the Palestinian refugee crisis. Washington viewed Israel's hardline position against repatriation as intransigent. It particularly angered Truman, who wrote to Mark F. Etheridge, the US representative at the United Nations Conciliation Commission for Palestine, saying he was "rather disgusted with the manner in which the Jews are approaching the refugee problem," adding that he "told the President of Israel in the presence of his Ambassador just exactly what [he] thought about it" (Truman, 1949).

The 1950s and 1960s brought two further sources of tension between Israel and the United States. The first was the 1956 war, during which Israel invaded the Sinai Peninsula in coordination with the United Kingdom and France. This aggression not only damaged the US–Israel relationship, but also weakened US and UK ties (Warner, 1991). While Israel's relationship with Washington may have been tense during this period, its relationship with France was strong and was becoming stronger. France played a key role in supplying Israel with advanced weapons and helped it develop nuclear weapons (Crosbie, 2015), a third issue that was a source of tension between Israel and the United States. The Eisenhower and Kennedy administrations both made efforts to prevent Israel's nuclear weapons development, though Washington ultimately accepted the reality once Israel crossed the threshold (Cohen, 1998).

During this period other issues divided Israel and the United States. For example, even though Washington supported Israel militarily, this assistance was minor compared to France's. Indeed, during the 1967 war, Israeli pilots flew French aircraft. Despite being an American ally, France operated a far more independent foreign policy during this period. It was not until after the 1967 war, arguably, that the Cold War enveloped the Middle East, which led to major changes, including the origin of Israel's airplanes.

The Post-1967 Era

Once the dust cleared following the second week of June 1967, the Middle East had been dramatically altered. Israel occupied the West Bank and the Gaza Strip as well as the Sinai Peninsula and the Golan Heights. Israel also managed to change perceptions, garnering respect for its military prowess in both Washington and Moscow. Moscow and Israel had grown further apart since 1948, and Moscow's closeness to Syria leading up to the 1967 war defined a clearer division between it and Israel. With the question of Palestine central to the region and Middle Eastern centrality to the global oil supply and the American economy, the region was now thrust into the center of the Cold War arms race, with Arab republics being supported by Moscow while Israel was primarily supplied weapons by the United States, replacing France (Kinsella, 1994).

Over this period, however, Israel's utility as an American instrument to counter Soviet influence in the region began to wane. The most significant moment in this shift occurred as a result of the Camp David peace treaty, which saw Israel return occupied Sinai to Egypt. The agreement with Egypt culminated a long-term US effort to break Egypt out of the Soviet sphere of influence. As part of the peace agreement, Egypt would begin receiving billions of dollars in American military aid. While Syria remained a Soviet client, Egypt, the most influential Arab country, had joined the American side of the divide (Quandt, 2015).

While Israel continued to enjoy a strong relationship with the United States, the 1979 peace agreement meant that the Cold War dimension of the Middle East was largely over. However, 1979 ushered in other trans-formational events, including the rise of Islamist politics and the Iranian revolution, where the pro-American shah was replaced by an anti-imperialist Islamist leadership.

New World Order and the "Clash of Civilizations"

The collapse of the Soviet Union ended the Cold War and the paradigm defining global alliances for the latter half of the twentieth century. What would follow was not immediately clear. American president George H. W. Bush declared a "new world order," structured around American global leadership. The first major test of this declaration was the 1991 Gulf War, where the United States led an international coalition against the Iraqi military advance on Kuwait. The American coalition included a wide range of Arab states that were in the American orbit during the Cold War, Egypt and, most importantly, Syria, which had the longest and strongest ties with Moscow. When the Iraqis launched missiles against Israel, Washington pressed the Israelis not to respond for fear that it would jeopardize the coalition. This left the Palestine Liberation Organization (PLO) in the precarious situation of siding with Iraq, even as much of the Arab world was opposing it; siding with the United States would have been akin to supporting Israel, which the PLO could not do (Mattar, 1994).

In the aftermath of the war, a new geopolitical reality dawned on the Middle East. As the frame of the Cold War faded into history, much of the Arab world was now angry with the PLO and Iraq, while Syria was opening towards Washington; this further isolated and weakened the PLO. Completing a process that had begun decades prior, current political realities led the PLO to finally become an American client. (For example, within a few years, the PLO's designation as a terror organization was reversed by the US State Department.) While this shift helped launch the Israeli-Palestinian peace process, it also meant that Israel and the Palestinians were no longer on opposite sides of the United States in the global divide.

While the new world order began taking shape during this period of uncertainty, another challenge grew out of the graveyard of empires that had helped bring the Soviet Union down. A headline of a 1993 article in *The Independent*—written by Robert Fisk—read "Anti-Soviet Warrior Puts His Army on the Road to Peace"; Osama Bin Laden began gaining a global voice. Fisk wrote, "When the history of the Afghan resistance movement is written, Mr. Bin Laden's own contribution to the mujahedin—and the indirect result of his training and assistance—may turn out to be a turning-point in the recent history of militant fundamentalism; even if, today, he tries to minimise his role."

The transnational attacks perpetrated by the Islamist network that came to be known as Al-Qaeda presented a new challenge to the emerging global order, and one that would preoccupy American policymakers for decades to come. A harbinger of future events, the first bombing of New York's World Trade Center took place in early 1993. At the same time, several prominent American writers advanced ideas about a new paradigm defining the global divide. "Communism versus capitalism" would be replaced by the confrontation between the so-called "Judeo-Christian" West and the Islamic world.

Samuel Huntington, whose controversial book *The Clash of Civilizations and the Remaking of the World Order* (1996), based on his 1993 *Foreign Affairs* article, roiled the international relations conversation throughout the 1990s and helped reinforce this message. While Huntington's book was heavily criticized, eventually to the point of derision, the book gained a second life following 9/11, and was elevated and celebrated.

Indeed, perhaps the most popular question framing the discussion in the post-9/11 moment was "Why do they hate us?" The answer most often put forward, as critics pointed out, was that "they" hate "us" because they are not like us, they are Muslim (Alsultany, 2012). Between Israel and the Palestinians, only one side fit into the popular American understanding of "us": the Israeli side. The Palestinian side was "them."

Reinforcing this flawed narrative was the confluence of both the American "War on Terror" and invasions of Afghanistan and Iraq in the aftermath of 9/11 and the Palestinian uprising against Israel, now known as the Al-Aqsa Intifada. Combatting terrorism became a topic that American and Israeli leaders could speak about to their own and one another's domestic audiences in one voice. *The New York Times* reported on Israeli and Palestinian reactions the day after the 9/11 attacks, quoting Israel's then-finance minister Benjamin Netanyahu:

> Asked tonight what the attack meant for relations between the
> United States and Israel, Benjamin Netanyahu, the former prime
> minister, replied, "It's very good." Then he edited himself: "Well, not
> very good, but it will generate immediate sympathy." He predicted
> that the attack would "strengthen the bond between our two peoples,
> because we've experienced terror over so many decades, but the
> United States has now experienced a massive hemorrhaging of
> terror." (Bennet, 2001)

Despite a brief period of time in the aftermath of the Cold War when there seemed to be an opportunity for realignment, an emerging global paradigm once again put the United States and Israel firmly on one side of the divide and Palestinians on the other.

This "us versus them" dynamic had important implications not only for the global divide, but also for the divide in American domestic politics. As the war on Iraq became the single most divisive and defining political issue in the United States at the time (Jacobson, 2010b), the "us versus them" narrative became more prominent and more politicized around the bases of America's major parties. The Republican Party's base was far more majoritarian in nature: racially it was overwhelmingly white, and it was home to America's influential evangelical constituency. The Democratic Party's base was far more racially diverse and less religiously committed. The "us versus them" narrative thus became more prominent in right-wing messaging not only because it was a narrative that supported American confrontation in the Muslim world, but also because it overlapped with important divides in American politics (Baumgartner, Francia, & Morris, 2008).

Despite the disaster of the war on Iraq, the American public had not yet fully turned against the war by the 2004 election. In fact, George W. Bush owed his victory in large part to white, evangelical voters, who supported America's military actions in Iraq. During the 2004 Democratic National Convention, however, America was introduced to a senator from Illinois who was African American, whose middle name was Hussein, and whose

Muslim father had come to the United States from Kenya and married a white woman from Kansas. As he said in his speech at the time, "we gather to affirm the greatness of our nation not because of the height of our skyscrapers, or the power of our military, or the size of our economy; our pride is based on a very simple premise, summed up in a declaration made over two hundred years ago: 'We hold these truths to be self-evident, that all men are created equal.'" Barack Hussein Obama's words and personal story starkly contrasted with the prevailing "us versus them" narrative. As support for the war declined, Obama rode opposition to it (and the party that embraced it) all the way to the Oval Office (Jacobson, 2010a).

Obama, Trump, and the Sputtering American Transformation

The legacy of institutionalized racism in the United States continues to be profound. But the election of an African American president was an important benchmark in a growing shift in American domestic politics where ethnic and racial minorities, since 2008, have seen more access to political power than ever before.

The political right's response to this shift was characterized by racism, nativism, xenophobia, and Islamophobia. Perhaps the right's most notable response to Obama's rise was birtherism—the unfounded allegation that Obama is not a citizen born in the United States, but rather was born in Kenya and had falsified his birth certificate. In fact, even after two terms as president, 2016 polls found that a vast majority of registered Republican voters still doubted Obama's citizenship.

Internationally, Obama's rise meant a shift away from a "with us or against us" mentality that had characterized the Bush administration and a reorientation towards multilateralism. The antiwar sentiment that propelled Obama to office, along with the material drain of years of war in Iraq and Afghanistan, shifted American foreign policy away from so-called nation-building. Obama also welcomed the opportunity for diplomacy with Iran, which the preceding administration infamously placed on an "axis of evil" list (along with Iraq and North Korea). Reorienting "War on Terror" policies away from mass deployments in places like Iraq and willingness to negotiate with Iran led to a narrative of criticism of Obama from the political right (often neoconservatives) that complemented and reinforced the narrative of birtherism; in short, there was something suspect, even traitorous, about this president (Munayyer, 2017).

It was during Obama's presidency, which was nearly concurrent with right-wing Israeli governments led by Benjamin Netanyahu's Likud, that support for Israel became an increasingly partisan political issue. Iran policy was often the key driver in this divide, with Netanyahu advocating for a more belligerent American stance alongside Obama's American Republican oppo-nents. This culminated in Netanyahu's 2015 speech to Congress, orchestrated by the Republican Speaker of the House without White House support, where he discussed his opposition to the Iran nuclear deal.

Other important events on the ground in Israel/Palestine also shaped perceptions of the United States-Israel relationship. Netanyahu's government expanded settlements, doubling down on the illegal policy despite America's vocal opposition. At the same time, Israeli civilian deaths from Palestinian acts of violence—common during the second Intifada—had declined sig-nificantly, while Israel continued to carry out massive bombardments against Palestinians, routinely leaving civilians as the majority of victims. The analogy in the days following 9/11—that Israel, like America, was a victim under attack—was clouded by the optics of an aggressive, recalcitrant Israel.

The reactionary response to the Obama presidency, which eventually came in the form of Donald Trump, presented exclusivist nationalism in response to the inclusivist multiculturalism seen during Obama's rise. The nationalist politics of Trump were also part of an ascendant populist wave sweeping different parts of the globe. This emerging global clash of ideas was not a clash between capitalism and communism or the West and Islam, but rather a clash between multiculturalism and ethnic nationalism, between in-clusivist and exclusivist political systems. The growing tension between Israel and America under Obama merely set the stage for what came next: a United States–Israel relationship defined by Trump and Netanyahu's warm embrace.

Today, Israel fits neatly alongside Trump's ethno-nationalist politics, even though the "Trump phenomenon" will likely be both reactionary and ephemeral in the United States because the key constituencies supporting and benefiting from ethno-nationalist politics are becoming a minority. While an ethno-nationalist political coalition energized in reaction to Obama's presidency might prove barely viable in the short term, such policies will prove too divisive to secure a winning coalition in the long term. In Israel, however, Jewish ethno-nationalism is the glue that binds society, increasingly deployed to keep a unified society behind a state that increasingly lurches to the right. As Aziza Khazzoom discusses in her essay (this volume), although "we often think of Israel as a creation of European Zionism populated by Jews from Europe (Ashkenazim), for much of the State of Israel's history, close to half its Jewish population has been of Middle Eastern origin." She exam-ines the potential affinity that could evolve between Jews of Middle Eastern origin and Palestinians, making clear that the state has worked to combat this possibility through the process of expecting Mizrahi immigrants to "change putatively eastern names, behaviors, accents, mentalities, traditions, musical tastes, family formations, and the like. Some entered intelligence occupations and went undercover in Arab countries, or monitored news broadcasts from Arab countries, looking for areas of weakness. In this sense they build on cultural commonality with Arabs to become not Arab, and therefore full members of the Jewish society." Thus, while ethno-nationalism may be a limited path to power in the United States, in Israel, where it is so tied to the interests of power, it is much harder to imagine a shift away from the politics of ethno-nationalism.

Conclusion

Across these four periods, Israel has found itself in various stages of affinity with the United States. The strongest periods in the United States-Israel relationship were those when Israel fit neatly onto the American side of a global divide for both strategic and perceived values-based reasons. In the pre-1967 period, although Israel gained US support, there were tensions in the relationship. The post-1967 period, which lasted through the end of the Cold War, was the strongest in terms of the United States-Israel "special relationship" because of Israel's strategic utility to the United States as well as the popular perception that it was on the US side of the global values divide between democracies and authoritarian states. In the post–Cold War "clash of civilizations" period, Israel's strategic value decreased, but it continued to be seen as a civilizational ally in the "Judeo-Christian" confrontation with Islam during the "War on Terror." As this global dichotomy's legitimacy waned under the Obama administration, Israel's strategic value to the United States never recovered to Cold War levels, and its moral affinity for the values of multiculturalism dissipated as the seeming permanence of its occupation became more apparent.

Today, in the Trump era, the United States is experiencing a reactionary moment in what is otherwise a longer trajectory towards a more diverse and equitable polity. Israel, however, is moving in the opposite direction, privileging its Jewishness over democratic principles, further entrenching the occupation and the denial of basic rights to millions of Palestinians. In the short term, the United States-Israel relationship will face tension again, as in the pre-1967 period.

Democrats, whose party base and politics are more inclined to inclusion, are already becoming more alienated from Israel. For example, Joey Ayoub (this volume) traces the growth of a burgeoning black-Palestinian solidarity to a shared politics of oppression. Republicans, on the other hand, have a base that is more sympathetic to both ethno-nationalism and Israel. Still, over time, while the American attitude towards inclusion has been fraught, it has been largely unidirectional, with a constantly expanding definition of what it means to belong in America. Barring radical changes in Israel's treatment of Palestinians, Israel will find itself increasingly alienated from the United States and more generally from a Western world that values inclusion over exclusion.

Yousef Munayyer is the executive director of US Campaign for Palestinian Rights. Prior to joining USCPR, he was the executive director of the Jerusalem Fund and Palestine Center and also served as a policy analyst for the American-Arab Anti-Discrimination Committee. His doctoral research focused on the intersection between foreign policy and domestic policy and its impact on terrorism and civil liberties; he received his PhD in government and politics from the University of Maryland. He frequently writes on matters of foreign policy in the Arab and Muslim world, and civil rights and civil liberties in the United States. His writings have appeared in every major metropolitan newspaper in the United States and many others internationally, as well as online. He is a frequent commentator on national and international media outlets, including CNN, MSNBC, Fox News, NBC, CBS, Al Jazeera English, C-Span, and others.

References

Alsultany, E. (2012). *Arabs and Muslims in the Media: Race and Representation after 9/11.* New York, NY: New York University Press.

Baumgartner, J.C., Francia, P.L., & Morris, J.S. (2008). "A Clash of Civilizations? The Influence of Religion on Public Opinion of US Foreign Policy in the Middle East." *Political Research Quarterly, 61*(2), 171–79. https://doi.org/10.1177/1065912907307288

Bennet, J. (2001, September 12). "A Day of Terror: The Israelis; Spilled Blood Is Seen as Bond That Draws 2 Nations Closer." *New York Times.* Retrieved from https://www.nytimes.com/2001/09/12/us/day-terror-israelis-spilled-blood-seen-bond-that-draws-2-nations-closer.html

Cohen, A. (1998). *Israel and the Bomb.* New York, NY: Columbia University Press.

Crosbie, S.K. (2015). *A Tacit Alliance: France and Israel from Suez to the Six Day War.* Princeton, NJ: Princeton University Press.

Fisk, R. (1993, December 6). "Anti-Soviet Warrior Puts His Army on the Road to Peace." *The Independent.* Retrieved from https://www.independent.co.uk/news/world/anti-soviet-warrior-puts-his-army-on-the-road-to-peace-the-saudi-businessman-who-recruited-mujahedin-1465715.html

Ganin, Z. (2005). *An Uneasy Relationship: American Jewish Leadership and Israel, 1948–1957.* Syracuse, NY: Syracuse University Press.

Huntington, S. (1996). *The Clash of Civilizations and the Remaking of the World Order.* New York, NY: Simon & Schuster.

Jacobson, G.C. (2010a). "George W. Bush, the Iraq War, and the Election of Barack Obama." *Presidential Studies Quarterly, 40*(2), 207–24. https://doi.org/10.1111/j.1741-5705.2010.03755.x

Jacobson, G.C. (2010b). "Perception, Memory, and Partisan Polarization on the Iraq War." *Political Science Quarterly*, *125*(1), 31–56. https://doi.org/10.1002/j.1538-165x.2010.tb00667.x

Judis, J.B. (2014). *Genesis: Truman, American Jews, and the Origins of the Arab/Israeli Conflict.* New York, NY: Farrar, Straus, Giroux.

Kinsella, D. (1994). "Conflict in Context: Arms Transfers and Third World Rivalries during the Cold War." *American Journal of Political Science*, *38*(3), 557–81. https://doi.org/10.2307/2111597

Mattar, P. (1994). "The PLO and the Gulf Crisis." *Middle East Journal*, *48*(1), 31–46. https://www.jstor.org/stable/4328660

Munayyer, Y. (2017, August 23). "How Your Favorite #NeverTrump Republicans Planted Seeds of His Rise to Power." *The Forward*. Retrieved from https://forward.com/opinion/politics/380633/never-trumpers-fueled-rise-of-white-supremacists-calling-obama-anti-israel/

Quandt, W.B. (2015). *Camp David: Peacemaking and Politics.* Washington, DC: Brookings Institution Press.

Truman, H.S. (1949). The President to Mr Mark F. Ethridge, at Jerusalem [Washington, April 29, 1949]. Office of the Historian. Retrieved January 15, 2018, from https://history.state.gov/historicaldocuments/frus1949v06/d617

Warner, G. (1991). "The United States and the Suez Crisis." *International Affairs*, *67*(2), 303–17. https://doi.org/10.2307/2620833

eight
BDS (Boycott, Divestment, and Sanctions)

One of the most common aspects of the question of social justice in Israel/ Palestine is the debate over BDS (Boycott, Divestment, and Sanctions against Israel). Given that international sanctions are a highly unlikely possibility, partially owing to the strength of the relationship between Israel and the United States, the debate mostly clusters around boycott (i.e., academic, cultural, and consumer) and divestment efforts (i.e., shifting investments away from companies that are perceived to support the occupation).

The debate over BDS hinges on two questions: Are the tactics themselves legitimate? And are the core demands of the movement fair and reasonable? How someone answers these two questions often reveals whether they see BDS as furthering the cause of social justice or as hindering it altogether.

Advocates of BDS answer in the affirmative to both questions. Because BDS is nonviolent, they argue, it is an appropriate and just method of resistance. They contend that because Palestinians—through a civil-society-wide call issued in 2005—have appealed for BDS, it is incumbent on human rights advocates to follow in turn. Even if BDS doesn't directly work, they say, Palestinians deserve to know that others are doing what they can in solidarity. They maintain that because no one knows definitively that this strategy won't work, we need to try, especially given the breadth of human rights violations entailed by the occupation, the civil rights deficit stemming from Israeli policies towards Palestinian citizens of Israel, and the injustice that stems, in this view, from not letting Palestinian refugees return.

As to the second of these questions—the justness of the BDS demands— BDS advocates argue that the call to end the occupation, the demand to bring about refugee return, and the demand to end inequality within Israel are all legal and ethical imperatives. On refugee return specifically, for example, they point to UN General Assembly Resolution 194, issued in December 1948. Among other things, this resolution states that "refugees wishing to return to their homes and live at peace with their neighbours should be permitted to do so at the earliest practicable date."

Critics of BDS point out problems with the movement's tactics and goals. Regarding tactics, they make the case that BDS singles out Israel when other and possibly much more egregious human rights abuses taking place elsewhere go unmentioned. Bristling at what they see as an attempt to delegitimize Israel, they claim that academic boycotts, specifically, undermine the value of academic freedom that undergirds the scholarly enterprise. Similarly, they note that cultural boycotts go against the spirit of the free flow of culture embodied in film, theater, and music.

Regarding the BDS movement's goals, critics claim that demanding refugee return would lead directly, and definitively, to the end of the Jewish state; Israel, they say, has a right to its core identity. (Some also point to the fact that Resolution 194, being a General Assembly rather than a Security Council resolution, is nonbinding.) They also argue that BDS does not draw a sufficient distinction between the State of Israel within the Green Line on one hand, and the occupied territories on the other.

The three essays in this chapter represent the scope of debate over BDS today. Tom Pessah and Amjad Iraqi each make the case for BDS. Pessah injects an added focus to the debate, however. He argues that anti-Semitism charges have been used as a weapon to delegitimize BDS; in addition to tracing the contours of the movement, his essay attempts to counter these charges. Iraqi's essay also adds a new element to the debate, by focusing on legislative attempts—in Israel, the United States, and elsewhere—to ban BDS. Finally, Rachel Fish's essay lays out the case against BDS, paying special attention to dynamics taking place on university and college campuses specifically and in the academy more broadly. She contends that the effects of BDS are not as benign as its proponents would have us believe.

BDS: A Diverse Movement in Support of Human Rights

TOM PESSAH

"BDS" stands for "Boycott, Divestment, and Sanctions." The term first appeared in a call to action issued on 9 July 2005 by a group of Palestinian civil society bodies. This statement called "upon international civil society organizations and people of conscience all over the world to impose broad boycotts and implement divestment initiatives against Israel similar to those applied to South Africa in the apartheid era" (BDS Movement, 2017). These initiatives are intended to force Israel to comply with international law in three main respects:

1. "Ending its occupation and colonization of all Arab lands and dismantling the Wall" [by "the Wall" they mean the barrier Israel has erected throughout the West Bank to facilitate the expropriation of Palestinian land];
2. "Recognizing the fundamental rights of the Arab-Palestinian citizens of Israel to full equality"; and
3. "Respecting, protecting and promoting the rights of Palestinian refugees to return to their homes and properties as stipulated in UN resolution 194."

According to the BDS movement's website (BDS Movement, 2017), the first goal, to end the occupation, refers to liberating the areas occupied since 1967—"the West Bank (including East Jerusalem), Gaza Strip and the Syrian Golan Heights." The second goal is to end discrimination against Palestinian citizens of Israel "proper." The third goal addresses the plight of the Palestinians who were displaced by Israel in 1948 by recognizing their families' right to return to the places where they resided in their ancestral homeland.

As regards the third goal, while successive Israeli governments have refused to discuss the possibility of a massive unconditional return of Palestinians to the country, Palestinians see this as a fundamental human right, anchored in international law (Awad, 2011). Many of the plans for accomplishing return do not involve massive displacement of the existing Jewish Israeli population. For example, Palestinian houses could be rebuilt on the sites of current parks and agricultural areas, many of which were literally built on top of Palestinian residences; and legal compromises could be reached in cases where Israelis directly occupy former Palestinian houses (Zochrot-Badil, 2012). Thus, as

Rachel Fish (this volume) notes, the aim is not merely to end the occupation; BDS proponents reject any Israeli demand to preserve a Jewish majority by violating *any* of these Palestinian rights. Maintaining the Jewish character of the state through such violations is seen as illegitimate.

The BDS call to action was signed by 170 bodies representing Palestinian labor federations, refugee networks, women's organizations, vocational associations, youth movements, cultural groups, and popular resistance committees based in the occupied territories, in Israel, and abroad. Since 2005, the list of supporting organizations has changed, but the movement has managed to maintain its independence from Israel, the Palestinian Authority (PA), Hamas, and the Arab states: none of these entities have ever endorsed BDS, nor do they dictate the movement's policies.

In November 2007, the first Palestinian BDS conference was held in Ramallah (occupied West Bank). This led to the consolidation of the Palestinian BDS National Committee (BNC), the body that became responsible for steering the international campaign. Since then, the Palestinian Campaign for the Academic and Cultural Boycott of Israel (PACBI), which is a member of the BNC, has issued guidelines for different types of boycotts (economic, cultural, and academic), detailing what is and what is not boycottable (BDS Movement, 2017).

For instance, Israeli artists performing abroad who are funded by the Israeli government to serve as "cultural ambassadors" are considered by BDS to be legitimate targets. But unlike their South African predecessors, individual Israeli artists—not funded by the Israeli state—are not to be targeted. Speakers from abroad should boycott Israeli universities complicit in human rights abuses (e.g., by enabling the development of weapons and legal doctrines that have been used against Palestinian civilians; Hever, 2009), yet there is no expectation that Palestinian and Jewish citizens of Israel refrain from participating in these institutions. Corporations complicit in the occupation are boycotted regardless of nationality, without singling out Israeli companies.

In addition to guidelines, the BNC issues specific calls for boycott which appear on their website and are publicized through social media. BNC members communicate with individuals worldwide regarding implementation.

The BNC cannot offer financial incentives for participation in boycotts. It is a small organization, whose main authority is moral, not legal. Grass roots groups of citizens from around the world mobilize in reaction to a specific call or demand that their church, for example, pull its investments from a corporation complicit in the occupation. These campaigns become valuable opportunities for sharing testimonies and information on the continual abuse of Palestinian human rights, thus keeping the issue in public consciousness despite Israel's efforts to the contrary.

Anti-Semitism and "Anti-Semitizing"

Previous Palestinian forms of resistance have been violently suppressed by Israel. There is no law guaranteeing the right to protest in the West Bank, and those who do so regularly face imprisonment. At the beginning of the second Intifada, hundreds of Palestinian protesters were shot despite not posing a threat to Israeli soldiers (Amnesty International, 2000). But because of BDS's international grass roots character, Israel cannot use such naked forms of force to stifle it. The most common alternative for the Israeli state and its supporters is to smear BDS activists as anti-Semitic.

"Anti-Semitism" is a term popularized in the late nineteenth century by those who genuinely believed in the existence of a malevolent Jewish "race" that "pure-blooded" Germans allegedly needed to defend themselves from. However, anti-Jewish prejudice is older than this term. The belief that Jews were collectively responsible for killing Jesus Christ was a standard part of Christian theology for centuries. In modern times, anti-Semites have attributed capitalism itself to rich Jewish bankers and their supposed quest for world domination. Even the well-documented genocide of over six million Jews during World War II is described by some anti-Semites as a falsehood created to further "Jewish power." Anti-Semitism functions as an ongoing set of tropes that have enabled persecution of Jews for centuries. Even in the absence of such visible scripts, we could assume some conscious or unconscious bias is present if Jews are treated differently for no evident reason. (For a deeper discussion, see Klug, 2014).

Yet, acknowledgement of this painful history does not preclude recognizing that accusations of anti-Semitism are often weaponized to smear critics of the Israeli state. Assertions that Israel is "worse than the Nazis" or that "the Zionists" are the biggest threat to global civilization are indeed modern-day variations on older anti-Semitic themes of omnipotent "Jewish power." But Israel's control over Palestinians, with its ongoing lethal results, cannot be hidden by invoking prejudice towards Jews. For instance, support for the right of Palestinian refugees to return to their ancestral homes cannot be reduced to anti-Semitism.

Israel's defenders sometimes suggest that Zionism means nothing other than Jewish self-determination, and that opposing Israel as a manifestation of this self-determination could only be a form of prejudice. Yet until the establishment of the State of Israel, most of the world's Jews did not support Zionism. Virtually all Orthodox Jews believed that only divine intervention—specifically the coming of the Messiah—could allow masses of Jews to gather in Palestine. The majority of Reform Jews saw their sacred mission as fulfilling their religious duties while advancing progress in the countries they resided in. In Tsarist Russia, extreme state oppression drove many Jews to become socialist revolutionaries aiming to overthrow the regime, not to establish a new state in the Middle East. Still others chose immigration to places other than Palestine or cultural assimilation. Even today most of the world's Jews choose to not reside in Israel.

In addition to the multiple non-Zionist visions of Judaism, many Jews and non-Jews have come to oppose Zionism on the basis of its treatment of Palestinians. From its beginning, Zionism was a project of colonization—granting Jews who settled in the country more rights than most of the existing population, who were expected either to become a minority in their own country or to be expelled. Palestinians have been displaced by Zionists since the late nineteenth century, a process that reached its peak in 1948, when military confrontation with the neighboring Arab countries became an opportunity for cleansing of an estimated 85 per cent of the Palestinian inhabitants of the area that became the State of Israel (Abu Lughod, 1971). The remaining Palestinians became second-class citizens in the State of Israel, losing much of their property; after 1967, those in the West Bank and Gaza became occupied subjects, suffering from ongoing state violence, home demolitions, and mass incarceration. Some were displaced from their lands in additional waves or incidents of ethnic cleansing that occur through to the present day. As mentioned, the Israeli regime has also forcefully prevented Palestinian refugees from returning to their homes. Clearly, disagreement with these dire consequences of Zionism cannot be reduced only to anti-Semitic sentiment, campus climate, and other reasons (Fish, this volume).

Fish argues that BDS supporters privilege opposition to Israel in relation to other progressive causes. In reality, BDS supporters are often active in other struggles, including labor issues, LGBTQ rights, lowering students' tuition, and opposing police brutality. Nevertheless, even if this were not the case, there are other legitimate reasons to focus on the Palestinian cause above others: having a Palestinian friend or family member; the centrality of Palestine within Christianity, Islam, and Judaism; seeing parallels with other forms of oppression (especially towards people of color); and more. As with all political issues, there is no "worst is first" rule: in order to get involved, it is not necessary to prove that the target is the world's worst abuser of human rights. In other words, most pro-Palestine activists are not driven by an anti-Jewish or anti-Israeli animus.

When such arguments against BDS fail, supporters of Israel and its policies attempt to "anti-Semitize" BDS supporters by painting their words and deeds as resembling traditional anti-Jewish tropes. Tying the BDS movement—including its calls for boycotting international companies providing weapons for the occupation—to Nazi-era boycotts of Jewish businesses, as Fish does in her essay, is an example of such "anti-Semitizing."

Addressing criticisms of Israel's policies on their merits would elicit a variety of reactions from the Jewish community, but anti-Semitizing pro-Palestine and BDS activists is more likely to mobilize the Jewish community against what are portrayed as existential threats. Such accusations also deflect attention from the criticism itself by focusing on the alleged character of the critics. In addition, these sensationalized reports are often guaranteed to receive media coverage, donors are more likely to support groups that present themselves as combating dangerous anti-Semitism, and it is easier to implement punitive measures against political opponents once their arguments are reduced to hate speech.

Activism on postsecondary campuses provides good illustrations of this phenomenon. In 2014, in an effort to raise awareness about Israel's house demolition policy in the West Bank, pro-Palestine students distributed mock eviction orders to all of the students residing in two New York University (NYU) dorms. At the bottom of each leaflet was a clear statement that "this is not a real eviction notice." Although the university has no separate dorms for Jewish students, the vice president of an NYU pro-Israel student group suggested that only Jewish students had been targeted. The NYU vice president for public affairs, the university's housing office, and the school's Jewish chaplain all denied the existence of a Jewish dorm. Nevertheless, the accusation was picked up by multiple media outlets, including the *New York Post*, *CBS New York*, and *The Times of Israel*. All these venues falsely reported that only Jewish students were served fake eviction notices, with the supposed aim of intimidating them (Nguyen, 2014). As this example demonstrates, rampant Islamophobia and anti-Arab sentiment in the media encourage the proliferation of such stories because they fit into existing stereotypes of fundamentalist, Jew-hating pro-Palestine activists.

There are hundreds of documented cases of false accusations of anti-Semitism made on campuses all over the United States. These include six high-profile investigations of universities by the Department of Education, none of which produced evidence of wrongdoing (Palestine Legal & Center for Constitutional Rights, 2015). These investigations demonstrate that—contrary to what Fish (this volume) suggests in her essay—such accusations are taken seriously by official bodies yet have usually been found to have no merit. Two recent academic studies provide further evidence that Jewish students in the United States feel safe and experience only low levels of prejudice (Kelman et al., 2017; Wright, Shain, Hecht, & Saxe, 2017).[1] Of course, this phenomenon of "anti-Semitizing" is not limited to the United States.

BDS Activists Combat Antisemitism

Both out of principle and because they are aware of the ways such accusations can derail their activities, BDS activists have been at the forefront of combating anti-Jewish prejudice within left-wing circles. In 2012, for example, a founder of the Free Gaza Movement, Greta Berlin, tweeted that "Zionists operated the concentration camps and helped murder millions of innocent Jews." Refusing to retract her statements, Berlin was shunned by BDS supporters in the United States, where she resides (Abunimah, 2012b).

The same year, leading BDS activists and several members of Students for Justice in Palestine were among the signatories of a Palestinian call to disavow Gilad Atzmon (Abunimah, 2012a). This ex-Israeli, ex-Jewish jazz musician has described the Holocaust as a myth, praised Nazism, and suggested that medieval fabrications about Jews' ritual murder of Christian children may have been true. Atzmon was denounced by these BDS activists despite attempting to promote himself as an ally to Palestinians.

In 2015, Alison Weir and her group If Americans Knew were removed from the membership of the US Campaign for Palestinian Rights, a coalition of hundreds of pro-Palestine organizations endorsing BDS. This step was taken after it emerged that Weir had made and promoted a series of anti-Jewish statements, including the idea that Jews themselves are the prime cause of anti-Semitism (US Campaign, 2015).

Jews and Israelis in the BDS Movement

Jews are actively engaged in many BDS-affiliated organizations. Jewish Voice for Peace, a major political group with over 60 chapters in the United States and 200,000 listserv subscribers, officially endorses BDS, as does the International Jewish Anti-Zionist Network and several Canadian and European groups of Jewish activists. Jews are also well represented in Students for Justice in Palestine, a movement with about 200 chapters in US universities and colleges.[2] Many leaders of the US Campaign for Palestinian Rights are Jewish, as well. If anti-Jewish sentiments within the BDS movement were as prevalent as Israel's supporters suggest, there would not be such a high proportion of Jews working alongside Palestinians and others to further the movement's goals. In fact, in contrast to most Zionist organizations, BDS supporters usually distinguish Zionism from Judaism and direct their criticism at the former, not the latter.

Israeli Jews are seen as potential allies by the BNC, whose website includes a translation of the BDS call into Hebrew. This document specifically invites "conscientious Israelis to support this Call, for the sake of justice and genuine peace" (Palestinian Civil Society, 2005). In the words of its co-founder, Omar Barghouti (paraphrasing renowned Brazilian educator Paolo Freire), the BDS movement strives to "restore the humanity of both oppressors and oppressed" (quoted in Horowitz & Weiss, 2015). In 2013, after British politician George Galloway refused to debate an Israeli student attending Oxford University, explaining his decision as based in his support of BDS (Williams, 2013), the BNC immediately issued a statement clarifying that "BDS does not call for a boycott of individuals because she or he happens to be Israeli" (BNC, 2013).

"Normalization" is a key term in the BDS movement's discussion of the role of Israelis. Its use became widespread in the Arab world after the Israeli peace treaty with Egypt (1978), to denounce informal social and economic initiatives treating Israel like a normal country, despite the fact that the oppression of the Palestinian people had not ended and was in fact deepening. At that time, antinormalization meant refusal to participate in any initiatives that Israelis are a part of. As a result of the failure of the Oslo accords and the continuation of the occupation, resistance to normalization in this sense is widespread today in the West Bank.

While the BDS movement shares this concern about treating unequal social and economic relationships with Israelis as normal, resulting in an acceptance of Palestinians' oppression, the solution it proposes is somewhat different. Rather than boycotting Israelis as such, based on their nationality, BDS supports a transition from normalization to "co-resistance." Co-resistance must be based on full support for Palestinian rights, whereby the relationship itself forms a means of resistance (e.g., a joint political action against the Separation Wall; Horowitz & Weiss, 2015; PACBI, 2012). As long as Israelis accept these conditions, they are welcome in the movement. This BDS interpretation of antinormalization is more widespread internationally, including in the United States and Europe. Israeli organizations that respect these conditions and promote BDS, based on full endorsement of Palestinian rights, include the Coalition of Women for Peace, the Israeli Committee against House Demolitions, the Alternative Information Center, and Boycott from Within.

However, given the social and political pressure against doing so, in the near future BDS is unlikely to be advocated for by more than the small minority of Israelis who have already done so.

As mentioned, Israel's official line is that BDS is nothing but a form of anti-Semitism. While this accusation is mostly false, it would also be an exaggeration to argue that the movement (like other movements with a non-Jewish majority) is entirely free of anti-Jewish animus. Some Jewish members report that outside speakers who expressed anti-Semitic sentiments have been hosted by BDS-affiliated groups and, on occasion, concerns about anti-Jewish language have not been taken seriously enough. BDS's commitment to universal principles of human rights does not suffice, in itself, to prevent bigotry within the movement, and constant vigilance against such bigotry remains crucial. Yet, most Jews in the movement do not report experiencing serious intolerance. It is worth emphasizing that the movement's sustained diversity and inclusion of both Jews and Palestinians stands in stark contrast to the relative religious and ethnic homogeneity of most Zionist groups.

Conclusion

The BDS movement is continuing to expand, despite Israel's efforts to suppress it by "anti-Semitizing" its participants. Much of the movement's strength derives from the diversity of its supporters, including the Movement for Black Lives and the Latin youth association MEXChA. Within this coalition, many Jews and some Israelis have found a place. The road towards accomplishing BDS's three major goals remains long, yet no other movement provides as much hope for supporters of Palestinians and universal human rights.

Tom Pessah is an Israeli sociologist and activist. He completed his BA in sociology and general history and his MA in sociology at Tel Aviv University. From 2005 to 2014 he studied at the University of California, Berkeley, where he received his PhD in sociology in 2014. His dissertation compared discussions of the cleansing of indigenous groups in several settler-colonial societies. Since returning to Israel he has taught at Ben-Gurion University and Hebrew University of Jerusalem. While at UC Berkeley, he was a member of the Students for Justice in Palestine chapter, participating in several divestment campaigns. He is currently a board member of Zochrot, an Israeli organization promoting recognition of the *Nakba* and the right of return.

Notes

1 Wright et al.'s (2017) study is based on a representative sample of Jewish students, unlike an earlier study (Saxe et al., 2016) cited by Fish, which surveyed only Birthright applicants and participants.

2 Students for Justice in Palestine is a decentralized, grass roots student movement. Typically, the funding of each of its chapters comes from local university student governments, together with fundraisers held for particular events. In addition, the movement receives free services from pro-Palestine NGOs such as Palestine Legal and Jewish Voice for Peace. Contrary to what Fish asserts in her essay, there is no evidence of any international funding directed at SJP chapters.

References

Abu Lughod, J. (1971). "The Demographic Transformation of Palestine." In I. Abu Lughod (ed.), *The Transformation of Palestine* (pp. 139–64). Evanston, IL: Northwestern University Press.

Abunimah, A. (2012a, March 13). "Palestinian Writers, Activists Disavow Racism, Anti-Semitism of Gilad Atzmon." *The Electronic Intifada*. Retrieved from https://electronicintifada.net/blogs/ali-abunimah/palestinian-writers-activists-disavow-racism-anti-semitism-gilad-atzmon

Abunimah, A. (2012b, October 18). "A Final Word on Greta Berlin and the Free Gaza Controversy." *The Electronic Intifada*. Retrieved from https://electronicintifada.net/blogs/ali-abunimah/final-word-greta-berlin-and-free-gaza-controversy

Amnesty International. (2000). *Israel and the Occupied Territories: Excessive Use of Lethal Force*. Retrieved from https://www.amnesty.org/en/documents/mde15/041/2000/en/

Awad, D. (2011, February 2). "Long Journey Home: The Right of Return, International Law, and the Fate of Palestinian Refugees." *Muftah*. Retrieved from https://muftah.org/the-long-journey-home-the-right-of-return-international-law-the-fate-of-palestinian-refugees-by-dina-awad/#.XC_GPs2xVPY

BNC. (2013, February 21). "BDS Movement Position on Boycott of Individuals." Retrieved from https://bdsmovement.net/news/bds-movement-position-boycott-individuals

Hever, S. (2009, October). *Academic Boycott of Israel and the Complicity of Israeli Academic Institutions in Occupation of Palestinian Territories* (Socioeconomic Bulletin no. 23). Jerusalem, Israel: Alternative Information Center. Retrieved from https://bdsmovement.net/files/2011/02/EOO23-24-Web.pdf

Horowitz, A., & Weiss, P. (2015, July 9). "The BDS Movement at 10: An Interview with Omar Barghouti." *Mondoweiss*. Retrieved from http://mondoweiss.net/2015/07/movement-interview-barghouti/

Kelman, A., Ahmed, A., Horwitz, I., Lockood, J., Shalev Marom, M., & Zuckerman, M. (2017). "Safe and on the Sidelines: Jewish Students and the Israel-Palestine Conflict on Campus." Sanford University Research Group of the Concentration in Education and Jewish Studies. Retrieved from https://sgs.stanford.edu/news/new-study-professor-kelman-finds-lower-levels-anti-semitism-us-universities

Klug, B. (2014, November). *What Do We Mean When We Say "Antisemitism"? Echoes of Shattering Glass*. Presentation at the conference Antisemitism in Europe Today: The Phenomena, the Conflicts, Berlin, Germany. Retrieved from https://www.jmberlin.de/sites/default/files/antisemitism-in-europe-today_2-klug.pdf

Nguyen, P. (2014, April 25). "Bait-and-Switch Anti-Semitism: NYU SJP Accused of Targeting Jews, or Not." *Mondoweiss*. Retrieved from http://mondoweiss.net/2014/04/semitism-accused-targeting/

PACBI (Palestinian Campaign for the Academic and Cultural Boycott of Israel). (2012, April 1). "Debating BDS: On Normalization and Partial Boycotts." Retrieved from http://www.pacbi.org/etemplate.php?id=1850

Palestine Legal & Center for Constitutional Rights. (2015). *The Palestine Exception to Free Speech*. Retrieved from https://palestinelegal.org/the-palestine-exception/

Palestinian Civil Society. (2005). "Palestinian Civil Society Call for BDS." Retrieved from https://bdsmovement.net/call

Saxe, L., Wright, G., Hecht, S., Shain, M., Sasson, T., & Chertok, F. (2016). *Hotspots of Antisemitism and Anti-Israel on US Campuses*. Waltham, MA: Steinhardt Social

Research Institute, Brandeis University. Retrieved from http://www.brandeis.edu/ssri/pdfs/campusstudies/AntisemitismCampuses101316.pdf

US Campaign for Palestinian Rights. (2015, July 16). "Statement on Complaint Filed Regarding Alison Weir and If Americans Knew." US Campaign to End the Israeli Occupation. Retrieved from https://uscpr.org/archive/article.php-id=4510.html

Williams, R. (2013, February 21). "'I Don't Debate with Israelis': George Galloway Accused of Racism after Walking out of Middle East Debate at Oxford." *The Independent*. Retrieved from http://www.independent.co.uk/news/uk/politics/i-dont-debate-with-israelis-george-galloway-accused-of-racism-after-walking-out-of-middle-east-8505232.html

Wright, G., Shain, M., Hecht, S., & Saxe, L. (2017). *The Limits of Hostility: Students Report on Anti-Semitism and Anti-Israel Sentiment on Campus*. Waltham, MA: Steinhardt Social Research Institute, Brandeis University. Retrieved from https://www.brandeis.edu/ssri/noteworthy/fourcampuses.html#.WjfOLSLuIEs.facebook

Zochrot-Badil. (2012). "Study Visit to Cape Town." *Zochrot*. Retrieved from http://zochrot.org/en/article/54464

BDS: Binaries, Divisions, and Silencing

RACHEL FISH

The Boycott, Divestment, and Sanctions (BDS) campaign has not occurred in a vacuum. A larger context of events provides an important backdrop for the emergence of the BDS movement. As Tom Pessah (this volume) writes, the BDS call to action uses activist language to change Israeli government policy through boycotting, which is an expression of nonviolence intended to address the inequalities Palestinians face.

On American college campuses, however, the reality of the BDS movement's influence is not as benign as Pessah and Amjad Iraqi (this volume) suggest. Iraqi argues that anti-BDS legislation attempts to limit protected speech under the First Amendment. However, the BDS legislative conversation is less about Palestinian political equality than about expressions of anti-Jewish politics and an undercurrent of delegitimization of the State of Israel.

History of Boycotts

The BDS movement emerged within a wider context of historical boycotts or sanctions against Jews, Jewish products, and the modern State of Israel. During different periods, Jewish products made by and services provided by Jewish communities were boycotted, most saliently in 1920s and 1930s Europe under Hitler's regime. In Palestine during the period of the *Yishuv* (the pre-state Jewish community in Palestine), Arab shopkeepers began an economic boycott of Jewish shopkeepers in 1921, around the time the first Arab riots erupted. These specific boycotts, aimed at the Jewish state generally rather than at any particular Israeli governmental actions, form the context in which the Boycott, Divestment, and Sanctions movement would emerge in the period immediately after the 2001 Durban conference.

WCAR

The World Conference Against Racism, Racial Discrimination, Xenophobia, and Related Intolerance (WCAR), held in Durban, South Africa, in 2001, a few months prior to the attacks of 9/11, created a platform for the demonization and delegitimization of Israel (Brackman, 2013), especially at the NGO (nongovernmental organization) Forum held in Kingsmead Stadium.

The WCAR Declaration of Principles condemned Israel for war crimes, ethnic cleansing, and genocide. Throughout the conference the label "apartheid state" was repeatedly applied to only one nation-state, Israel. With this pejorative term, Israel replaced South Africa, similarly shamed among the world's NGO community (UN, 2001), as an international pariah. The strategy was to isolate Israel in all possible arenas—diplomatic, economic, military collaboration, social, and welfare—calling for all states to sever their links with Israel via embargoes or sanctions. Meanwhile the distribution of the notorious anti-Semitic pamphlet *The Protocols of the Elders of Zion* and other anti-Semitic paraphernalia fanned the flames of hatred against and bigotry towards Jews (BBC, 2002; Elliot, 2001).

In the immediate wake of the Durban conference, boycott and divestment movements against Israel began to emerge. By 2002, a group of European academics were advocating for an academic boycott of Israel (*The Guardian*, 2002). At the same time, divestment petitions began circulating on American college campuses, including Harvard, MIT (where the divestment movement against Israel began), Princeton, Columbia, and throughout the University of California system. In 2003 and 2004, European churches as well as mainline Protestant churches of the United States were calling for divestment from Israel. By co-opting language more commonly seen in social justice movements and adopting successionist anti-Jewish versions of liberation theology, a new understanding of the Palestinian-Israeli conflict emerged.

BDS

Palestinian organizations voiced their BDS platforms beginning in 2002 through the "Palestinian NGO Network," calling for a comprehensive boycott of Israel. Thereafter, in 2004, the Palestinian Campaign for the Academic and Cultural Boycott of Israel (PACBI) was founded (BNC, 2017).

The language of the BDS movement's core documents does not frame its goals in a spirit of coexistence, shared society, or peace building. The principles of the BDS movement claim that Israel was built "mainly on land ethnically cleansed of its Palestinian owners and that a majority of Palestinians are refugees, most of whom are stateless." The document proceeds to demand that Israel: (1) end its occupation and colonization of all Arab lands and dismantle the security barrier or Wall; (2) recognize the fundamental rights of the Arab-Palestinian citizens of Israel to full equality; and (3) respect protecting and promoting the rights of Palestinian refugees to return to their homes and properties as stipulated in UN Resolution 194 (BNC, 2017). This language suggests that all of Israel is on Arab land that must be reclaimed by the Palestinians. There is no delineation between events from 1948 and 1967. The reference to the "Wall" does not address why the security barrier was built—not as a border but as a way to limit terrorism and infiltrators seeking to harm Israeli civilians. The issue of refugees remains an unresolved final status issue in future negotiations between Israelis and Palestinians.

BDS emphasizes the renewal of a Palestinian presence throughout the land of Israel while simultaneously rejecting the existence of a Jewish state. BDS advocates, including those on American university and college campuses, see Israel's "original sin" as rooted not in the 1967 war, when Israel gained control of East Jerusalem, the West Bank, Gaza, the Sinai Peninsula, and the Golan Heights, but in the wake of 1948—the establishment of the State of Israel itself. This view considers Zionism fundamentally a colonialist movement that displaced Arabs, rather than a national movement for political liberation and self-determination for the Jewish people. These two narratives are nonintersecting parallel lines and cannot be reconciled.

A Climate of Hostility on American College Campus

Each university environment is unique; each campus community decides whether or not BDS should have a place on campus and to what degree. On many North American campuses, small, extremely vocal groups of students and faculty advocate BDS in local chapters of nationally and internationally funded advocacy organizations and supporters, such as Students for Justice in Palestine (Bard, 2015; NGO Monitor, 2015; Schanzer, 2016; Schiffmiller, 2016). The BDS framework—with its refusal to normalize any aspect of Israel—puts students and faculty with connections to Israel on the defensive; BDS discourse intentionally flattens any complexity or nuance in discussions about Israel or in explorations of related issues.

In general, two different types of groups on college and university campuses engage in BDS activism. The first are those who are personally deeply engaged with Israel/Palestine. Some of them claim that the entire Jewish national project is illegitimate, either because they do not believe in the creation of any nation-state, or because they do not believe the Jewish people in particular have a claim to statehood, or they feel that Palestinian injustice needs to be rectified. In contrast, others are connected to Israel but are, or have become, harsh critics of Israeli policies. Those in this latter group may have been critical of the occupation or other Israeli policies for a long while, and in frustration have moved from connected criticism, or partial boycott, to support for the BDS campaign.

This second audience largely consists of those on campus identifying as progressive and/or liberal. Their understanding is that the BDS movement is generally aligned with their social justice worldview. But they also go much further—their rhetoric emphasizes that Israel is the most salient state violator of human rights, ignoring human rights abuses in other countries altogether.

This has the paradoxical effect of aligning progressives who support BDS with advocates of repressive regimes they might otherwise oppose.

On campus the majority of progressive student groups ranging from Black Lives Matters to students of color, LGBTQ, feminist, religious, and other similarly identified groups, partially due to the language of intersectional oppression, unite their distinct positions into a monolithic voice against Israel in ways that privilege BDS over other progressive causes. Such campus progressives do not compare the status of LGBTQ individuals, women, ethnic or religious minorities in Muslim-majority countries or the Palestinian territories to those constituencies in Israel. Similarly, there is little focus on the Syrian regime's genocide against its own citizenry nor on female genital mutilation and child marriage, both of which occur in parts of the Islamic world. Instead, Palestinianism has become an indispensable component in the suite of litmus tests for campus progressives.

In an era of identity politics, students who are the "other" in relation to gender, race, feminism, immigrant status, or socioeconomic class seem to have been afforded an enhanced status on campus. Those who identify as Zionists, however, are an exception to this rule. Many if not most campus Zionists, like other American Jews, are themselves active in some of these same progressive causes. But to BDS advocates, any support of Israel is deemed to be a form of oppression. Students or faculty who vocalize support for Israel are routinely labeled imperialists, colonialists, apartheid advocates, and even "Nazis," often finding themselves excluded from social justice spaces.

From Postmodernism to Silencing Debate

Systemic features of modern university life, especially in connection with the humanities, tend to transform multi vocal critiques of Israeli policy into a kind of BDS advocacy that shuts down meaningful conversations. The primary postmodern tenet in this context is all "truths" are equal and "facts" are subordinate to one's "truth." The intellectual elements that make up a culture hostile to the Jewish state explore implicit power dynamics, such as ideas stemming from Orientalism, Marxism, postcolonialism, postnationalism, and multiculturalism.

Edward Said's (1978) influence through his book *Orientalism* has helped shape this discourse not only in Middle East studies specifically but in the humanities generally. Arguably, its core tenet is that Westerners cannot understand, explain, or properly study Arab-majority and Muslim-majority countries. Said contends that colonial views exoticize and oppress indigenous populations, shaping the political realities of colonized people in the process. As a corrective to Orientalism, Said and those influenced by him argue that the truth about a given culture and society can come only from people within it. Consequently, Western critical thought about the Arab and Islamic worlds are often perceived as racist or supremacist.

Marxist critique, in the twenty-first century, as applied throughout the humanities, is less often about economic approaches and more about power dynamics. Campus discourses, influenced by scholarship that focuses on power dynamics, produce caricatures of it, in which wealth and power are inherently evil, the poor are inherently moral, and the intellectual's task is to weaken the powerful and empower the weak. Race, class, and gender are the primary lenses for analysis within the humanities. In this paradigm, the "weaker" group is privileged in scholarship. In this equation, the Palestinians' lesser state power means they are more appropriate recipients of scholarly advocacy.

Post colonialism is a view that condemns all actions of the Western world and lionizes indigenous people as the only ones able to understand themselves and to dismantle the effects of the colonial. Associating Israel primarily with early European Zionists of the late nineteenth and early twentieth century while eliding the largely Middle Eastern background of the majority of Israeli Jews, BDS advocates on campus see Israel as an imperial, white European outpost in the Middle East where all the other peoples are deemed "indigenous": one can hear the echo of the twentieth century anti-Semitic critique of Jews as "rootless cosmopolitans."

Post nationalism, on the other hand, blames the nation-state for the problems of the world and lauds internationalism and the idea of a "flat world" where globalization is deemed the ideal. A nation-state such as Israel, which privileges or prioritizes one particular people at the expense of another, is deemed anachronistic. This is particularly true of Jews who are often seen as holding purely a confessional identity, as being part of a religious group only, and not also as possessing an historical identity as a people.

Taken together, these intellectual currents formulate a political culture that permeates the university environment, creating fertile ground for the demonization of the State of Israel. Without dismantling this reigning cognitive paradigm, or at least mounting a credible, serious assault upon it, the chances of Israel getting fair treatment in the academy are dim.

Structural Challenges in the University

As a result of the near-complete victory of this dominant ideology, systemic or structural factors within academia contribute to the vilification of Israel that BDS has shaped. Three of these structural aspects are: area studies, faculty, and the administration.

Area Studies

The emergence of area studies within the academy has created an interdisciplinary approach that emphasizes identity politics and claims. Area studies arose in the 1960s and 1970s partially in response to the exclusion of specific populations and perspectives from the academy; consequently, it has always included a measure of activism alongside its scholarship. This is most evident in Middle East studies programs.

Funding from Arab countries, governments, and leaders for programs in Middle Eastern studies, Arab studies, and Islamic studies often encourage a one-sided perspective regarding Israel and Israeli history. Multi million dollar gifts to institutions such as Harvard, Georgetown, and Columbia University indicate the scope of this trend. However, many universities do not disclose such gifts, making the financial influence less visible. Harvard has accepted $20 million from the Saudi Prince Al-Walid bin Talal bin Abdul Aziz for the Center for Middle East Studies. Al-Walid bin Talal has also given Georgetown University $20 million for the Center for Muslim-Christian Understanding. University of Arkansas has an endowment from King Fahd of Saudi Arabia for $20 million for the Center for Middle East and Islamic Studies. Columbia University has received endowments from both the UAE and Saudi donors for the Edward Said chair for over $2 million. All one has to do is review the "Disclosures of Foreign Gifts," document reported under Title 20, section 1011f on the US code. In addition to the outright purchasing of chairs and centers, many Middle Eastern leaders and governments provide other forms of support that are more difficult to document, including scholarship programs, travel grants, and publication grants. Some "outreach" activities provide classroom materials and use Saudi-sponsored material in teacher-training seminars and trips for public school educators to Middle Eastern countries to learn about the Arab world and Islam (Stotsky, 2004). Typically, these materials offer a skewed presentation of the Islamic world or a highly polemical portrayal of Israel rather than a nuanced understanding of either.

Faculty

Naturally, faculty members across a range of disciplines hold a spectrum of political views on subjects, including Israel/Palestine. Faculty members who articulate positions supportive of Israel's right to exist as a Jewish and democratic state, however, often encounter professional and personal consequences, even if their fields are entirely unrelated to the issue (Flaherty, 2014; Leger Online, 2015; Pessin & Ben-Atar, 2018; Sales, 2017). On a professional level, they may not be invited to speak at particular conferences, publish with specific presses, or they may be silenced within campus discourses about Israel. Consequently, some faculty who believe in articulating a nuanced and sophisticated position about Israel often remain silent and avoid campus politics, fearful of being labeled the "AIPAC Professor" on campus.

Faculty are also faced with the increased challenge of confronting BDS in their professional academic associations, including not only the Middle East Studies Association but also the Modern Language Association, the American Studies Association, and the American Anthropological Association, where resolutions to adopt an academic boycott against Israel have been put to a vote. As in progressive student politics, academics far afield from their area of expertise may find that BDS is a litmus test: opposing it risks isolating them from colleagues and other scholars. Those opposed to BDS have described feeling intimidated in such encounters, expressing that they feel BDS advocates have created hostile environments and cultivated a mob mentality in these academic associations (Nelson, 2018).

University Administrations

Unlike private donations, gifts to American universities by the governments of Saudi Arabia, the UAE, and others typically come with precise accompanying directives. Understandably, university administrations often want to meet these terms, thus preserving these relationships. They are also interested in avoiding confrontation with Muslim students. Both of these pressures, along with the general culture on college campuses regarding political correctness, make many administrators insensitive towards Jewish concerns. Inherently conflict averse, administrators often hide behind the academic freedom of their faculty members to avoid having to address hostility towards Israel-supporting faculty or students directly.

Moreover, university presidents appropriately committed to protecting free speech find it challenging to distinguish free speech from hate speech in the context of Israel. Many university presidents exercise a double standard that does not recognize Jews as a minority but only as part of a larger powerful white majority, therefore not in need of, or entitled to, the sensitivity and protection given to other minorities.

In contrast, former president of Harvard University Larry Summers labeled the divestment movement against Israel as "antisemitic in effect if not intent" on the first day of class in September 2002 (Arenson, 2002). It was a powerful statement, since many university administrators facing the BDS movement—the divestment movement's successor—were and remain unwilling to speak publicly in their condemnation of hate speech towards the Jewish state.

Conclusion

In their essays, Tom Pessah and Amjad Iraqi (this volume) each emphasize the legitimacy of boycott as a tactic for pressuring the State of Israel. There is no boycott taking place on American campuses, nor are universities really endorsing it. But the rhetoric around BDS does have a real consequence and it is not benign: it puts Israel-supporting faculty and students, especially those who are Jewish students, on the defensive, even outside of political conversations. BDS prevents constructive and educational conversations. The long-term cost of the BDS movement on campuses is that students find themselves shrinking from opportunities to engage in conversations about Israel. Voices are silenced, due to both self-censorship and intimidation; conversations are deemed to be overly polarizing, highly polemical, and thus attract extremes on each side (Fish & Borenstein, 2018).

Rachel Fish is a senior advisor and resident scholar of Jewish/Israel philanthropy at the Paul E. Singer Foundation in New York City. Most recently she was the executive director of the Schusterman Center for Israel Studies at Brandeis University. She completed her doctoral degree in 2013 in the Near Eastern and Judaic Studies department at Brandeis University, where she researched the history of the idea of binationalism and alternative visions for constructing the State of Israel. She has taught at Brandeis University, Harvard University, UMass Amherst, and Tzion and Me'ah, adult Jewish education programs. In 2015 she held the Rohr Visiting Professorship at Harvard University, where she lectured on modern Israel and received the Derek Bok Certificate of Teaching Excellence. She is co-editor, with Ilan Troen, of the book *Essential Israel: Essays for the Twenty-First Century* (Indiana University Press, 2017).

References

Arenson, K.W. (2002, September 21). "Harvard President Sees Rise in Anti-Semitism on Campus." *New York Times*. Retrieved from https://www.nytimes.com/2002/09/21/us/harvard-president-sees-rise-in-anti-semitism-on-campus.html

Bard, M. (2015, October 14). "BDS Money Trail Suggests Opaque Funding Network." *New York Jewish Week*. Retrieved from http://jewishweek.timesofisrael.com/bds-money-trail-suggests-opaque-funding-network/

BBC. (2002, November 21). "Mary Robinson, UN Human Rights Chief: Talking Points Special." *BBC News World Edition*. Retrieved from http://news.bbc.co.uk/2/hi/talking_point/forum/1673034.stm

BNC (Boycott Divestment Sanctions National Committee). (2017). "Boycott Divestment Sanctions National Committee." Retrieved May 25, 2018, from https://bdsmovement.net/bnc

Brackman, H. (2013, March). *Boycott, Divestment, Sanctions against Israel: An Anti-Semitic, Anti-Peace Poison Pill*. Simon Wiesenthal Center. Retrieved from http://www .wiesenthal.com/atf/cf/%7B54d385e6-f1b9-4e9f-8e94-890c3e6dd277%7D/ REPORT_313.PDF

Elliot, M. (2001, September 9). "The Racism Conference, the Disgrace in Durban." *Time Magazine Online*. Retrieved from http://content.time.com/time/world/ article/0,8599,174283,00.html

Fish, R., & Borenstein, M. (2018, March 13). "The Case for Rigorous Israel Education for High School Students." *eJewish Philanthropy*. Retrieved from http://ejewishphilanthropy .com/the-case-for-rigorous-israel-education-for-high-school-students/

Flaherty, C. (2014, August 15). "In a Hurricane." *Inside Higher Ed*. Retrieved from https:// www.insidehighered.com/news/2014/08/15/cary-nelson-faces-backlash-over -his-views-controversial-scholar

The Guardian. (2002, April 6). "More Pressure for Mid East Peace." Retrieved from https://www.theguardian.com/world/2002/apr/06/israel.guardianletters

Leger Online. (2015, April 22). "Conn College Took the Low Road in the Case Of Andrew Pessin." *Connecticut Jewish Ledger*. Retrieved from http://www.jewishledger.com/ 2015/04/conn-college-took-the-low-road-in-the-case-of-andrew-pessin/

Nelson, C. (2018, January 6). "Judith Butler Plans a Stealth MLA Presidency." *Jewish Journal*. Retrieved from http://jewishjournal.com/opinion/229428/judith-butlers -plans-stealth-mla-presidency/

NGO Monitor. (2015, November 22). "BDS on American Campuses: SJP and Its NGO Network." Retrieved from https://www.ngo-monitor.org/reports/bds_on _american_campuses_sjp_and_its_ngo_network/

Pessin, A., & Ben-Atar, D.S. (eds). (2018). *Anti-Zionism on Campus: The University, Free Speech, and BDS*. Bloomington, IN: University of Indiana Press.

Said, E. (1978). *Orientalism*. New York, NY: Pantheon Books.

Sales, B. (2017, September 20). "University of Maryland Professor Says She Was Fired for Being Pro-Israel." *Times of Israel*. Retrieved from https://www.timesofisrael.com/ university-of-maryland-professor-says-she-was-fired-for-being-pro-israel/

Schanzer, J. (2016, April 19). "Israel Imperiled: Threats to the Jewish State." Foundation for Defense of Democracies. Retrieved from https://docs.house.gov/meetings/FA/ FA18/20160419/104817/HHRG-114-FA18-Wstate-SchanzerJ-20160419.pdf

Schiffmiller, Y. (2016, November 25). "The Rockefeller BDS Empire, the New Israel Fund, and Campus Anti-Semitism." *Jewish News Syndicate*. Retrieved from https://www.jns .org/the-rockefeller-bds-empire-the-new-israel-fund-and-campus-anti-semitism/

Stotsky, S. (2004). *The Stealth Curriculum: Manipulating America's History Teachers*. Washing- ton, DC: Thomas B. Fordham Foundation. Retrieved from https://files.eric.ed.gov/ fulltext/ED485533.pdf

Taraki, L. (2004, August 19). "Boycotting the Israeli Academy." *Znet*. Retrieved from https://zcomm.org/znetarticle/boycotting-the-israeli-academy-by-lisa-taraki/

United Nations. (2001, January 31). *Durban Declaration and Programme of Action*. Retrieved from http://www.un.org/WCAR/durban.pdf

Weiss, M. (2017, August 25). "Arab League Boycott of Israel." Congressional Research Service. Retrieved from https://fas.org/sgp/crs/mideast/RL33961.pdf

The Right to Boycott Is Nonnegotiable

AMJAD IRAQI

In March 2017, Benjamin Cardin, a Democratic senator from Maryland, introduced a congressional bill prohibiting people in the United States from engaging in boycotts against Israel. Written as an amendment to the 1979 Export Administration Act, which originally aimed to counter the Arab League's ban on economic relations with Israel, the Israel Anti-Boycott Act proposes that offenders be punished with civil fines of up to $250 thousand, or criminal penalties of up to $1 million (COTUS, 2018). The original version of the bill, which was partially amended in March 2018 following heavy pushback from civil society groups and lawmakers, even imposed prison sentences of up to 20 years for engaging in such boycotts.

Cardin's bill is part of a wave of US laws aiming to counter the Palestinian-led Boycott, Divestment, and Sanctions (BDS) movement. As of early 2018, 24 state legislatures have enacted some form of anti-BDS legislation, with more bills being considered in other states and at the federal level (Palestine Legal, 2018). Governors are also considering issuing executive orders that will require their states to blacklist and divest from companies and institutions that engage in boycotts of Israel; Maryland, New York, and Wisconsin have already done so. After signing his order in June 2016, New York governor Andrew Cuomo (2016) declared in the *Washington Post*: "If you boycott Israel, New York will boycott you."

The implementation of these laws has often been taken to ludicrous levels. After Hurricane Harvey struck Texas in August 2017, residents in the city of Dickinson had to declare that they would not participate in boycotts of Israel as a condition for receiving relief grants (Gajanan, 2017). In December 2017, the ACLU filed a lawsuit on behalf of Mikkel Jordhal, an attorney in Arizona, after he was obliged to sign a similar agreement in order to contract with the state to represent local indigent prisoners (Yachot, 2017). In January 2018, following another ACLU petition, a federal judge issued an injunction against Kansas's anti-BDS law after Esther Koontz, a public school teacher, refused to sign the same declaration as a condition for employment. (Koontz is a member of the Mennonite Church, which endorses BDS.) "You don't need to share my beliefs," said Koontz, "or agree with my decisions to understand that this law violates my free speech rights. The state should not be telling people what causes they can or can't support" (Eidelman, 2018).

The Palestine Exception

The scale of the anti–BDS crackdown is startling. Historically, boycotts are a legitimate form of political expression, praised in textbooks and modern politics as an example of how nonviolence can be a powerful, moral, and strategic tool for advancing human rights struggles. In the United States, political boycotts are meant to be stringently protected under the First Amendment, backed by years of clear Supreme Court jurisprudence.

Now, in a perverse twist, the very countries that purport to uphold civil liberties have become the main forces undermining them. Governments, universities, and local authorities are rewriting laws and regulations that effectively impose a price tag on citizens' right to boycott for the Palestinian cause (Greenwald & Fishman, 2016). Criticism of Israel now falls under the purview of new definitions of anti-Semitism in the United Kingdom and United States. Several BDS activists in France have been criminally convicted and bank accounts of BDS groups have been shut down, while BDS-affiliated accounts in Germany are also facing closures. Local councils in the United Kingdom have also been threatened with penalties if they opt to boycott Israeli goods or divest from the Israeli defense industry.

This "Palestine exception" to the right to boycott follows a long legacy of attempts by states, corporations, and other institutions to thwart the potential of nonviolence to challenge abuses of power (Iraqi, 2017). In claiming a unique status as the only Jewish state in the world, Israel and its supporters portray the Palestinians' use of boycotts as a hostile campaign driven by anti-Jewish hatred, with some equating it to violence and even terrorism; this view is also echoed by Rachel Fish (this volume). Why, they ask, would anyone disparage the "only democracy in the Middle East" if not out of anti-Semitism? Even many liberals argue that although boycotts may be lawful, they should not be exercised against Israel because they impose a discriminatory double standard and undermine peace. A simple glance at world history, and at the intentions behind these accusations, show that this is far from the case.

History of Boycotts

Although today's BDS movement was officially launched in 2005, as Tom Pessah (this volume) describes, boycotts and other forms of civil disobedience have been used by Palestinians and solidarity groups throughout the past century, as Fish (this volume) also notes (Munayyer, 2011). The first Intifada (1987–93), in which Palestinians in the West Bank and Gaza launched general strikes and an economic boycott of Israeli products and institutions, particularly serves as a major inspiration for Palestinian nonviolence and grass roots resistance to this day.

These efforts were hindered in the 1990s by the political and economic configurations of the Oslo Accords, which saw Israeli goods flood the Palestinian market while Israeli settlements expanded their control over Palestinian resources (Arafeh, 2017). The newly formed Palestinian Authority (PA), whose elites gained lucrative benefits from the colonial economy, attacked Palestinian critics of the accords and suppressed nonviolent protests in coordination with the Israeli army (Tartir, 2017). It was only after the second Intifada (2000–2005), the subsequent Palestinian political vacuum, and Israel's retrenchment of its occupation that Palestinian civil society was able to re-mobilize and revive its boycott strategies on a mass scale, culminating in the BDS declaration in 2005 and the creation of the BDS National Committee (BNC) in 2007.

The BDS movement is not only a continuance of Palestinian political tradition, but also derives its inspiration, directly and indirectly, from countless local and international boycott campaigns throughout history. The most famous of these include the Indian Swadeshi movement against British colonial rule in the early 1900s; the Montgomery bus boycott against racial segregation in the United States in 1955–56; and the BDS campaign against apartheid in South Africa in the 1960s–80s. Other examples include a Jewish civil society boycott of Nazi Germany in the 1930s; the Delano grape strike for workers' rights in California in the 1960s; long-term consumer boycotts of clothing lines that use sexist advertisements or exploit foreign workers; boycotts against the trading of conflict or "blood diamonds" from African countries; and divestment campaigns against the fossil fuel industry. The list goes on.

"Different Standards"

The historical intolerance of states towards boycott campaigns served as warning signs for the Palestinians, who expected heavy reprisals for their BDS efforts. When European and American Jewish organizations called for an economic boycott of Nazi Germany, the Reich launched its own boycott of Jewish businesses and intensified its anti-Jewish persecutions (Jewish Virtual Library, 2018.). The Swadeshi movement's boycott of British goods in India was met with brutal violence and divide-and-conquer tactics by the colonial power. Black Americans who joined the Montgomery bus boycott were beaten and arrested by law enforcement authorities, and scores of civil rights leaders were criminally indicted (*Stanford Daily*, 1956). Performers and activists who called for boycotts and sanctions against apartheid South Africa were blacklisted and targeted by Pretoria's intelligence services. Arguably, no act of political nonviolence has ever gone unpunished.

Ironically, Israel's demand for an exception to this revered history of boycotts is itself unexceptional. In a 1989 op-ed in *The Christian Science Monitor*, academic Anne-Marie Kriek, echoing the South African government's talking points, chastised the world for its apparent obsession with the apartheid regime. Praising white-minority rule for bringing unparalleled standards of living and peace to the continent, Kriek (1989) claimed that the anti-apartheid movement's goal was to "condition hatred for South Africa" based on "sensationalized and distorted" criticisms of the country. "Why," she asked, "is South Africa so harshly condemned while completely different standards apply to black Africa?"

The same narrative, which is employed almost word-for-word by Israel advocates today, is also found in Fish's essay (this volume). Her analysis leaves the impression that Palestinians have little cause for discontent against Israel, except for racist animosity. Her attempt to link the tactics of BDS—a nonviolent, grass roots, and rights-based movement—with the anti-Semitic motives of the Nazi regime—a militaristic, fascist, and genocidal state—is meant to conceal the knowledge that boycotts have a proven record of promoting struggles that most in the twenty-first century recognize as just. It would be hard to imagine Fish describing the boycotts in India, the United States, or South Africa as founded upon anti-white hatred, or the Jewish-led boycott of the Reich as anti-German propaganda, instead of a strategy to defend black, brown, and Jewish human rights. Palestinian BDS is no different. As Pessah (this volume) notes, there is no "worst is first" rule when boycotting human rights abusers: if there is injustice, there will be resistance.

"Political Terror"

Initial legal victories have signaled that many of today's anti-BDS laws may not survive judicial scrutiny. A British administrative court ruled in June 2017 that the government's attempt to block local councils from boycotting Israel was unlawful and done with "improper purpose" (Jamal, 2017). The US federal judge who froze Kansas's law in January 2018 found that the state was imposing a "plainly unconstitutional choice" on citizens: "This is either viewpoint discrimination against the opinion that Israel mistreats Palestinians or subject matter discrimination to the topic of Israel. Both are impermissible goals under the First Amendment" (Foundation for Middle East Peace, 2018).

Bizarrely, Israel's Supreme Court reached a similar conclusion when it examined the country's own anti-boycott law, enacted by the Knesset in

2011—but, in contrast, it ruled that BDS, not the Israeli government, was responsible for the offense. The court approved the law in a 5–4 ruling in April 2015, thus allowing Israeli citizens to sue individuals or groups that call for a boycott of "a person, or other entity, solely because of their affiliation with the State of Israel, one of its institutions, or an area under its control, in such a way that may cause economic, cultural or academic harm" (Supreme Court of Israel, 2015). The first such lawsuit was filed in January 2018 against New Zealand activists Nadia Abu-Shanab and Justine Sachs (the former Palestinian and the latter Jewish), after they wrote an open letter that persuaded the singer Lorde to cancel her concert in Tel Aviv (Eglash, 2018).

The petitioners against the anti-boycott law—a coalition of Palestinian and Jewish human rights organizations and activists in Israel—argued that it was a blatant attack on civil rights aimed at chilling political dissent. The judges, however, openly embraced this goal. The court admitted that the law violated freedom of expression, but believed that this violation was reasonable and proportionate because the law was pursuing a "worthy aim": to protect Israelis from the "discrimination" of boycotts, and to "prevent harm to Israel's standing in the world, or harm to its relations with other countries" (Adalah, 2017).

Justice Hanan Melcer, who wrote the leading opinion for the majority, claimed that boycotts could be considered a form of "political terror." Justice Elyakim Rubinstein, citing biblical texts and Jewish history, wrote that "there is nothing wrong in anchoring laws passed by the Knesset in the struggle against those who wish to destroy us." Justice Yitzhak Amit, who quipped that BDS could stand for "Bigoted, Dishonest, and Shameful," declared, "There is something Orwellian in the petitioners' claim that the law restricts freedom of speech"; boycotts, he said, were not a product of free expression but a strategy to silence it, "to make one opinion and one 'truth'" (Marom, 2015). He seemed immune to the conspicuous irony that he, a representative of the country's highest legal authority, was the very subject of Orwell's warnings.

"One Truth"

The Supreme Court's ruling contains a more important revelation. By accepting the government's commitment to protect the "areas under its control" from BDS, the judges admitted that, as far as Israeli law is concerned, the settlements in the West Bank are an integral part of Israel's national consciousness. It is hardly the first time that the court has expressed this view—several judges hail from settlements themselves—but it is one of its most explicit acknowledgements. And there, embedded in the ruling, lies the real motive behind Israel's anti-boycott campaign: after five decades of occupation, it has little to no interest in abandoning its hold of the Palestinian territories, nor the discriminatory system that privileges Jews over non-Jews (Thrall, 2017).

In fact, emboldened by its impunity, the Knesset has been passing laws to formally annex large swaths of the West Bank. The newly opened US embassy in Jerusalem straddles the invisible Green Line that once delineated the occupied east from the west, symbolically entrenching Israel's claim to the city as its "eternal and undivided capital." Israeli center-left parties, echoing the far-right's rhetoric, are vowing to maintain Israel's presence in "Judea and Samaria." The colonial ideology that subjugates Palestinians, including those with Israeli citizenship, has festered into a fierce intolerance for Jewish critics of Israel as well (Shatz, 2016). Thus, in rejecting the right to boycott, the Supreme Court was simply reflecting, in Justice Amit's words, Israel's "one opinion and one truth": to question the occupation is to challenge the state.

Ironically, these confessions from Israel's highest echelons are catalyzing BDS's expansion. The movement is now seen as one of the few actors countering the conflict's status quo, at a time when Israel is doing everything it can to preserve it. Today, as Pessah (this volume) describes, BDS is supported and led by Jewish activists alongside Palestinians and other allies. Student unions, churches, and academic associations are divesting from Israeli companies involved in the occupation. More celebrities are publicly refusing to visit or perform in Israel, in moves reminiscent of the UN "Register of Performers" that boycotted apartheid South Africa. Grass roots movements like Black Lives Matter are developing intersectional narratives to bolster Palestine solidarity (see Joey Ayoub, this volume). Major policy actors are adopting accountability measures long promoted by BDS, including the UN database of businesses operating in settlements and the European Union's differentiation mechanisms (Lovatt, 2016). It is no wonder that the Israeli government is investing vast resources into undermining people's right to boycott worldwide: BDS is working.

"It Doesn't Add Up"

This is not to say that the BDS movement is in any way immune to criticism. The decentralized nature of the campaign has stirred serious debates among Palestinians and allies around its discourse, guidelines, and impact (Barghouti, 2016). Fish (this volume) rightly raises the fact that some activists have abused BDS for politically ignorant or racist reasons, including on college campuses. However, as Pessah (this volume) also shows, these are hardly the majority of activists, nor do they reflect the tenets of BDS. The three objectives of the movement—to end an occupation, to repatriate refugees, and to achieve equality—would not be controversial demands in any part of the world, and there is no justification for making an exception for Israel. To believe that these principles threaten the existence of the "Jewish state" is to admit that Israel's *raison d'etre* is inherently antithetical to those values. "How can you be for equality in the US," asks Dima Khalidi, director of the Chicago-based Palestine Legal, "when you defend Israel's discriminatory laws and apartheid policies? It doesn't add up" (Iraqi, 2017).

Critics of BDS do not want to admit this serious contradiction. Fish's interpretations of intersectionality, postcolonialism, postmodernism, and post-nationalism—intellectual frameworks that have been central to restoring the voices of oppressed and disenfranchised people, and to challenging inequalities of power—inadvertently expose the fear among Israel advocates that the world is increasingly recognizing the two faces of Zionism (a trait shared by all nationalisms in different ways). Zionism is indeed a "national movement for political liberation and self-determination for the Jewish people." But it is also a settler-colonial ideology that uprooted a nation and planted an apartheid regime. Fish further omits the fact that decades of Palestinian civil disobedience have been crushed by Israel just as viciously as armed attacks, deeming every form of opposition to its rule as unacceptable, whether nonviolent or not.

So how else should Palestinians act against their injustices? Palestinians cannot be denounced when they employ violence yet be equally chastised when they use nonviolence. We cannot praise the power of boycotts yet criminalize them when used on a particular country. At the very least, one should not have to tell the governments and courts of self-proclaimed democracies that the right to boycott is a nonnegotiable human right. Those who refuse to learn that lesson today will learn it from history books tomorrow.

Amjad Iraqi is an advocacy coordinator at Adalah—The Legal Center for Arab Minority Rights in Israel, where he has worked since 2012. He is also a policy analyst with Al-Shabaka: The Palestinian Policy Network, and a contributing editor at *+972 Magazine*. He serves as a consultant for several policy and human rights groups in Israel-Palestine, and has published articles in the *London Review of Books* and *Le Monde Diplomatique*, among other outlets. Amjad has an MA in public policy from King's College London, and an Honours BA in peace and conflict studies from the University of Toronto.

References

Adalah. (2017, September 25). Discriminatory Laws Database. Retrieved from www .adalah.org/en/content/view/7771

Arafeh, N. (2017, May). "50 Years of Occupation: Ongoing Colonial Economic Domination." *This Week in Palestine*, no. 241. Retrieved from https://thisweekinpalestine.com/50-years-occupation-2/

Barghouti, O. (2016, June 14). "BDS: Discussing Difficult Issues in a Fast-Growing Movement." *Al-Shabaka: The Palestinian Policy Network*. Retrieved from https://al-shabaka.org/commentaries/bds-discussing-difficult-issues-in-a-fast-growing-movement/

COTUS (Congress of the United States). (2018 [2017]). S.720. Israel Anti-boycott Act. 115th Congress, 2017–2018. Retrieved from www.congress.gov/bill/115th-congress/senate-bill/720/text

Cuomo, A. (2016, June 10). "If You Boycott Israel, New York State Will Boycott You." *Washington Post*. Retrieved from www.washingtonpost.com/opinions/gov-andrew-cuomo-if-you-boycott-israel-new-york-state-will-boycott-you/2016/06/10/1d6d3acc-2e62-11e6-9b37-42985f6a265c_story.html

Eglash, R. (2018, January 31). "Singer Lorde Cancelled Her Concert in Israel. Now Those Who Told Her Not to Are Being Sued. *Washington Post*. Retrieved from www.washingtonpost.com/news/worldviews/wp/2018/01/31/singer-lorde-canceled-her-concert-in-israel-now-those-who-told-her-not-to-go-are-being-sued/

Eidelman, V. (2018, January 30). "Laws Targeting Israel Boycotts Fail First Legal Test" [American Civil Liberties Union blog post]. Retrieved from www.aclu.org/blog/free-speech/rights-protesters/laws-targeting-israel-boycotts-fail-first-legal-test

Foundation for Middle East Peace. (2018, January 31). "Federal Court Prelim Ruling Ks Boycott Bill—Key Excerpts." Retrieved from https://fmep.org/resource/federal-court-prelim-ruling-ks-boycott-bill-key-excerpts/

Gajanan, M. (2017, October 20). "A Texas City Will Only Give Your Hurricane Aid If You Promise Not to Boycott Israel." *Time Magazine Online*. Retrieved from http://www.time.com/4992101/hurricane-harvey-texas-dickinson-israel/

Greenwald, G., & Fishman, A. (2016, February 16). "Greatest Threat to Free Speech in the West: Criminalizing Activism against Israeli Occupation." *The Intercept*. Retrieved from http://www.theintercept.com/2016/02/16/greatest-threat-to-free-speech-in-the-west-criminalizing-activism-against-israeli-occupation/

Iraqi, A. (2017, October 18). "A Legal Shield for the Palestine Movement in the US." *+972 Magazine*. Retrieved from https://972mag.com/a-legal-shield-for-the-palestine-movement-in-the-u-s/130289/

Jamal, B. (2017, June 26). "This Ruling Allows Councils to Boycott Israel. It's a Crucial Victory." *The Guardian*. Retrieved from www.theguardian.com/commentisfree/2017/jun/26/israel-palestine-bds-campaign-judicial-review

Jewish Virtual Library. (2018). "US Policy during World War II: The Anti-Nazi Boycott (1933)." *Jewish Virtual Library*. Retrieved May 26, 2018, from www.jewishvirtuallibrary.org/1933-anti-nazi-boycott

Kriek, A.-M. (1989, October 12). "South Africa Shouldn't Be Singled Out." *Christian Science Monitor*. Retrieved from www.csmonitor.com/1989/1012/ekri.html

Lovatt, H. (2016, October 31). "EU Differentiation and the Push For Peace in Israel-Palestine." European Council on Foreign Relations. Retrieved from www.ecfr.eu/publications/summary/eu_differentiation_and_the_push_for_peace_in_israel_palestine7163

Marom, Y. (2015, April 17). "High Court on BDS: Somewhere between Terror and Holocaust Denial." *+972 Magazine*. Retrieved from https://972mag.com/high-court-on-bds-somewhere-between-terror-and-holocaust-denial/105656/

Munayyer, Y. (2011, May 18). "Palestine's Hidden History of Nonviolence." *Foreign Policy*. Retrieved from http://foreignpolicy.com/2011/05/18/palestines-hidden-history-of-nonviolence-2/

Palestine Legal. (2018). "Anti-BDS Legislation by State." Retrieved January 16, 2018 from https://palestinelegal.org/righttoboycott/

Shatz, A. (2016). "Israel's Putinisation." *London Review of Books, 38*(4), 11–12. Retrieved from www.lrb.co.uk/v38/n04/adam-shatz/israels-putinisation

Stanford Daily. (1956). "115 Negroes Indicted in Montgomery." Retrieved February 23, 2018 from https://stanforddailyarchive.com/cgi-bin/stanford?a=d&d=stanford 19560223-01.2.18

Supreme Court of Israel. (2015). Summary of Decision in Uri Avery et al. v. The Knesset et al., April 15 (HCJ 5239/11, HCJ 5392/11, HCJ 5549/11, HCJ 2072/12) [Translated from the original Hebrew by Adalah]. Retrieved from https://www.adalah .org/uploads/Boycott_decision_apri_2015_english_summary.pdf

Tartir, A. (2017, May 16). "The Palestinian Security Forces: Whose Security?" *Al-Shabaka*. Retrieved from https://al-shabaka.org/briefs/palestinian-authority-security-forces -whose-security/

Thrall, N. (2017, May 16). "Israel-Palestine: The Real Reason There's Still No Peace." *The Guardian*. Retrieved from www.theguardian.com/world/2017/may/16/the -real-reason-the-israel-palestine-peace-process-always-fails

Yachot, N. (2017, December 8). "ACLU Files Second Lawsuit Challenging Laws Suppressing Boycotts of Israel" [American Civil Liberties Union blog post]. Retrieved from www.aclu.org/blog/free-speech/rights-protesters/aclu-files-second -lawsuit-challenging-laws-suppressing-boycotts

Index

Index

Jews and Palestinian Arabs
  British Mandate, memories of friendship, 19
  self-determination, opinion polls favoring,
    39
Jews from Arab countries, 137, 138, 145,
    151–58
  compensation and reparation, 151, 152, 155
  Holocaust survivors, attitude toward, 154–55
  immigrant (*olim*)/refugee dichotomy, Zionist
    position, 151, 152–56, 158, 168
  Jewish indigeneity, 19
  refugee recognition, international context,
    157
  See also displacement and dispossession
Jews, persecution, 7–8, 10, 22
Jordan
  East Jerusalem and West Bank, Jewish
    eviction, 119
  East Jerusalem and West Bank, sovereign
    claim, 102, 103, 108, 119
Joseph's Tomb, 126–27
Judaization. *See* Palestine
Justice for Jews from Arab Countries (JJAC),
    152, 154, 155, 157

King David Hotel bombing (Jerusalem)
  multiple experiences, memorability, 15
Kurdish minority
  Iraq, 40
  Turkish suppression, 40

Law of return. *See* Israel
laws of occupation
  arbitrary application, 120–21

Mamilla Cemetery (Jerusalem)
  Dijani family ancestor, tomb property rights,
    193
Mandela, Nelson, 197
Middle East and North Africa Jews, 156
  See also Jews; Mizrahi Jews
Mindanao Christians, Philippines settlements
  European settler colonialism, similarities, 65
minority rights, 39–40
Mizrahi and Ashkenazi Jews
  relationships to Palestinians, 216, 222, 223n
Mizrahi Jews
  Ashkenazi Jews, relationship, 217, 218–19
  de-Arabization, 219–20, 223n, 230–31
  indigenous conceptions of Jewish society,
    221
  Palestinian solidarity, 214, 216, 217–18, 219,
    220, 221, 230

  push and pull factors, 216, 221
  shared common culture, 210
  See also European colonialism; Zionism
Mizrahi/Ashkenazi Jews
  Black-Palestinian bond example, 211
Muslim Umayyad dynasty, 18
Muslim-Jewish relations
  Medieval Andalusia, 18

Nakba (disaster), 11, 14–15, 33, 52, 57, 80, 84,
    87, 143, 199n
  Arab radio broadcasts, differentiated pasts
    affecting, 15, 16, 27
  Israel, responsibility, acknowledgement, 31,
    58
  See also Bedouins; Israel
Naksa (setback), 56
narratives
  constructed fallacies, 15, 16, 24
  constructed truths, 24, 26, 37, 163
  false, reconciliation, impact, 15
  identities, construction, individual and group,
    role, 3
  Jewish mainstream, 9, 10
  multiple, framework
    external stakeholders, influence, 24
    fact, perspective, narrative, truth,
      interrelation, 23–24
    Palestine/Israel example, 23
  Palestinian mainstream, 9, 10, 11
  political action, leading to, 3
  power, financial, military, political, moral,
    influencing, 17
  United States, "us vs them" mentality, 228,
    229
  See also Israel/Palestine; Israeli-Palestinian
    conflict
nation-state
  ascriptive characteristics, 35, 36, 54
  citizenship rights, 38, 53–54
  human rights transcending, 54–55
  development, historical dimensions, 43–44
  emergence, origins, evolution, 35–38, 43–44
  identity community, hegemonic group,
    dominance
    examples, 37–38, 48
  identity community, hegemonic group,
    minority treatment, 40, 48
  identity group, immigrants and indigenous
    people affecting, 36–37
  minority rights, 37
national identity. *See* Jewish-Israeli national
    identity, development

270

Reflections on
Self —
Delusion
9th Terantino?
New Yorke